T0208013

MYSTERY OF THE EUCHARIST

TYPOLOGY'S TRIUMPH
OVER INTERPRETIVE ALLEGORIZATION

Hilary Arthur Nixon, PhD

WESTBOW
PRESS®
A DIVISION OF THOMAS NELSON
& ZONDERVAN

WestBow Press books may be ordered through booksellers or by contacting:

WestBow Press
A Division of Thomas Nelson & Zondervan
1663 Liberty Drive
Bloomington, IN 47403
www.westbowpress.com
844-714-3454

Because of the dynamic nature of the Internet, any web addresses or links contained in this book may have changed since publication and may no longer be valid. The views expressed in this work are solely those of the author and do not necessarily reflect the views of the publisher, and the publisher hereby disclaims any responsibility for them.

Back cover and interior image design by Rebekah Campbell.

Unless noted otherwise, all Scripture quotations are taken from The New American Standard Bible®, Copyright © 1960, 1962, 1963, 1968, 1971, 1972, 1973, 1975, 1977, 1995 by The Lockman Foundation. Used by permission.

Scripture quotations marked NIV are taken from The Holy Bible, New International Version®, NIV® Copyright © 1973, 1978, 1984, 2011 by Biblica, Inc.® Used by permission. All rights reserved worldwide.

Scripture quotations marked NKJV are taken from the New King James Version®. Copyright © 1982 by Thomas Nelson. Used by permission. All rights reserved.

Scripture quotations marked KJV are taken from the King James Version.

ISBN: 978-1-6642-7491-4 (sc)
ISBN: 978-1-6642-7492-1 (hc)
ISBN: 978-1-6642-7490-7 (e)

Library of Congress Control Number: 2022914499

Print information available on the last page.

WestBow Press rev. date: 10/7/2022

The weapons of our warfare are not of the flesh,
but divinely powerful for the destruction of fortresses.
We are destroying speculations and every lofty thing
raised up against the knowledge of God,
and we are taking every thought captive
to the obedience of Christ.
2 Corinthians 10:4–5B

Communion focuses on three associations.
Bread and body
Wine and blood
Cup and new covenant

A synecdoche represents a part for the whole. (Synecdoche is a specialized form of metonym.)

The cup is only a small inaugural part of the new covenant.

Still we understand that the cup **represents** the whole new covenant.

Alloeosis, another figure of speech, reinterprets an initial idea because of later context.

Since	This cup	**represents** the new covenant.
then by alloeosis	This bread	**represents** My body.
	This wine	**represents** My blood of the covenant.

This book looks at how figures of speech and literal interpretation help us understand God's Word. Through the ceremony of the Lord's Supper, they enable us to encounter anew the Father, Son and Holy Spirit. They also reconnect us to the virtues, the benefits, Christ won for us when He suffered on the cross.

CONTENTS

Noteworthy

INTRODUCTION, APPROACH AND DATA

This book explains how God uses Communion to remind us of Messiah's sin bearing passion. This renews believers to Christ's blessings (which he earned at the cross). The Lord's Supper is the renewal ceremony of the new covenant. Through it, believers encounter God and fortify their relationship with Him. This book answers how bread and wine, and flesh and blood, and Father, Son and Holy Spirit are tied together.[1]

Eucharist derives from a Greek word which means "giving thanks." The Eucharist is the sacramental mystery where a ceremony with bread and wine link us to Jesus and his blessings. Twice in the ceremony, a Eucharistic prayer of thanks is given to God — once for the bread and once for the cup. Figures of speech clarify how grammar understands the ceremonial words. "The problem that ... we still face — is the role and function of figurative language. How may it be recognized? What does it mean?"[1] Proper methods of interpreting God's Word (hermeneutics) and how one understands "the raised human body of Jesus" are also needed to unlock the mystery of the Eucharist. This mystery is solved when you understand three relationships: bread and Christ's body, wine and Christ's blood, and finally the cup's relationship to the new covenant. But *knowing* about the ceremony falls short of *experiencing* Christ in Holy Communion and receiving renewed energy to live as his disciple.

The Bible uses several terms to identify the ceremony. "When you meet together, it is not to eat the Lord's Supper," 1 Corinthians 11:20. "You cannot partake of the table of the Lord and the table of demons" 1 Corinthians 10:21. Communion derives from Latin and corresponds

---

[1] The answer is a modern paraphrase of the idea with which Zwingli ends his work on the Lord's Supper. *Zwingli and [H.] Bullinger*, Editor: G.W. Bromiley, Library of Christian Classics vol. XXIV, (Philadelphia: Westminster Press, 1953), p. 238

to the Greek word κοινωνια (koinonia) often translated as fellowship. "The cup of blessing which we bless, is it not the communion of the blood of Christ? The bread which we break, is it not the communion of the body of Christ? For we being many are one bread, and one body: for we are all partakers of that one bread" 1 Corinthians 10:16–17 (KJV). I use the term Holy Communion to identify the ceremony. "They were continually devoting themselves to the apostles' teaching and to fellowship, to the breaking of bread and to prayer" Acts 2:42. The Catholic Church use the term Mass which means "sending". (They see the sending of Christ when transubstantiation occurs). Lutherans use the term Sacrament of the Altar.[2]

This treatise starts with the biblical verses on and about the Lord's Supper. Next, the words of institution are explained in their literal, historical and grammatical context. Simplicity enables comprehension. Historical interpretations then get introduced and critiqued. This is much more technical. Just as a diamond looks different in various lights, so Holy Communion has several valid motifs. Those that adhere to the biblical text and biblical methods of interpretation receive favorable comment. This permits a multidimensional approach to the Eucharist. Throughout, I strive to be accurate, maintain a tone of respect and present solid biblical analysis. While catechisms present denominational distinctions with simplicity and biblical authority, they fail to fully interact with other views. We interact, show the faults in some views, but above all strive to learn the uplifting spiritual lessons about how we unite with God and find his grace through the Eucharist.

The appendix contains nine sections. A. Provides interpretive definitions. "Literal" takes the original author's intent. (Hence figures of speech are part of literal interpretation.) "Letteral" removes an author's intended use of a speech figure. B. Presents and evaluates historical "Methods of Interpretation." Typology should exclusively be used, even though its mechanism is more difficult. "Allegorical interpretation" adds ideas not intended by the original author — hence it is **not** a legitimate method of interpretation. C. Outlines "Figures of Rhetoric."

---

[2] *Dr. Martin Luther's Small Catechism* with an American Translation text, (New Haven, Missouri: Leader Publishing Co., 1971), p. 193. Question "296 By what other means is the Sacrament of the Altar known?"

Language uses words, grammar and syntax to communicate meaning. Figures of rhetoric describe methods to present that meaning. The result is either spoken or written. D. *NYM words (like synonym or antonym) are *word-to-word associations*. E. Deals with "Figures of Speech" which technically are *word to phrase associations*. (But this distinction is new, so many word-to-word associations show up in this list.) Four attempts at organization provide an overview. An alphabetical list of "Figures of Speech" follows. Every type of biblical figure of speech is presented but every incident is not shown. This list demonstrates that alloeosis, synecdoche, and metonym are not obscurities, but are a standard part of figures of speech. Included are 25 figures of speech Zwingli identified. Google has not yet caught up with these. F. Symbolism of Items in the Ark. G. Glossary is a convenient dictionary for unfamiliar words. H. Bibliography cites works referenced. I. Lists Alphabetical Index of Biblical References.

Footnotes hold scholarly arguments and references, along with Greek, Hebrew, and Jewish terminology. The advanced reader should carefully work through the footnotes. (For instance, the text simply states: "their Thursday[10] celebration of the Passover." Footnote '10' resolves a very longstanding synoptic problem on the timing of the Passover meal — requiring Hebraic intimacy of the Old Testament and nearly a full page to do so.

Bible quotations are **mainly** from The New American Standard Bible (NASB). Other versions include: King James Version (KJV), New International Version (NIV), and New King James Version (NKJV). If Bible verse lacks version, it is from NASB.

This author works within the hermeneutic (or an interpretative framework) of literal, historical, grammatical interpretation. He adheres to the concept of one author intended interpretation.[3] He seeks to be unbiased in the presentation and evaluation of the historical views. He accepts motifs that arise from the biblical text (exegesis); he rejects ideas that are read into the text (eisegesis). His devotion to the Bible as God's Word, his expertise in methods of interpretation and his PhD in

---

[3] I am not a follower of *sensus plenior* where multiple author intended interpretations of one text are found. However typology permits many applications of that one author intended meaning.

historical theology help us grow in our faith and understanding. In Holy Communion, the community of faith renews its covenant with God. As we faithfully remember what Christ has won for us, we are empowered by the Holy Spirit to renew our life in Christ. Those who think it is an empty ceremony, (where God is not spiritually present), are in for an awakening. Those who think they eat the body and blood of Christ will be guided to a different understanding.

BIBLICAL VERSES INSTITUTING THE LORD'S SUPPER

Matthew 26:26–30 While they were eating, Jesus took *some* bread, and after a blessing, He broke *it* and gave *it* to the disciples, and said, "Take, eat; this is My body." And when He had taken a cup and given thanks, He gave *it* to them, saying, "Drink from it, all of you; for this is My blood of the covenant, which is poured out for many for forgiveness of sins. But I say to you, I will not drink of this fruit of the vine from now on until that day when I drink it new with you in My Father's kingdom." After singing a hymn, they went out to the Mount of Olives.

Mark 14:22–25 While they were eating, He took *some* bread, and after a blessing He broke *it*; and gave *it* to them, and said, "Take *it*; this is my body." And when He had taken a cup, *and* given thanks, He gave *it* to them, and they all drank from it. And He said to them, "This is My blood of the covenant, which is poured out for many. Truly I say to you, I will never again drink of the fruit of the vine until that day when I drink it new in the kingdom of God." After singing a hymn, they went out to the Mount of Olives.

Luke 22:14–20 When the hour had come, He reclined *at the table*, and the apostles with him. And He said to them, "I have earnestly desired to eat this Passover with you before I suffer; for I say to you, I shall never again eat it until it is fulfilled in the kingdom of God. And when He had taken a cup *and* given thanks, He said, "Take this and share it among yourselves; for I say to you, I will not drink of the fruit of the vine from now on until the kingdom of God comes." And when He had taken *some* bread *and* given thanks, He broke *it*, and gave *it* to them, saying, "This is My body which is given for you; do this in remembrance of Me." And in the same way *He took* the cup after they had eaten, saying, "This cup which is poured out for you is the new covenant in My blood."

1 Corinthians 11:23–34B For I received from the Lord that which I also delivered to you, that the Lord Jesus in the night in which He was betrayed took bread; and when He had given thanks, He broke it, and said, "This is My body, which is for you; do this in remembrance of Me." In the same way *He took* the cup also after supper, saying, "This cup is the new covenant in My blood; do this, as often as you drink it, in remembrance of Me." For as often as you eat this bread and drink the cup, you proclaim the Lord's death until He comes. Therefore whoever eats the bread or drinks the cup of the Lord in an unworthy manner, shall be guilty of the body and the blood of the Lord. But a man must examine himself, and in so doing he is to eat of the bread and drink of the cup. For he who eats and drinks, eats and drinks judgment to himself, if he does not judge the body rightly. For this reason many among you are weak and sick, and a number sleep. But if we judged ourselves rightly, we should not be judged. But when we are judged, we are disciplined by the Lord so that we will not be condemned along with the world. So then, my brethren, when you come together to eat, wait for one another. If anyone is hungry, let him eat at home, so that you may not come together for judgment.

BIBLICAL VERSES EXPLICITLY ABOUT HOLY COMMUNION

1 Corinthians 10:14–22B Therefore, my beloved, flee from idolatry. I speak as to wise men; you judge what I say. Is not the cup of blessing which we bless a sharing in the blood of Christ? Is not the bread which we break a sharing in the body of Christ? Since there is one bread, we who are many are one body; for we all partake of the one bread. Look at the nation Israel; are not those who eat the sacrifices sharers in the altar? What do I mean then? That a thing sacrificed to idols is anything, or that an idol is anything? No, but I say that the things which the Gentiles sacrifice, they sacrifice to demons, and not to God; and I do not want you to become sharers in demons. You cannot drink the cup of the Lord

and the cup of demons; you cannot partake of the table of the Lord and the table of demons. Or do we provoke the Lord to jealousy? We are not stronger than He, are we?

BIBLICAL VERSES SOME REGARD AS REFERENCES TO THE EUCHARIST

1 Corinthians 5:7–8. For Christ our Passover also has been sacrificed. Therefore let us celebrate the feast, not with old leaven, nor with the leaven of malice and wickedness, but with the unleavened bread of sincerity and truth.

John 6:55–56. For My flesh is true food, and my blood is true drink. He who eats My flesh and drinks My blood abides in Me and I in him.

A SYNOPTIC ON THE WORDS OF INSTITUTION

Verses Referenced	Abbreviation
Matthew 26:26–30	Mt
Mark 14:22–25	Mk
Luke 22:14–20	Lk
1 Corinthians 11:23–26B	Paul

	Mt	Mk	Lk	Paul
(Before the meal, Christ vows not to drink of cup nor eat another Passover meal until fulfilment occurs in the kingdom.)			Lk	
Take	Mt	Mk		
eat;	Mt			
This is My body	Mt	Mk	Lk	Paul
which is	Lk			Paul
given			Lk	
for you; do this in remembrance of Me			Lk	Paul
Drink from it, all of you	Mt			
for	Mt			
This	Mt	Mk	Lk	Paul
/ is My blood of the covenant	Mt	Mk		
\ cup is the new covenant in My blood			Lk	Paul
which is poured out	Mt	Mk	Lk	

/	for many	Mt	Mk	
\	for you			Lk

for the forgiveness of sins   Mt

do this as often as you drink it, in remembrance of Me   Paul

("As often as you eat this bread and drink the
cup, you proclaim the Lord's death until He
comes." 1 Corinthians 11:26.)   Paul

(After the meal, Jesus vows not to drink of
the cup until he drinks it with his disciples in
God's kingdom)   Mt   Mk

THE BREAD

Take. Eat.
This is My body
which is given for you;
do this in remembrance of Me.

PRELUDE TO JESUS CHRIST'S WORDS ABOUT THE BREAD

Jesus gave thanks and blessed God for the bread.[4] Perhaps He prayed: "Blessed are You, O Lord our God, King of the Universe, who brings forth bread from the earth."[5]

Mark 14:22 begins, "He took *some* bread, and after a blessing broke *it* and gave *it* to them." Notice italics on the word "*some*" and three times on "*it*." Italics are put on words implied by the text even though they are not explicitly in the Greek text. When the mind has to think and fill in what was broken, given and taken, we have encountered a figure of speech called <u>ellipsis</u>. Translators show the ellipsis, the implied words, *by putting them in italic* [or sometimes brackets]. Hence "He took bread … broke [it] and gave [it] to them." Without these filler words, Mark 14:22 becomes: "He took bread, and after a blessing broke [ ] and gave [ ] to them." Can you feel how the letteral translation becomes hesitant? The rhythm gets lost and the mind is forced to fill

---

[4] Concerning Christ's blessing, two different Greek Words are used.

In Mark 14:22, ευλογησας letterally means "to speak well of" hence Testament "to bless, ascribe praise and glorification." So Jesus ascribed praise to God for the bread.

In 1 Corinthians 11:24 ευχαριστησας [transliterated as eucharist] means to give thanks. So Jesus expressed thanks to God for the bread.

[5] The standard Jewish prayer for daily bread is part of the Haggadah (Passover ceremony. Eric-Peter Lipson, *Passover Haggadah*. A Messianic Celebration, (San Francisco: JFJ Publishing,1986), p. 57. Henceforth referred to as Lipson.

in implied words. Clearly the text says "he took bread". But the mind supplies what he broke and what he gave. Grammatically the last stated thing continues to be implied. He took bread, broke [it] and gave [it].[6]

TAKE [IT]. EAT

He took [some] bread, and after a blessing broke [it] and gave [it] to them and said, "Take [it] …" Mark 14:22. Grammatically the ellipsis continues into the command to "take." What we are to "take" is that bread, consecrated, broken and given to the disciples. Paul clearly writes that bread is taken, blessed, broken and eaten.

> The Lord Jesus … took bread; and when He had given thanks, He broke it, and said, "This is My body, which is for you; do this in remembrance of Me." … For as often as you eat this bread … whoever eats the bread … so let him eat of the bread. 1 Corinthians 11:23–24B, 26, 27, 28 [My underlines.]

Take communion and one may bring on judgment! The bread is linked to Christ's body.

> For as often as you eat this bread and drink the cup, you proclaim the Lord's death until He comes. Therefore whoever eats the bread or drinks the cup of the Lord in an unworthy manner, shall be guilty of the body and the blood of the Lord. But a man must examine himself, and in so doing he is to eat of the bread and drink of the cup.1 Corinthians 11:26–28.

Church history is full of references to eating bread and partaking of Christ during the Eucharist. Both aspects are in Pope Gelasius I, 492–496 AD: "the substance or nature of the bread and wine does not cease to exist, although the elements, the Holy Spirit perfecting them,

---

[6] Ellipsis is called brachyology, when square brackets are used. On implied words either *italics* (ellipsis) or brackets (brachyology) may be used. When a parchment is fragmented and words are missing from the text, only brackets may be used.

pass over (*transact*) into a divine substance, as was the case with Christ himself."[7] Notice that the "nature of the bread … does not cease to exist" and that the Holy Spirit somehow brings about "a divine substance." *Both* eating bread and partaking of Christ must be part of an orthodox understanding of the Eucharistic. Exactly how the bread and the body of Christ relate, that is the goal of this grammatical and historical study.

Historically the first clear attempt to explain the bread/Christ combination by transforming (or swapping out) the nature of the bread for the nature of Christ arose with Paschasius Radbertus *De Corpore et Sanguine Domini* (831, revised 844). The real presence of Christ in Holy Communion is the very same flesh that was born of Mary, suffered on the cross and was resurrected. At each consecration it is miraculously multiplied by the omnipotence of God. But Radbertus differentiated Christ's body in heaven because this consecrated "presence was in a spiritual mode" which he did not define. Ratramus and Rabanus Maurius vehemently opposed this Real Presence taught by Radbertus. In the eleventh century, Berengar of Tours taught Real Presence in the Supper but denied that any change in the elements was needed. This led Catholics in 1215 AD to officially accept transubstantiation[8] where the

---

[7] The authenticity of this quote is disputed by Catholics, since it runs contrary to their later teachings. Still it succinctly illustrates the tension of ideas. It is part of the historical record: de duabus naturis in Christo, Thiel. Ep. Pontif, p. 541f. A modern work with the quote is Reinhold Seeberg, *Text-book of the History of Doctrines*, 2 vols, translated by Charles E Hay, (Grand Rapids, Michigan: Baker Book House), vol. II, p. 34.

[8] Do not be confused by this point, that bread is eaten. From the first, the church has simultaneously believed in two axioms: Christ is present and bread is eaten. Reinhold Seeberg, *Text-book of the History of Doctrines*, (Grand Rapids, Michigan: Baker Book House, 1966), book 2, p. 34. Divergence developed in one attempt to reconcile these two axioms into the theory of transubstantiation — where the substance of the bread gets miraculously replaced by the substance of Christ. Paschasius Radbertus, *De corpore et sanguine domini*, 831 AD, is the first to try in writing to formulate how transubstantiation might account for these two positions. The first Creed to profess transubstantiation as a doctrine of the church is in 1215 at the fourth Lateran Council, under Innocent III. Following Thomas Aquinas they held that the miracle does not annihilate the substance of the elements, but converts it into the substance of the Lord. See Thomas Aquinas, Sum. Theol. P. III. qu. 75, art. 3. They did not follow Scotus who held that the substance of the elements is annihilated. They did not follow Occam who used impanation or consubstantiality, which the Lutherans later modified into their

substance of the bread becomes miraculously replaced by the substance of Jesus. In transubstantiation, the believer partakes of the substance of Christ, even though the accidents (or specie) of bread appear to be eaten. Since 1215, Catholicism officially affirms the believer eats Christ's body and blood and tacitly that bread (in its substance) is not eaten.

The current words of institution are "Take [it], eat." The prior ellipsis of Christ's action with bread, continues in his command "Take, eat." In Matthew 26:26, Jesus took [some] bread, and after a blessing, He broke [it] and gave [it] to the disciples, and said, "Take [it], eat [it]." Of the synoptic Gospel accounts, Matthew alone shares Christ's command to "eat." But Paul also uses the verb, "For as often as you <u>eat this bread</u> … whoever <u>eats the bread</u> … so let him <u>eat of the bread</u>. 1 Corinthians 11:26, 27, 28 [My underlines.] Today in the Lord's Supper, clergy take bread, say thanks, break the bread and give it out with the commands: "Take. Eat."

THIS IS MY BODY

The original words spoken in Aramaic are letterally, "This [] my body." What does "this" refer to? Carlstadt taught that Jesus, pointing to his own body, said, "This is my body." In contrast everyone else teaches, "This [bread] is my body." Grammar alone does not resolve the interpretation.[9] But a historical consensus overwhelmingly connects Christ's body with the bread.

---

view of consubstantiation. See George Park Fisher, *History of Christian Doctrine*, (N.Y.: Charles Scribner's Sons, 1899), p. 257.

[9] "Τουτο εστιν το σωμα μου" "This is my body" is in the Synoptic Gospels. In 1 Corinthians 11:24 it is "Τουτο μου εστιν το σωμα". "This" is a pronominal adjective so it must agree in gender and number with the noun it modifies. "This" [τουτο] connects to a singular <u>neuter</u> noun. According to Dana and Mantey, *A Manual Grammar of the Greek New Testament*, (N.Y.: The Macmillan Co, 1957), p. 35: It is to be carefully observed that there is not only "sense gender"—that which is relative to actual sex, but "grammatical gender"—that which is determined purely by grammatical usage.

If one interprets strictly by grammatical gender, "this" modifies the neuter word "body" [σωμα, σωματος, το]. That is Carlstadt's approach. If one interprets it by actual gender, then bread is intended. Although bread [αρτος, αρτου, ο] is grammatically masculine, its actual gender is neuter since it is non–personal.

To the disciples, "This is my body" ruptured their Thursday[10] celebration of the Passover.

With food in their bellies, the disciples may have begun to rest easy, almost into comfortable drowsiness, as they listened to the familiar Passover liturgy — now developed for more than fourteen centuries. They remember with thanksgiving God's deliverance of Israel. But Christ Jesus breaks with tradition; he shatters the expected words with

---

[10] "The first day of Unleavened Bread on which the Passover lamb had to be sacrificed" Luke 22:7 (similarly Matthew 26:17 and Mark 14:12). These passages identify the day as Thursday the 14th of Nissan. This is the day of preparation when the Passover lambs were sacrificed and prepared in the afternoon. The Passover meal occurs after dark that evening — the 15th of Nissan. Jewish days begin at sunset and continue until the next sunset.

John's Gospel presents a different time frame. The Jews who took Jesus from Caiaphas to Pilate did not enter into the unclean Gentile Praetorium [the governor's mansion] "in order that they might not be defiled, but might eat the Passover" John 20:28. Likewise John writes: "Now it was the day of preparation for the Passover, it was about the sixth hour [about 6 A.M. Roman time]. And he [Pilate] said to the Jews, "behold your king" John 19:14. So John has Christ's death coincide with the time when the paschal lambs were slaughtered. This means Jesus's Passover meal was 1 day earlier.

Now John's account compared to the other synoptic accounts is one thorny and seemingly unreconcilable problem. Making the best of the situation, Joachim Jeremias seeks a middle of the road solution. Whether the meal occurred on the feast day or the day before, the Lord's Supper is "surrounded by the atmosphere of the Passover." The Lord's Supper first becomes fully understandable when it is "set within the context of the Passover ritual." Joachim Jeremias, *The Eucharistic words of Jesus* (New York: Scribner, 1966), p. 88,84.

From a Jewish perspective a solution is available. The passages refer to the Paschal lamb itself, slaughtered Thursday afternoon (14th Nissan) and eaten at the Passover meal that evening. (After 5 PM Thursday, the next day Friday 15th Nissan has begun). So by Friday morning "whatever is left of it until morning, you shall burn with fire" Exodus 12:10, see also Deuteronomy 16:4.

On the 15th of Nissan there are some additional traditional peace offerings — unfortunately also called "Pesach" in Hebrew. Multiple sacrifice**s** [Pesachim] are spoken of in the Talmud "What is the meaning of Pesachim? ... "The Peace offerings (*sh'lamim*) of Pesach" (Rosh Hashanah 5a). Therefore John refers to "the paschal peace offerings prepared and eaten during day of 15th Nissan. These offerings could be taken from flock or herd, be male or female and, unlike the Paschal lamb, could be boiled. Compare 2 Chronicles 35:13: 'they roasted the Passover offerings with fire according to the ordinance; but the other holy offerings they boiled in pots.'" See Lipson, 5–6.

his new declaration, "This is my body which is given for you. Do this in remembrance of me." He begins to hint to them of the next day's dark events when his physical body will be sacrificed at Calvary. Befuddled, the disciples witness the unfolding redemptive events, but they are not immediately clear about the significance. About 20 years later, Paul with crystal clarity presents the message, "I make known to you, brethren, the gospel … Christ died for our sins," 1 Corinthians 15:1,3. It is fact that *Jesus died*. It is theology that he died *for sin*. It is saving faith to personally believe, "He died for *my* sins." The gospel succinctly stated is "Christ died for our sins."

Likewise Paul writes, "For Christ our Passover also has been sacrificed. Therefore let us celebrate the feast, not with old leaven, nor with the leaven of malice and wickedness, but with the unleavened bread of sincerity and truth," 1 Corinthians 5:7–8. Paul makes a Christian moral application about Passover; in Jewish terminology, Paul employs halakah on the Passover. Just as the angel of death passed over a household with the blood appropriately applied to the lintel; so likewise Christ's blood appropriately applied by faith, staves off eternal death. In this sense, Christ is our Passover. God acted at the original Passover to redeem the Jews from physical bondage. God acted through Christ's death at Passover, to spiritually redeem believers from bondage to sin and death. (At our current stage of redemption, the spiritual aspects are greater than the physical aspects of Christ's redemption. For instance spiritually we know death is conquered in Christ, but we still face physical death. We have redemption, but the fullness of it is not yet manifest.) Since Christ is our Passover, wickedness and malice (and within the context of 1 Corinthians 5 immorality) are to be put away. In like manner, leaven is to vanish during Passover celebrations. With sincerity and truth we are to do the Christian walk.

What I've done in the previous paragraph is to explain, to the best of my ability, what Paul means by "Christ is our Passover." Paul's terse phrase provides a loaded hint toward those thoughts. It is akin to reading between the lines — to get an understanding of what the author intends. But I am careful to limit myself to agree with Paul's words of how Christ is our Passover. The exact correlation between Passover and Christ is a difficult study in typology. There are similarities. At

Passover, God acted to redeem His people; Christ's death happened during the Passover Feast, when faithful Jews were required to be in Jerusalem. There are differences. The Passover sacrifice pertains to a hybrid *peace offering* which is roasted, eaten by all with its remains burned the next morning as a whole burnt offering.[11] Christ's sacrifice is a *sin offering*[12] whose blood is presented inside the heavenly temple. According to tabernacle/temple law, no one is to eat anything of that sin offering. (But more about this in the next phrase "My body which is given for you." Everything in the Jewish Seder has symbolic "memorial" meaning. For now, we focus on the changes Christ made in Passover.

Traditional Passover elements consist of unleavened bread, bitter herbs, and an unblemished year-old male kid — either a sheep or a goat. The head of the household slaughters the kid. The family roasts, then eats the kid, as a peace offering. They totally burn whatever remains on the next morning, offering it as a whole burnt offering.[13] Since this is a meal, the Jews logically added wine to the ceremony. By the time of Christ, Passover's tradition incorporated five cups of wine in the Passover ceremony.[14]

There are similarities in the celebrations of Passover and the Eucharist. Both use bread and wine. Both are a memorial[15] in that believers ceremonially recreate the original occasion in an attitude of

---

[11] Exodus 12:3–10.

[12] Hebrews 9:26, "He [Christ Jesus] has been manifested to put away sin by the sacrifice of Himself." Hebrews 13:10 "We have an altar, from which those who serve the tabernacle have no right to eat. For the bodies of those animals whose blood is brought into the holy place by the high priest as an *offering* for sin, are burned outside the camp." See also the numerous references in Leviticus 4 about sin offerings with blood in the temple. See Leviticus 16:27 regarding the sin offerings on day of atonement. Whenever the sin offering's blood was presented inside the tabernacle/temple no one is permitted to eat of it.

[13] Exodus 12:3–13B.

[14] See any Jewish liturgy on the Passover, which they call the Passover Haggadah. The Passover meal, they call the Seder. Current practice has only 4 cups of wine as explained in the section: The Wine.

[15] Exodus 12:14, "Now this day will be a memorial to you." Luke 22:19, "This is my body which is given for you; do this in remembrance of Me." "Do this in remembrance of me" 1 Corinthians 11:24–25. The New Testament Greek Word for "remembrance" (αναμησις) is also used in Hebrews 10:3, "But in those sacrifices

memorial remembrance with thanksgiving. Several elements differ. In the Lord's Supper, there are no bitter herbs; the type of bread is *not scripturally mandated* as unleavened (although the first ceremony undoubtedly used unleavened bread); there is no animal sacrificed, no kid roasted, no animal flesh eaten, no remainders of the peace offering burned in the morning as a whole burnt offering. Holy Communion is not necessarily confined to once a year.

A monumental transition is underway — the Passover Seder — the Jewish ceremonial meal — changes to the commemoration of the Lord's Supper. It is not the addition of another layer of tradition. The old Covenant Passover (or Seder in Jewish terms) is cut off and totally replaced by the new covenant memorials of bread, wine and cup. Every time one participates in the Eucharist, a New Covenant renewal ceremony takes place. Formerly the Israelites sacrificed, roasted and ate the Paschal lamb as a peace offering; now in Holy Communion, believers shed no blood, they roast no peace offering, they eat no meat and they burned no remainders of a sacrifice as a whole burnt offering. In Christ's Last Supper no physical meat procurement took place — no physical sacrifice happened, and, no blood was used. But Jesus' words were loaded with implications of his sin sacrifice at Calvary which would happen within the next 24 hours.

Jesus is the Lamb of God who takes away the sin of the world (John 1:29). Yes he died for sin at Passover time. Yes he is our Passover, but that does not make him a substitute for the Paschal lamb which is roasted, eaten, with the remaining portions burned the next morning. The disciples did not think they physically ate Jesus' body. Although they had roasted meat as part of the Passover meal, they ate no flesh in the new ceremony of the Lord's Supper. They did not think of the Eucharist as a recreation of the Passover feast (but coincidentally the inauguration of the Eucharist did occur at the time of Passover). They took the Lord's Supper as a new covenant replacement for the old covenant Passover. When Jesus said, "This is my body," the disciples understand "This [bread] is my body." The old Passover meal ceased; the Eucharist is what they continued to do.

[those the law commanded] there is a reminder of sins year by year." See also footnote 33 for Old and New Testament use of "remembrance.'

"This is my body" is understood in different ways. For now a partial list is given, but explanations follow in the section on Historical Interpretations.

Zwingli and Calvin:	This [bread] *represents* my body.
Catholic Church:	This [bread] *becomes* my body.
Luther:	This [bread] is [with] my body.

Where is Jesus now? *In his deity, he is always with us.* "Lo, I am with you always, even to the end of the age" Matthew 28:20. And where is the risen body? On the first Easter Sunday, the angel told the women: "He is not here" (Matthew 24:6, Mark 16:5, Luke 24:6). *This means the resurrected body of Jesus is not everywhere.* The Bible *predicted* that Messiah would be seated at the right hand of God in heaven (Psalm 110:1; Mark 12:26, 14:62; Matthew 22:44, 26:64; Luke 22:69.) After Jesus ascended up into heaven, the Bible states as **fact** that he is seated at the right hand of God (Romans 8:34; Colossians 3:1; Ephesians 1:20; Hebrews 8:1, 12:2). *All orthodox Christians believe that Jesus in his resurrected ascended humanity is seated at the right hand of God in heaven.* In the section on Historical Interpretations we will see why Lutherans and The Catholic Church endeavor to see the resurrected body of Jesus in more places than just seated at the right hand of God in heaven.

WHICH IS GIVEN FOR YOU

Consider the type of sacrifice Jesus made at Calvary. In the Old Testament, every sin offering whose blood entered the tabernacle/temple was burned outside the camp — *no one* ate of it. See Leviticus 4:1–26B (especially verses 11–12). Day of Atonement sin offerings follow the same requirement.

> The bull of the sin offering and the goat of the sin offering, whose blood was brought in to make atonement in the holy place, shall be taken outside the camp, and they shall burn their hides, their flesh, and their refuse in the fire. Leviticus 16:27

Christ's death at Calvary is a sin offering. "He, having offered one sacrifice for sins for all time, sat down at the right hand of God," Hebrews 10:12. The purpose of this sin sacrifice is to sanctify believers: "We have been sanctified through the offering of the body of Jesus Christ once for all," Hebrews 10:10. Christ's blood entered heaven's temple.

> When Christ appeared as a high priest of the good things to come, He entered through the greater and more perfect tabernacle, not made with hands, that is to say, not of this creation; and not through the blood of goats and calves, but through His own blood, He entered the holy place once for all having obtained eternal redemption. Heb. 9:11–12.

> … without the shedding of blood there is no forgiveness. Therefore it was necessary for the copies of the things in the heavens to be cleansed with these, but the heavenly things themselves with better sacrifices than these. For Christ did not enter a holy place made with hands, a mere copy of the true one, but into heaven itself, now to appear in the presence of God for us; nor was it that He should offer Himself often, as the high priest enters the holy place year by year with blood not his own. Otherwise, he would have needed to suffer often since the foundation of the world; but now once at the consummation of the ages He has been manifested to put away sin by the sacrifice of Himself. Hebrews 9:22–26.

The Bible explicitly teaches that Christ's sin sacrifice is not to be eaten by anyone.

> We have an altar from which those who serve the tabernacle have no right to eat. For the bodies of those animals whose blood is brought into the holy place by the high priest as an offering for sin, are burned outside the camp. Therefore Jesus also, that He might sanctify the people through His own blood, suffered outside the gate. Hebrews 13:10–12.

By context Calvary is the Christian altar of Hebrews 13:10. At that altar, which was outside the camp,[16] no one ate of the flesh of His sacrifice — for His blood was to be taken as a propitiation inside the heavenly sanctuary, the true tabernacle. So the physical body, which Christ used to bear the believer's sin, is not ever for human consumption. Rather His offering is a sin sacrifice to atone for sin. It appeases God's wrath and justice. Communion enables us to think about the sin sacrifice which He made once for all time at Calvary. As we approach God by faith, the Holy Spirit unites us to Christ Himself and with all the virtues (or benefits) Christ has won for us.

Communion does not enable us to letterally eat Christ. Surprisingly the Bible does not prohibit people from eating dead humans. In fact it is one of the curses of breaking God's law. "Further, you shall eat the flesh of your sons and the flesh of your daughters you shall eat," Leviticus 26:29. See Deuteronomy 28:53–55 which promised sieges on cities of such magnitude that people would consume their own dead children!

What is prohibited is eating any living flesh — that has blood or life's force at work in it. "Only be sure not to eat the blood, for the blood is the life [or soul], and you shall not eat the life [or soul] with the flesh. You shall not eat it; you shall pour it out on the ground like water," Deuteronomy 12:23–24. The Jerusalem Council continues the admonition to abstain from blood (Acts 15:29). This prohibition rationally places a major stumbling block before those who believe they letterally eat Christ's flesh and drink His blood in communion. Opponents have hurled epitaphs at the "flesh eaters," like Cannibal, Capernatic and Sarcophagi.[17] Christ's own words in John 6 have helped confuse matters.

> I am the living bread that came down out of heaven; if
> anyone eats of this bread, he shall live forever; and the
> bread also which I shall give for the life of the world is My
> flesh. The Jews therefore began to argue with one another

---

[16] Hilary Arthur Nixon, *The Mystery of Ezekiel's Temple Liturgy. Why Ezekiel's Temple Practices Differ From Levitical Law*, (Bloomington, Indiana: Westbow Press, 2018 [rev(ision) date 05/08/2019]), p. 130–131.

[17] Two Greek words when combined mean "flesh eaters" — (σαρχ φαγειν). By extension, a marble coffin which houses flesh eating organisms is a sarcophagus.

saying, "How can this man give us His flesh to eat?" Jesus therefore said to them, "Truly, truly, I say to you, unless you eat the flesh of the Son of Man and drink His blood, you have no life in yourselves. He who eats My flesh and drinks My blood has eternal life, and I will raise him up on the last day. For My flesh is true food, and My blood is true drink. He who eats My flesh and drinks My blood abides in Me and I in him. As the living Father sent Me, and I live because of the Father, so he who eats Me, he also shall live because of Me. John 6:51–57

By allegory, Jesus substituted his flesh and blood for the bread (51,53). Then stated, "Unless you eat the flesh of the Son of Man and drink His blood, you have no life in yourselves"(53). This even offends his disciples (John 6:61). Those who interpret Jesus literally here, invariably associate the Eucharistic bread and wine with chewing on Christ's flesh and drinking His blood. But this is not what Jesus taught his disciples! (John 6 is at least one year before Christ instituted the Lord's Supper.) This is what Jesus taught. "It is *the **Spirit** who gives life*, the flesh profits nothing; *the **words** that I have spoken to you are spirit and are life*" John 6:63. Peter says "Lord, to whom shall we go? You have ***words** of eternal life*," John 6:68. (My italics and bold words.) Notice Peter does not request an ear lobe or a knuckle sandwich to munch on; Peter seeks Christ's **words** which bring eternal life. An alloeosis is a figure of speech where an initial idea (physical eating) gets changed or reinterpreted by later context (not eating). "The flesh profits nothing." This alloeosis changes all previous thought about eating flesh. Physical eating is not meant. Instead, the Holy Spirit and the word of God bring life. Belief is what gives eternal life. "Everyone who beholds the Son and believes in Him will have eternal life, and I Myself will raise him up on the last day" John 6:40. "Truly, truly, I say to you, he who believes has eternal life" John 6:47. Belief not manducation (eating) is the key!

Another approach to this passage distinguishes mortal flesh from immortal resurrected flesh. Hence the "[mortal] flesh profits nothing (John 6:63)." In this case, spiritually eating Christ's crucified vivified, resurrected and glorified body, does make eternal life available to the believer. But nowhere does the context of this passage define "flesh" as post-resurrection flesh. Reading ideas into the text (eisegesis) is not valid interpretation. When ideas arise from the text (exegesis), then we must hold onto them. Especially when it means altering initial ideas.

In review, Jesus's human body is a sin sacrifice at Calvary. No one is permitted to eat any of the flesh of that sin sacrifice because Christ's blood is propitiated inside the heavenly tabernacle. Prohibitions exist about drinking blood. Therefore, whenever we encounter words, about feasting upon Christ, we understand them in a spiritual and figurative sense. When the words of institution state, "This [bread] is my body which is given for you," we associate the bread that we eat with the sacrifice that Christ made at Calvary. The bread/Christ connection is tied to the words of Christ, which makes the bread into a symbol or sign of Christ. How do the benefits of Christ and His sacrifice become ours? As we eat bread, by faith we remember Christ's body which was broken for us. In the Holy Spirit, we are united with our Lord and Savior Jesus Christ in fellowship and communion.

DO THIS IN REMEMBRANCE OF ME

When we "do this," we are to remember Christ as our Lord and Savior. As we meditate on Christ's redemption, His love, God's atonement, the forgiveness of our sin, the fellowship of the Holy Spirit — we connect by faith to Christ. The benefits he won for us, He brings down and applies to our lives. The Spirit also connects us by faith with the whole community of faith (on earth and in heaven).

Just as a Jew, faithfully celebrates Passover (remembering God's redemptive work to bring the Jewish people out of Egyptian slavery), even so the Christian remembers what Christ has done for him. This mental exercise invokes wonder, worship and recollection of God's redemptive realities. Our spirit basks in the fellowship of the saints and spiritually unites with the triune God. Our conscience gets re-energized to live with and for Christ. This is not mental brainwashing; it is a memorial process that triggers the spiritual communion of loving and being loved by God through Christ Jesus in the power of the resurrection and the Holy Spirit.

Faith and remembrance are the keys for the Holy Spirit to unite us to Christ and his benefits. Must there be bread and wine for the Holy Spirit to link us? No, but it is God's ordained new covenant renewal ceremony, so the Holy Spirit can use it.

THE WINE

Drink from it, all of you
for this   /   is My blood of the covenant
                \   cup is the new covenant in My blood
which is poured out   /   for many
                        \   for you
for the forgiveness of sins
do this as often as you drink it, in remembrance of Me

PRELUDE TO THE JESUS CHRIST'S WORDS ABOUT THE WINE

Jesus lifts a common cup from the table. Perhaps it is just a wine bowl[18] made of pottery or wood. By tradition, five Passover cups of wine are poured, but only four are shared by all participants. Each cup retells God's promised action (Exodus 6:6–8; Malachi 4:5.)[19]

1. **I will bring you out**. The Cup of Sanctification (Kiddush), at the Seder's start.
2. I **will rescue you.** The Cup of Telling–forth, of Praise and of Deliverance, which is taken after singing the first part of the Hallel (Psalm 113–114B) before the main meal.
3. **I will redeem you.** The Cup of Blessing and Redemption, taken after the meal.
4. **I will take you as My people**. The Cup of Completion, near the Seder's end.
5. **I will send you Elijah the prophet,** Malachi 4:5. Before the 1900's, Elijah's Cup was filled but not drunk. It awaited the

---

[18] In ancient times, a master gave a "wine bowl of freedom" to each slave he freed. Eric–Peter Lipson, p. 15.
[19] Lipson, pp. 15–16.

prophet. The youngest child opened the front door looking for Elijah. But mob assaults against Jews have caused this tradition with the fifth cup to cease. Riots flamed up on Passover Eve in York in 1190 and in Russia from 1881–1905. "For centuries Jews in many lands have been afraid to open their doors at Passover–Easter time for fear of … the violence of ungodly people."[20]

At either the first or second Passover cup,[21] Christ utters a Nazirite vow to abstain henceforth from grape products.

> Luke 22:14–18 When the hour had come He reclined *at the table*, and the apostles with him. And He said to them, "I have earnestly desired to eat this Passover with you before I suffer; for I say to you, I shall never again eat it until it is fulfilled in the kingdom of God. And when He had taken a cup *and* given thanks, He said, "Take this and share it among yourselves; for I say to you, I will not drink of the fruit of the vine from now on until the kingdom of God comes."

In similar fashion at the fourth cup[22] Christ reiterates his vow of abstinence from grape vine products. "But I say to you, I will not drink of this fruit of the vine from now on until that day when I drink it new with you in My Father's kingdom" (Matthew 26:29). "Truly I say to you, I shall never again drink of the fruit of the vine until that day when I drink it new in the kingdom of God" (Mark 14:25).[23]

---

[20] Lipson, p. 66.

[21] Ibid., p. 15.

[22] "The final cup, relating to the fourth promise, that of the restoration of Israel, will not be taken by Jesus until the establishing of the Kingdom of God." Robert L. Thomas editor, Stanley N. Gundry, Associate Editor. *A Harmony of the Gospels*, (Chicago: Moody Press, 1978), p. 213.

[23] I have presented my solution to a thorny synoptic problem. I accept Luke's record that Christ vows not to eat of the fruit of the grape before the supper. Therefore I do not think Christ drank of the cup during Holy Communion. I accept Matthew and Mark's account as Christ's reaffirmation of his abstinence from the fruit of the grape after the meal. This solution maintains the accuracy of each synoptic account. One attempt which does not maintain the accuracy

The main meal follows the second cup. Jesus reveals the betrayer, Judas, by giving him a portion of this main meal. Judas leaves before the main meal is completed.[24] Therefore, Judas was not around for the third and fourth cups.

The third Passover cup is called the *Cup of Blessing and Redemption*. At the time of the third cup, Christ again broke with tradition and instituted the cup of wine in Holy Communion. We are sure of this because Paul uses the "cup of blessing" synonymously with the "cup of the Lord."

> Is not the *cup of blessing* which we bless a sharing in the blood of Christ? Is not the bread which we break a sharing in the body of Christ? Since there is one bread, we who are many are one body; for we all partake of the one bread. ... You cannot drink the *cup of the Lord* and the cup of demons; you cannot partake of the table of the Lord and the table of demons. 1 Corinthians 10:16–17, 21 [My italics].

Jesus gives a Eucharist thanks, probably with this traditional blessing: "Blessed are You, O Lord our God, King of the Universe, who creates the fruit of the vine."

> And when He [Jesus] had taken a cup and given thanks, He gave *it* to them, saying, "Drink from it, all of you; for this is My blood of the covenant, which is poured out for many for forgiveness of sins. But I say to you, I will not drink of this fruit of the vine from now on until that day

---

of Luke's order is A. T. Robertson, *A Harmony of the Gospels*, (N.Y.: Harper and Row, 1950), section 148 footnote: "Luke here departs from the order of Mark (and Matthew) and mentions the institution of the supper earlier in the evening. It seems best to follow the chronology of Mark, who places it after the departure of Judas".

[24] John 13:21–30. I use the cups in Jewish Passover to determine when the main meal occurred and hence when Judas left. Different attempts at these synoptic problems have been attempted. E.g., Burton H. Throckmorton Jr. editor, *Gospel parallels*. A Synopsis of the First Three Gospels. (New York: Thomas Nelson and Sons, 1952), 2nd edition, sections 235–237.

when I drink it new with you in My Father's kingdom."
Matthew 26:27–29.

Drink from It, All of You

The cup passes to all present. Judas had already left. These are Christ's apostles, his inner family with whom He shares His last Passover meal. Yet they are also His followers, His faithful believers with whom Jesus gives new meaning to fellowship with this cup. All are to partake. Today the celebration of the Eucharist offers the cup to all the faithful, except in Catholicism where the cup is exclusively reserved for the clergy. Doctrinally they admit that offering the cup to all makes the best sense, but they have traditionally withheld the cup since the Middle Ages.[25]

For this Cup Is the New Covenant in My Blood — Luke, Paul

For this Is My Blood of the Covenant — Matthew, Mark

The shape of the original cup was a bowl.[26] In the Old Testament on the Day of Atonement, the high priest took a *bowl* of blood and sprinkled that blood before and on the mercy seat to ceremonially cleanse himself and his people from their sin (Leviticus 16:14–15.) The blood showed a substitute's life was taken to atone for sin. "For the life of the flesh is in the blood, and I have given it to you on the altar to make atonement for your souls; for it is the blood by reason of the life that

---

[25] *Catechism of the Catholic Church*, second edition, 2019, Libreria Editrice Vaticana-United States Conference of Catholic Bishops, Washington, D.C., section 1390. (Hereafter abbreviated CCC.)

Since Christ is sacramentally present under each of the species, communion under the species of bread alone makes it possible to receive all the fruit of Eucharistic grace. For pastoral reasons this manner of receiving communion has been legitimately established as the most common form in the Latin rite. But "the sign of communion is more complete when given under both kinds, since in that form the sign of the Eucharistic meal appears more clearly."[GIRM 240]. This is the usual form of receiving communion in the Eastern rites. 1390

[26] A cup with a handle first appeared in Germany in 1701 AD. Earliest Eucharistic chalice is made of metal and was used in Antioch during the sixth century AD. The famed Lycurgus Cup is a Roman goblet (with foot, stem and liquid holder) from 400 AD.

makes atonement" Leviticus 17:11. Just as the bowl held the blood of the now dead sacrifice, so the Eucharistic cup (which was a bowl) causes us to remember Christ's death inaugurated a new covenant.

> For this reason He is the mediator of a new covenant, so that, since a death has taken place for the redemption of the transgressions that were committed under the first covenant, those who have been called may receive the promise of the eternal inheritance. For where a covenant is, there must of necessity be the death of the one who made it. For a covenant is valid *only* when [*sacrifice is*] *people are* dead, for it is never in force while the one who made it lives. Therefore even the first covenant was not inaugurated without blood. Hebrews 9:15–18. [My interpolation. Covenants usually inaugurate with death of sacrificial animals. Wills go into effect with death of the person.]

Messiah's passion fulfils his role as the suffering servant. The Old Testament predicted Messiah would suffer.

> He was despised and forsaken of men,
> A man of sorrows and acquainted with grief;
> And like one from whom men hide their face
> He was despised, and we did not esteem Him.
> Surely our griefs He Himself bore,
> And our sorrows He carried;
> Yet we ourselves esteemed Him stricken
> Smitten of God, and afflicted.
> But He was pierced through for our transgressions,
> He was crushed for our iniquities;
> The chastening for our well-being fell upon Him,
> And by His scourging we are healed. Isaiah 53:3–5.
> But the LORD was pleased, To crush Him, putting Him
> to grief;

> If He would render Himself as a guilt offering, Isaiah
> 53:10 a.

The Old Testament predicted that as sin-bearer Messiah would suffer death.

> My Servant, will justify the many,
> As He will bear their iniquities. Isaiah 53:11 b.
> Because He poured out Himself to death,
> And was numbered with the transgressors;
> Yet He Himself bore the sin of many,
> And interceded for the transgressors. Isaiah 53:12 b.
> By oppression and judgment He was taken away;
> And as for His generation, who considered
> That He was cut off out of the land of the living
> For the transgression of my people, to whom the stroke
> was due?
> His grave was assigned with wicked men, Isaiah 53:9–10a.

On the cross, Jesus said in Matthew 27:46, "My God, My God, why have you forsaken me?" This quotes Psalm 22:1. This psalm prophetically describes crucifixion at least three hundred years before the rulers of Carthage first began to crucify criminals.

> I am poured out like water,
> And all my bones are out of joint;
> My heart is like wax;
> It is melted within me.
> My strength is dried up like a potsherd,
> And my tongue cleaves to my jaws;
> And You lay me in the dust of death.
> For dogs have surrounded me;
> A band of evildoers has encompassed me;
> They pierced my hands and my feet.
> I can count all my bones.
> They look, they stare at me. Psalm 22:14–17

Psalm 22:6 says, "I am a worm." The scarlet worm, coccus ilicis, was used to create scarlet (or crimson) dye. The female worm lays her eggs under her body and once hatched the young feed on the living body of the mother — killing her. As she dies, crimson (or scarlet) dye oozes from her body staining everything. Her young get stained for life. Scarlet thread dyed using this worm abounds in the Tabernacle: veil (Exodus 26:31), tabernacle curtain walls (Exodus 26:1) and screen for tabernacle door (Exodus 26:36). Scarlet dyed thread was in the High Priest's ephod (Exodus 39:2–3) and the pomegranate hem on his blue robe (Exodus 38:31–33.) A further coincidence occurred on the third day after the worm's death, the body turns into a white wax and falls to the ground. "Though your sins are as scarlet, They will be as white as snow; Though they are red like crimson, They will be like wool" Isaiah 1:18.

So "I am a worm" means: I was born to be crushed. I live to be God's sacrifice. I am the Redeemer, the Lamb of God who will take away the sin of the world. I was born to die bearing your sin. I am the Christ, God's suffering Servant.

Jesus speaks openly of his cup of sorrows. "Are you able to drink the cup that I drink, or to be baptized with the baptism with which I am baptized?" Mark 10:38. "The cup which the Father has given Me, shall I not drink it?" John 18:11. "My Father, if it is possible, let this cup pass from Me; yet not as I will, but as You will" Matthew 26:39. "My Father, if this cannot pass away unless I drink it, Your will be done" Matthew 26:42. "Remove this cup from Me; yet not what I will, but what You will" Mark 14:36. "Father, if You are willing, remove this cup from Me; yet not My will, but Yours be done" Luke 22:42.

> At the first Eucharist, Jesus spoke in Aramaic. A letteral translation of these words are:
> > "This cup [] the new covenant in my blood."
> > The listener has to supply the verb!
> Is the cup letterally the new covenant?
> > No! The new covenant is more than just the cup.
> > The cup's function is only a small part in the inauguration of the new covenant.
> Is the cup the new covenant?

> No! But by Christ's passion, the cup of suffering,
> inaugurates the new covenant.
>
> Is the cup transubstantiated into the new covenant?
>   No!
> Is the cup [with] the new covenant?
>   No, not quite right. But the cup is part of the new
>   covenant.
> Is the cup representative of the new covenant?
>   Yes indeed!

The cup is a symbol (or biblical type) of the new covenant. Saint Augustine never confused the symbol with that which it symbolizes.[27]

From Luke and Paul, the simple words[28] plainly mean: "This cup [represents] the new covenant in my blood." We have already seen the contiguity (or close the association) between the cup and the new covenant. This as a figure of speech — a metonymy, where a part represents the whole. (We have already seen where the death of Jesus inaugurates the new covenant. Hence the cup by metonymy represents all of the new covenant.)

Like Zwingli, I use this metonymy as the *rational* key to other associations of bread/body and of wine/blood. The figure of speech to do this is alloeosis — which letterally means "other" as in "change to make other." Essentially initial understanding is changed by explanation in later context.

> Since the cup represents the new covenant,
> then the bread represents the body,
> and the wine represents the blood.

---

[27] For Augustine (in *De Doctrina Christiana*, 2.1.1.) the sign, *signum*, shows "a thing which, beyond the impression that it conveys to the senses, makes something else known." For instance an animal's tracks signifies the former presence of the animal. But the track is not the animal, it signifies the animal had been there.

[28] 1 Timothy 6:3–5B If anyone advocates a different doctrine and does not agree with sound words, those of our Lord Jesus Christ, and with the doctrine conforming to godliness, he is conceited and understands nothing; but he has a morbid interest in controversial questions and disputes about words, out of which arise envy, strife, abusive language, evil suspicions, and constant friction between men of depraved mind and deprived of the truth, who suppose that godliness is a means of gain.

Unfortunately, not all accept the <u>reasonableness</u> of (Zwingli's) grammatical approach. Reason does not usually settle an issue if our heart is attached elsewhere. When the heart loves a point of view, all sorts of support for that view arise in the mind — even if it is not logical or reasonable. We do not like to heed that which does not fit with our way of thinking. Consequently those, who do not appreciate this approach, run to Matthew and Mark. But before we move there, establish this fact as eternal truth. *In Luke and Paul, a figure of speech called metonymy forces us to see the cup as a representation of the new covenant!* It is universally agreed: the cup symbolizes the new covenant. The cup is part of the new covenant. But the *new covenant is not just the cup.* (This is to say, the cup is a part of the new covenant and can stand as a symbol for it. But the cup is not the entirety of the new covenant. In a synecdoche, a specialized metonymy, a part represents the whole. But a part is not the whole!)

> The association of wine with Christ's blood is clearly stated in both Matthew and Mark: "this [] is my blood of the covenant." Paul emphasizes this fellowship. "The cup of blessing which we bless, is it not the communion of the blood of Christ?" 1 Cor 10:16

The new covenant is a new relationship between God and man. The Old Testament (or old covenant) established law written on tablets of stone. The new seeks the law written in the believer's heart. "I will make a new covenant with the house of Israel ... I will put my law within them and on their heart I will write it; and I will be their God, and they shall be My people." Jeremiah 31:31,33. Hebrews 8:8–12 quotes this passage to show Christ Jesus inaugurates the new covenant, which could make the worshiper perfect in conscience (Hebrews 9:9 and 14), by Christ's reformation (Heb. 9:10).By the blood of Jesus, the new covenant takes effect. The new covenant between God and me is written in the blood of Jesus. Hallelujah. The communion cup symbolizes that new covenant relationship between the believer and God. The wine represents Christ's blood.

Hilary Arthur Nixon, PhD

[BLOOD] WHICH IS POURED OUT FOR MANY (FOR YOU)

This euphemistic phrase "[Blood] which is poured out" connotes Christ's death. Just as animals die, when their blood stops pouring out of them — even so, Jesus died when blood stopped flowing from his side.

> And for this He is the mediator of a new covenant, in order that since a death has taken place for the redemption of the transgressions that were committed under the first covenant, those who have been called may receive the promise of the eternal inheritance. For where a covenant is, there must of necessity be the death of the one who made it. Hebrews 9:15–16

But more than death is intended. Uses of blood in Old covenant sacrifices and ceremonies should take a book, but allow a brief summary. After the death of the sacrifice, its blood was used to show patterns of consecration, cleansing, sanctification, expiation and/or propitiation. Brief definitions follow. Consecration makes something or someone "set apart" from sin and set apart unto God. In consecration, a dedication to a holy purpose occurs as in the dedication of the tabernacle, its furniture or the high priest. Cleansing purifies (or washes) away defilement and sin. Sanctification is the process of making one holy. Expiation removes sin and transgression as if by covering over or washing the sin away. Propitiation involves presentation of sacrificial blood before God to appease God's wrath. Together expiation and propitiation allow atonement (at–one–ment or reconciliation) of the sinner/covenant–breaker with the Holy God. These Old Testament patterns and the death of the sacrifice are expressed by the phrase, "[blood] which is poured out." [29]

---

[29] The new believer should study these topics in a good Bible dictionary such as *The New Bible Dictionary* or *The Zondervan Pictorial Encyclopedia of the Bible*. The advanced student can learn much from the excellent (though dry and quite technical) Leon Morris, *The Apostolic Preaching of the Cross*, (Grand Rapids: Eerdmans, 1974). The chapter titles include: Redemption, Covenant, the Blood, Propitiation, Reconciliation, Justification.

Both the Old and New Testament prohibit eating blood. We are not to eat blood because an animal's life is intertwined "in" or "with" its blood.

> You shall not eat flesh with its life, that is, its blood.
> Genesis 9:4
> You shall not eat any fat or any blood. Leviticus 3:17
> You shall not eat any blood. Leviticus 7:26
> The life of the flesh is in [with][30] the blood, and I have given it to you on the altar to make atonement for your souls; for it is the blood by reason of the life that makes atonement. Leviticus 17:11
> The life of all flesh, its blood is identified with its life …
> You are not to eat the blood of any flesh, for the life of all flesh is its blood. Leviticus 17:14
> "Abstain from … blood" Acts 15:20 (The Jerusalem Council continues the prohibition.)

How should we interpret Christ's words in John 6:53–56? "Unless you drink His [the Son of Man's] blood, you have no life in yourselves … He who drinks My blood abides in Me and I in Him."[31] For Zwingli and most Protestants, Christ speaks here in hyperbole — in exaggerated overstatement. The context reveals the alloeosis key in verse 63. "the flesh profits nothing" {even if one could physically drink Christ Jesus' physical blood}. Instead (v.63) "It is the Spirit who gives life … the words that I [Christ] have spoken to you are spirit and are life" Peter does not want a drink of blood, he wants Christ's "words of eternal life" (v. 68). So later verses clarify earlier misunderstandings.

---

[30] The Hebrew language preposition, ", can be translated as "in" or "with."

[31] The Law prohibits eating **animal** blood (e.g., Genesis 9:4). Some see this as mortal blood; these are letterally convinced that Christ wants them to drink his blood. So they dodge this prohibition by saying Christ's **immortal** blood is commanded to be drunk. These clever distinctions fail to understand the figurative language of John 6.

25

FOR THE FORGIVENESS OF SINS

Christ's death expiates (wipes out) our sin. Christ's blood propitiates God — assuaging His wrath. It cleanses us and provides us with a status of "forgiven" in God's eyes. It is effective for a limited number of people — those who believe. These are the *many,* a limited number. As Isaiah 53:12 predicted, "He Himself bore the sin of many." The offer of atonement is universal, for Hebrews 2:9 says, "Jesus ... because of the suffering of death, ... might taste death for everyone." Although the court brazen altar was available to every Israelite, it was effectual only to those who made use of it. Likewise, Christ tasted death for everyone, but His death is effectual only to the many who make use of it. So, the good news is genuinely and sincerely presented to all mankind. However, the effectiveness of Christ's atonement is limited to those many who utilize His forgiveness for their sins. You are one of the many, if you believe that Christ died for your sins. (Cf. 1 Corinthians 15:3).[32] Hence the synoptic variations (For many/ For you) are compatible.

DO THIS AS OFTEN AS YOU DRINK IT, IN REMEMBRANCE OF ME

Whenever you partake of the cup, remember[33] Christ Jesus, His

---

[32] For further reading on this Amyraldian position (which is still considered as one of the viable options within the Calvinistic view on limited atonement), see James Oliver Buswell, *A Systematic Theology of the Christian Religion*, Zondervan, Grand Rapids Michigan, 1962, vol 2, p. 135–136.

[33] A discerning reader understands the author takes a decidedly Zwinglian approach to the word "remember." There are very few biblical references to the Greek noun, αναμησις. Leviticus 24:7 where both frankincense and the showbread are a memorial portion to be offered by fire to the Lord. Here the showbread acts as a covenant reminder both to God and to man. In seeing the showbread God is reminded about His promise to the Israelites about their land. The Jews had to farm the land, harvest the grain, remove the chaff, bake the bread and follow God's commandment about the tabernacle's table of showbread. Therefore the showbread acted as a covenant reminder to the Jews that God was faithful in his promise to them about the land. In Numbers 10:9–10B, the trumpets serve as memorials to God, reminding him of His covenant people. He hears the trumpets and remembers to help His people against their warring adversaries. Likewise when the monthly feast of trumpets has trumpet blasts over burnt and peace offerings, the blown trumpets serve the Jews "for remembrance before your God."

Twice αναμησις occurs in Psalm titles (Psalm 38 and 70) but the context is not useful in understanding the word. The Apocrypha has it to remind men Sirach 16:6 "But for admonition, they were troubled ... to put them in remembrance of the commandment of thy law." Hebrews 10:3 "But in these sacrifices there is a reminder of sin year after year." Here a remembrance to God shows the old covenant had not really dealt with the sin problem because of the yearly sacrificing. Also the humans were reminded they were sinners, by the ceremonial action they *confess* their sin and *confess* their need for cleansing. They still had "consciousness of sins" Hebrews 10:2.

In the remainder of this footnote, I condense the NT meaning of K. H. Bartels article "remember" from the *New International Dictionary of New Testament Theology*, editor Colin Brown, Zondervan, Grand Rapids, Michigan,1978. Vol 3. p. 240–247.

The word group for "remember" is used in the NT in ways also found in pagan literature. 1) To remember or call to mind, 2) to consider, to remember for good so that it benefits the person (as God remembers His holy covenant Luke 1:72), 3) to be mindful, 4) to mention.

The word group for "remember" is also used in *unique* biblical ways. A) To mention in prayer or **remember in prayer** as intercession (1 Thessalonians 1:2 f.) or a memorial before God (Acts 10:4). B) To **proclaim and exhort** — "I intend always to remind you" 2 Peter 1:12 f. John 14:26 it is the Holy Spirit who brings to your remembrance all that Christ said. The woman who anointed Jesus (Mark 14:9) has her story told "in memory of her". I remind you to rekindle the gift of God (2 Timothy 1:6). Remind them to be submissive to rulers and authorities (Titus 3:1). C) To **confess**. Hebrews 10:3 "These sacrifices served as a reminder of sin year after year." "As the OT sacrifices cannot remove sin, their effect is to expose it, so that he who brings an offering for sin year by year, is thereby confessing that he is, and remains, a sinner" (cf. K. H. Bartels, *Gedächtnis*, 26 and notes 209 f.).

The Other usage of "remembrance" is in the Eucharist. Any and all of the previous understandings are part of this understanding. Traditionally "do this in remembrance of me" within the context of the ceremony of the Eucharist is Christ's appointed means of being present in the hearts and minds of the community of the church. Historically several different emphases have arisen.

1) Zwingli — since the human body of the ascended Jesus is only at the right hand of God — Jesus' human body is not present in the Lord's Supper. Since the Holy Spirit gives life (John 6:63), we spiritually have access to Christ through the spirit — as we remember what Christ has done for us. Here thinking about what Christ accomplished in the past, connects through the Holy Spirit to the current union with Christ and His benefits.

2) Catholic Church transubstantiation — Remembrance is understood as making present or re-creation of the sacrifice of Christ at Calvary. Thus the remembrance re-creates the atoning death of Christ, so that the Eucharistic elements become the same sacrifice as at Calvary. Thus Christ himself is made present and the benefits of forgiveness of sin and the atoning death of Christ are made present. Here the historical remembrance is replaced with an re-entry into Christ's sacrifice and current presence.

death, and His new covenant. Remember with Christ's propitiated blood, God's wrath is turned away. Remember our sin is now expiated, because of his sacrificed blood. We are forgiven. As we meditate upon Christ, we receive his benefits and the Holy Spirit unites us with Him.

We commune spiritually with him both in heaven and on earth. Communion is one means of making us aware that God "raised us with Him [the risen Christ Jesus], and seated us with Him in the heavenly places, in Christ Jesus" (Ephesians 2:6). Simultaneously communion is one way to make us aware that Christ and the Father abide within us, on earth. "I [God] dwell on a high and holy place [in heaven] and also with the contrite and lowly of spirit" (Isaiah 57:15b). Jesus said, "If anyone loves Me, he will keep My word; and My Father will love him, and We will come to him, and make Our abode with him" (John 14:23). This dwelling place is the mansion (of John 14:2)!

---

3) Gregory Dix, *The Shape of the Liturgy*, 1945, p. 243 thinks the early church saw the Eucharist as "the recalling before God of the one sacrifice of Christ in all its accomplished and effectual fulness so that it is here and now operative by its effects in the souls of the redeemed." This Catholic stresses the benefits of Christ's work.

4) Max Thurian, a member of the Taize community, stresses the trinity's response to the ceremony. He uses remembrance as both Godward and manward. Manward has subjective reflection. Godward (by the Church's liturgical action) God is made present and reminded of the sacrifice of His Son and His Son's intercession on the Church's behalf. "The Eucharistic memorial is a proclamation by the Church; it is a thanksgiving and intercession of Christ for the Church." *Eucharistic Memorial, II, The New Testament, Ecumenical Studies in Worship* 8, 1961, 35 f.

5) J. Jeremias stresses the Godward aspect of enacted prayer. Here there is no real presence or Eucharistic sacrifice. There is an eschatological emphasis of God acting because He is called to remembrance by prayer. Jeremias stresses that much of the OT and Palestinian memorial formulae using the word "remember" is mostly concerned with God remembering. Here is the Passover Haggadath prayer, whose traditional roots extend at least back to the time of Christ. "Our God and God of our fathers, may there arise, and come, and come unto, be seen, accepted, heard, recollected and remembered, the remembrance of us and the recollection of us, and the remembrance of our fathers, and the remembrance of the Messiah, son of David, thy servant, and the remembrance of Jerusalem, thy holy city, and the remembrance of all thy people, the house of Israel. May their remembrance come before thee, for rescue..." *The Eucharistic Words of Jesus*, 1966, 246–49.

6) Within the early church, "remembrance" was expanded in the sense of creedal statements.

Partaking of communion bread and contents within the cup, are aids for us to connect to Christ and receive his benefits. Christ ordained these as a means so that we can spiritually rejoice in Christ and relate with God. Other means of grace also exist. We pray, meditate on the Bible, live as disciples of Christ. How we bask in our union with Christ is not exclusively limited to participation in the Eucharist. Still, the Eucharistic service is a wonderful and God–ordained means toward aiding our remembrance and participation within that new covenant relationship. Let us therefore keep the feast, in celebration with joy, in thanksgiving with prayer, in confession of sins with proclamation that Jesus is our Savior and Lord. For our good news is that Jesus died for our sin. The Eucharist ceremony is one way in which we can feast by faith because we remember what Christ has done and realize anew what He is doing to bring about our salvation.

This ends the layman's commentary on the biblical words of institution of the Eucharist. In the next section, the reader encounters various theological perspectives on the Lord's Supper. Prepare for rigorous analysis and sharp distinctions; the intent is to educate and expand on the pious truths already learned. From simplicity we move to historical complexity.

HISTORICAL
INTERPRETATIONS

The Eucharist controversy is not about the words of Jesus — for we all hold fast to His words. The controversy is about what He intended, when he said, "This is my body." Seven historical views arise. After an introduction, a critique may arise. Each holds to a presence of Christ in Holy Communion; they differ as to the nature of that presence, and the nature of the ascended Lord.

A. CARLSTADT

Carlstadt (Andreas Bodenstein of Carlstadt) taught that Jesus, pointing to His own body (NOT the bread), said "This is my body." His interpretation eternally *dissociates* the body of Jesus from the bread; yet Carlstadt letterally retains the words - "This is my body." Jesus is humanly present only at that first last supper. In subsequent celebrations, Carlstadt always avoids association of the bread with Jesus' human body. Therefore, bread and wine are reminders of that supper. Here the spiritual is totally separated from the physical (bread/wine). Carlstadt dissociates bread from the body of Jesus. Grammatically that is a possible interpretation. However, Carlstadt is wrong. 1 Corinthians 10:16 *links* body and bread, "The bread ... is it not the communion of the body of Christ?"

Historically only Quakers have done away with the ceremony; Carlstadt and all other Christians retain it, because the Bible says, "Do this in remembrance of me." For Carlstadt, the supper is a reminder of the Christ event on the cross. With or without bread, remembrance can trigger the Spirit to bring the benefits of Christ to the believer. Access to God's means of grace is spiritually triggered by prayer, Bible reading, confession, remembrance, and/or meditation. The Eucharist and Baptism are ceremonies that help us remember and link us to Christ. Even foot washing reminds us of Christ's humility.

B. ZWINGLI

For Zwingli, Jesus spoke Aramaic to his disciples; so Christ quite letterally said "This [] My body." The listener could supply the copulative verb "is" or "signifies". The latter fits best because of the cup's association. "The cup [signifies] the new testament in my blood." Using reason, Zwingli argued succinctly: a human body occupies finite space. Today Jesus' resurrected human body occupies finite space, for He is seated at the right hand of God in heaven. Romans 8:34 proclaims, "Christ Jesus is He who died, yes, rather who was raised, who is at the right hand of God, who also intercedes for us." The Apostle's Creed states the same, "He was crucified dead and buried … The third day he arose again from the dead and is seated at the right hand of God the Father Almighty." Scripture further supports the finiteness of Jesus' resurrected human body. But being full of the Holy Spirit, he [Stephen] gazed intently into heaven and saw the glory of God, and Jesus standing at the right hand of God; and he said, "Behold, I see the heavens opened up and the Son of Man standing at the right hand of God." Acts 7:55–56B.

All forms of Christian orthodoxy affirm that Jesus in his humanity is currently seated at the right hand of God in heaven. Orthodoxy differs however with respect to the manner in which Christ and the benefits he procured at the cross are present or effectively applied through the Eucharist elements. Consider Zwingli's position.

> This [human] nature was a guest in heaven, for no flesh had ever previously ascended up into it. Therefore when we read in Mark 16:19 that Christ was received up into heaven and sat on the right hand of God we have to refer this to his human nature, for according to his divine nature he is eternally omnipresent, etc. But the saying in Matthew 28:20 "Lo, I am with you always, even unto the end of the world," can refer only to his *divine nature, for it is according to that nature that he is everywhere*

present to believers with his special gifts and comfort. [34]
[My italics.]

Early Zwingli viewed the Lord's Supper as memorial; at Marburg (1529), he embraced Christ's spiritual presence in communion. (See footnote 94.) The following quotation is Bromiley's synthesis of the third section of Zwingli, *On the Lord's Supper*, Vol. XXIV of the Library of Christian Classics. In it we find that Zwingli taught Christ in His divinity is *present* in the Eucharist for the believer. (This is barely known within Zwinglian circles and unheard of outside of those circles!)

> Zwingli had no intention of denying a spiritual presence of Christ in the sacrament. Indeed, in the course of the Christological discussion, in the second part he had freely allowed a presence of Christ after his divine nature. This presence certainly means that the communion is more than a "bare" sign, at any rate to the believing recipient. But what Zwingli cannot allow is that the presence is in any way to be identified with the element itself. The importance of the elements is that they are a sign of the body and blood of Christ offered up for us: and that is why they are called a sacrament. This does not mean that the elements are necessarily nothing more than a reminder of the death and passion of Christ. For in the sacrament we have to do not merely with the elements but *with the spiritual presence of Christ himself* and the sovereign activity of the Holy Spirit. What it does mean is that in themselves the elements are nothing more than a representation of the body and blood of Christ. The words: "this is my body," simply mean: "This represents my body." There is no literal identity between the sign and the thing signified. [35] [My italics.]

---

[34] *Zwingli and Bullinger*, p. 213.
[35] *Zwingli and Bullinger*, p. 179.

believer's faith allows the Holy Spirit to connect the believer with Christ. Faith can be manifested either in the mind of the memorializing believer or through the human's spirit.

> "I believe that in the holy communion the true body of Christ is present *in the mind of* the believer. But that the actual, real body of Christ is present in the communion or is consumed by our mouth and teeth as is maintained by the papists and some who long for the flesh pots of Egypt [i.e. Lutherans], is something that we not only deny but we consistently maintain that it is an error and contrary to the Scriptures."[36] [My italics.]

> Grace, forgiveness, consideration and help must come as God's gift directly to the spirit of the recipient. It could not be brought (*conferre, adferre, dispensare*) by sensible means, not even by the wind or the word, still less by water, bread and wine or the oil of extreme unction. *Spiritus fait, qui tulip, non sensibilis* [The Spirit goes where He wills, not by sensible things] was the basis of Zwingli's confession.[37] [My underline.]

For Zwingli, the bread acts as a symbol. By thinking on what the bread represents, our memory opens up to those things which Christ Jesus has accomplished for that believer. Faith triggers this memorialism and enables the Holy Spirit to spiritually unite Christ Jesus with the believer. In one sense, it brings Christ's divine spiritual presence *down* to the believer on earth. Yet the human nature of Jesus remains up in heaven. In another sense, the spirit of the believer is brought up into

---

[36] G. R. Potter, *Zwingli*, Cambridge University Press, New York, 1976, p. 337–338. The underlined words "in the mind of the believer" are in Latin "*fidei contemplatione*" and are used for the first time in April 1529. The primary source for this is *Huldreich Zwinglis Sämtliche Werke*, h. v. E. Egli, G. Finsler, W. Köhler, O. Farner, F. Blanke, L. v. Muralt, E. Künzli, R. Pfister, J. Staedtke, F. Büsser. Corpus Reformatorum 88f (Berlin/Leipzig/Zurich, 1905 –) (In progress), VI ii, 806.

[37] Potter, p. 337 synthesizing Zwingli, *Fidei Ratio*, June 1530.

the heavenly places and communes with Christ Jesus there. This results in spiritual communion with Christ both in heaven and on earth.[38] Few Anabaptists realize that Zwingli was as much a virtualist as John Calvin. In virtualism, the bread and wine remain unchanged, but while receiving the elements, the faithful receive the virtue, the benefits, the power of the new life in Christ Jesus. Both make the connection to Christ by the Holy Spirit. Zwingli also makes the connection with the believer's mind — remembrance of what Christ has done, triggers the Holy Spirit to connect the believer with Christ.[39] [My italics.]

> "This is my body" means "the bread signifies my body," or "is a figure of my body." For immediately afterwards in Luke 22:19 Christ adds: "This do in remembrance of me," from which it follows that the bread is only a figure of his body to remind us in the Supper that the body was crucified for us.[40]

For Zwingli, the Holy Spirit was not bound to the elements of the Eucharist, nor to a select priesthood. Faith in Christ alone brings about the divine encounter even when no elements are at hand. Just as the Jews in the Passover ceremony, annually remembered what God had done for them, so Zwingli memorialized the Lord's Supper. The bread and the wine become reminders for us; as we memorialize, the Holy Spirit can connect us to the virtues of Christ and Christ himself.

---

[38] The Essenes who wrote the Dead Sea Scrolls also juxtaposed heaven and earth. But their trigger was worship by the righteous. "Perhaps the most intriguing feature of the Qumran community is the belief that worshipers could enter heaven and that heaven or its representatives were present on earth during worship." Craig Evans, *Holman QuickSource Guide to the Dead Sea Scrolls* (Nashville, Tenn.: B&H Publishing Group, 2010), p. 243.

[39] The reader probably understands this author is favorable to the Zwinglian position. Zwingli mandated the independence of the Holy Spirit from the ceremonial elements, but he also left the Holy Spirit free to use the elements if He so chose. The full model of virtualism was fully developed by Calvin at least 20 years later. All the elements of virtualism are in seed form in Zwingli; Calvin presented the full bloom of Zwingli's approach. Calvin also emphasized communion as corporate fellowship.

[40] Zwingli, On the Lord's Supper, in *Zwingli and [H.] Bullinger*, p. 225.

Zwingli's favorite speech figure is *alloeosis*: a first set of lines get clearly explained by a later set of lines. Using reason, the understanding of the first set gets altered.

Unless you eat the flesh of the Son of (first set of alloeosis.)
Man and drink His blood, you have no   John 6:53
life in yourselves.

It is the Spirit who gives life; the flesh   (explaining set.)
profits nothing; the words that I have   John 6:63.
spoken to you are spirit and are life.

Zwingli interpreted the "flesh" to mean the "physical body." The explaining set of lines showed Christ did not intend his listeners to imbibe in either cannibalism or blood drinking. His explanation is reasonable for "the flesh [body] profits nothing." Christ's words were the means to find life–giving truths; the Holy Spirit gives life.

I believe Zwingli and Calvin both have the best approach to the Eucharist. Both have, at root, a theology of the Holy Spirit that unites the believer to Christ Jesus. Both retain the finite ascended resurrected human body of Jesus seated at the right hand of God in heaven. Both understand Christ's spiritual divine presence. Calvin seems to emphasize that the spiritual union takes place in heaven; Zwingli seems to emphasize the union on earth. But, this is an oversimplification of their views. Both hold to Scripture which indicates the union takes place both in heaven and on earth.

The differences between Calvin and Zwingli are nuances on how the Holy Spirit brings about the communion. For Zwingli it is the memorialism, the thinking about Christ. Calvin emphasizes the fellowship of the body of Christ (the Church) where the commingling of our spirit with those united in faith and the Holy Spirit. At heart, Calvin's theology has the Holy Spirit commingle with the believer's spirit; Zwingli with his rationalistic and humanistic background sees the believer's mind with correct memorialism and faith as the element which the Holy Spirit honors. {In contrast, Luther binds Christ to the elements *with* the Words of institution (consubstantiation). Catholics transubstantiate, which means the substance of Christ replaces the substance of the properly consecrated elements.}

Zwingli Critiqued

Critiques think the weakest part of Zwingli is in the damnation of the unworthy partaker. "Whoever eats the bread or drinks the cup of the Lord in an unworthy manner, shall be guilty of the body and the blood of the Lord" 1 Corinthians 11:27. But Zwingli has wiggle room, because later in the context, judgment arises from "not judging the body correctly." One eats the elements, but is condemned for not discerning how the elements point to Christ's body.

> For as often as you eat this bread and drink the cup, you proclaim the Lord's death until He comes. Therefore whoever eats the bread or drinks the cup of the Lord in an unworthy manner, shall be guilty of the body and the blood of the Lord. But let a man examine himself, and so let him eat of the bread and drink of the cup. For he who eats and drinks, eats and drinks judgment to himself, if he does not judge the body rightly. For this reason many among you are weak and sick, and a number sleep. But if we judged ourselves rightly, we should not be judged. But when we are judged, we are disciplined by the Lord in order that we may not be condemned along with the world. 1 Corinthians 11:26–32.

A person must examine himself, so that God does not judge him as an unworthy partaker of the Eucharist. What makes one unworthy is that he does not "judge the body rightly" — i.e. he does not discern the symbolic element as representing Christ. When one partakes of the elements, their public action openly declares their inward belief that Christ died for their sin and they look forward to Christ's return.

When unbelievers partake, God curses them for the spiritual confusion: outwardly they claim to believe, but inwardly they don't. These frustrate the Holy Spirit with their unbelief . yet their outward participation in the ceremony proclaims their belief. Zwingli's approach to damnation is indirect and involves spiritual "guilt." While this is satisfactory to Zwinglians, it isn't strong enough in the eyes of Catholics who view the elements as directly connected to Christ's substance. For them, the unbeliever letterally partakes of Christ and is therefore "guilty of the body and blood of the Lord." But Zwingli, Calvin and Luther all agree that the recipient's faith is involved in correctly feasting on Christ. They explain God's judgement in varying ways, but they all hold to the judgement. Views, which go beyond the Bible's explanation, should be left in the realm of conjecture, not elevated to the point of dividing the church, which is one aspect of the body of Christ.

A second criticism of Zwingli's position is that he divides the nature of Christ. Zwingli does not. Zwingli emphasizes that the ascended finite physical body of Jesus sits at the right hand of God in heaven. In fact, since the ascension, the body is NOT found on this earth. As all theologians, Zwingli treads very carefully on these matters.[41] For the divine nature of Christ cannot be separated from or mixed with the human nature of Jesus. Orthodoxy simultaneously maintains the unity of the person of Christ in his divine and human natures.[42] Zwingli

---

[41] Cyril of Alexandria pushed to get Theodore and Nestorius labeled a heretic. But modern opinions wary widely about that label's propriety. Emphasis on the distinct functions of the two natures of Christ was pushed to extremes by opponents who stressed the unity of the God-man. Both repeatedly affirmed the oneness of Christ, but there is unguarded language upon which his enemies pounced, even though the enemies did not yet have the concepts or vocabulary to resolve the dual natures either. In fact the church councils went farther to protect the full humanity and full deity (the natures) of Jesus Christ (argument of Nestorius), than Cyril wanted. But the councils also maintained the unity of the one person (Cyril's emphasis). See J.N.D. Kelly, *Early Christian Doctrines* (New York: Harper and Row, 1960), p. 304–317 for details of the interactions against Theodore (p. 308–9 decidedly orthodox) and Nestorius. Kelly (p.312) writes about Nestorius, "Modern students are sharply divided, some regarding him as essentially orthodox but the victim of ecclesiastical politics, others concurring in differing degrees in the traditional verdict."

[42] The Christological controversies are extensive and have sharply delineated what is orthodox. In the section on Luther the most extensive statement will be given from the Helvetic Confession (See footnote 87), but for now consider an earlier universally accepted statement — from Editor John H. Leith, *Creeds of the Churches*, (Richmond, Virginia: John Knox Press, Revised edition 1973).
The Definition of Chalcedon (451 AD)
Following, then, the holy fathers, we unite in teaching all men to confess the one and only Son, our Lord Jesus Christ. This selfsame one is perfect both in deity

localizes the humanity of the risen Lord Jesus Christ *only* at the right hand of the Father in heaven. Catholicism adds to this, all the properly consecrated elements. Even so the Catholics still maintain some sort of a finite space that is occupied by the current physical body of Jesus. [The Lutherans view Christ's human body as omnipresent — not quite ubiquitous or everywhere. Lutherans are more open to this charge than any other position.]

Zwingli initially favored memorialism, but moved to spiritual presence. (See footnote 94.)

> The bread in communion was an outward and visible sign of an inward and spiritual grace, but no more. There was a substantial real presence of Christ when the elements were distributed, but in the hearts of the faithful only. Christ was spiritually present, but that was no miracle: Christ was not 'in' the bread, since in his humanity he must be in heaven until the judgment day. Hence unbelievers could not in any sense, even to their own damnation, receive anything but bread. Similarly the cup could not be the New Testament for

---

and also in human–ness; this selfsame one is also actually God and actually man, with a rational soul and a body. He is of the same reality as God [*homoousion to patri*] as far as his deity is concerned and of the same reality as we are ourselves [*homoousion hemin*] as far as his human–ness is concerned; thus like us in all respects, sin only excepted. Before time began he was begotten of the Father, in respect of his deity, and now in these "last days" for us and on behalf of our salvation, this selfsame one was born of Mary the virgin, who is God–bearer [*theotokos*] in respect of his human–ness [*anthropoteta*].

We apprehend this one and only Christ–Son, Lord, only–begotten — in two natures [*duo physesin*]; without confusing the two natures [*asunkutos*], without transmuting one nature into the other [*atreptos*], without dividing them into two separate categories [*adiairetos*], without contrasting them according to area or function [*achoristos*]. The distinctiveness of each nature is not nullified by the union. Instead, the "properties" [*idiotetos*] of each nature are conserved and both natures concur [*suntrechouses*] in one "person" [*prosopon*] and in one hypostasis. They are not divided or cut into two prosopa, but are together the one and only and only- begotten Logos of God, the Lord Jesus Christ. Thus have the prophets of old testified; thus the Lord Jesus Christ himself taught us; thus the Symbol of the Fathers has handed down to us.

the forgiveness of sins since this came from the death
of the Savior.[43]

Ulrich[44] Zwingli served as pastor at Zurich, but his influence brought
Basle, St. Gall and Schaffhausen into the Reformation. The Swiss Cantons
had governments akin to the ancient Greek City–states. However, the
Reformation ideals were bitterly opposed by the five Forest Cantons
(Lucerne, Zug, Schwyz, Uri, Unterwalder) who remained Catholic. In
1531 Zwingli served as chaplain with a small group of soldiers, when
he was killed by the Forest Canton forces. Johann Heinrich Bullinger
succeeded Zwingli at Zurich. H. Bullinger wrote the second Helvetic
Confession in 1562, revised 1564 and adopted in Scotland 1566. H.
Bullinger and Calvin wrote *Consensus Tigurinus*, a work on the Lord's
Supper in 1549. H. Bullinger and Calvin greatly aided the Protestants
who fled from England. His influence is evident in the Westminster
Confession of Faith, (which is presented later under Calvin).

C. THE CATHOLIC CHURCH

Catholic[45] references are to sections of *Catechism of the Catholic
Church*, second edition, copyright © 2019. (Hereafter abbreviated CCC.)
Twenty years after Vatican II, this catechism was developed by a Synod
of Bishops who were ordered to consolidate all faith and morals. The
second edition added endnotes [which I display as footnotes]. This
will continue to be their standard catechism for the next century. This
catechism shows a labor of love and has many beautiful insights. I
quote frequently to accurately show their position. I thank them for
the permission to do so. Focusing on the distinctive teachings helps
keep this presentation brief. Unfortunately, the few differences tend to
take away from the vast areas of agreement — how all believers need

---

[43] Potter, p. 312–13.
[44] Also spelled Huldreich, Huldrych, Huldricus, Huldrychus, Udalricus, and Huldrici.
[45] The church centered at the Vatican call themselves The Catholic Church. The
word "catholic" means "universal." Protestants see themselves as part of the
universal church, so they use the term Roman Catholic to designate the Vatican
branch. The Catholic Church, Catholic and Roman Catholic all refer to the same
church.

to receive the full benefits Christ procured on Calvary — especially through the grace of Holy Communion. Catholics call their service Mass which means "sending." They believe: in the epiclesis (when their clergy call upon God), the essences of both bread and wine transubstantiate into the essence of the body and blood of Christ. (See Glossary: Mass).

Understanding the Catholic Eucharist

Catholics acknowledge Christ Jesus has many ways of being present to the believer — especially in the Eucharist.

> "Christ Jesus, who died, yes, who was raised from the dead, who is at the right hand of God, who indeed intercedes for us," is present in many ways to his Church:[46] in his word, in his Church's prayer, "where two or three are gathered in my name,"[47] in the poor, the sick, and the imprisoned,[48] in the sacraments of which he is the author, in the sacrifice of the Mass, and in the person of the minister. But "he is present ... *most especially in the Eucharistic species.*"[49] CCC section 1373

Catholics teach about the divine spiritual presence of Christ. "...it is he himself [Christ] who presides invisibly over every Eucharistic celebration." [50] Catholics differ from Protestants. Catholics teach the corporeal body of Jesus is both "at the right hand of God" and "most especially in the Eucharistic species."[51] To Zwingli the Eucharistic

---

[46] Romans 8:34; cf. LG 48.

[47] Matthew 18:20.

[48] Cf. Matthew 25:31-46.

[49] SC 7.

[50] A line from CCC Section 1348.

[51] My underlined phrases from CCC Section 1373. "Christ Jesus, who died, yes, who was raised from the dead, who is at the right hand of God, who indeed intercedes for us," is present in many ways to his Church: in his word, in his Church's prayer, "where two or three are gathered in my name," in the poor, the sick, and the imprisoned, in the sacraments of which he is the author, in the sacrifice of the Mass, and in the person of the minister. But "he is present...most especially in the Eucharistic species."

presence in the species, by reason must alter or divide Jesus' human nature. But Catholics insist, they do not divide, join or mix the divine and human natures of Jesus Christ. It is a mystery, but in their view the resurrected body of Jesus Christ is not finitely limited the way our human body is. Here is their formal statement.

> The mode of Christ's presence under the Eucharistic species is unique. It raises the Eucharist above all the sacraments as "the perfection of the spiritual life and the end to which all the sacraments tend."[52] In the most blessed sacrament of the Eucharist "the body and blood, together with the soul and divinity, of our Lord Jesus Christ and, therefore, *the whole Christ is truly, really, and substantially contained.*"[53] "This presence is called 'real' - by which is not intended to exclude the other types of presence as if they could not be 'real' too, but because it is presence in the fullest sense: that is to say, it is a *substantial* presence by which Christ, God and man, makes himself wholly and entirely present."[54] CCC Section 1374.

So technically Catholics understand, "This is my [human and divine] body." Each transubstantiated element by itself, whether body or blood, includes the entire corporeal human and divine natures. "In the Eucharist Christ gives us the very body which he gave up for us on the cross, the very blood which he 'poured out for many for the forgiveness of sins.'"[55] When Catholic laity receive only the one element — the bread, they understand they receive both the body and the blood of Christ Jesus in his deity and humanity.

Catholic Understanding of "This Is My Body."

The phrase "This is My body" means: This [sign of bread now transubstantiated] is [has become] My [real corporeal and spiritual

---

[52] St. Thomas Aquinas, STh III,73,3c.
[53] Council of Trent (1551): DS 1651.
[54] Paul VI, MF 39.
[55] CCC Section 1365.

risen] Body. Everything about the current Lord Jesus Christ is present in the "substance" of the Eucharist: this includes his human body and blood, his human soul, and his divinity.

> By the consecration the transubstantiation of the bread and wine into the Body and Blood of Christ is brought about. Under the consecrated species of bread and wine Christ himself, living and glorious, is present in a true, real, and substantial manner: his Body and his Blood, with his soul and his divinity (Cf. Council of Trent: DS 1640; 1651) CCC Section 1413.

The Latin Mass traditionally offers only the changed bread to the laity. Doctrinally they understand Christ is totally present under each species of bread and wine.

> Since Christ is sacramentally present under each of the species, communion under the species of bread alone makes it possible to receive all the fruit of Eucharistic grace. For pastoral reasons this manner of receiving communion has been legitimately established as the most common form in the Latin rite. But "the sign of communion is more complete when given under both kinds, since in that form the sign of the Eucharistic meal appears more clearly."[56] This is the usual form of receiving communion in the Eastern rites. CCC Section 1390

> The Eucharistic presence of Christ begins at the moment of the consecration and endures as long as the Eucharistic species subsist. Christ is present whole and entire in each of the species and whole and entire in each of their parts, in such a way that the breaking of the 2 bread does not divide Christ.[57] CCC Section 1377

---

[56] GIRM 240.
[57] Cf. Council of Trent: DS 1641.

So Catholics teach that "This is my body" means:

> This [specie of bread, but now transubstantiates in substance into Christ] is [has become] My [real corporeal risen] Body [blood, soul, spirit and divinity.]

Christ's Substance in the Catholic Eucharist

Embracing transubstantiation (and its Neo–Platonic world view), Catholics understand that they eat the substance of Christ under the species of bread; they do not believe they eat the substance of bread when they take communion. Catholics emphasize the crucifix, because they believe Christ's sacrifice at Calvary remains ever present when the church celebrates the Eucharist. Although they embrace the mental aspects of historical memorialism[58], they expand the idea into a present reality.

> In the New Testament, the memorial takes on new meaning. When the Church celebrates the Eucharist, she commemorates Christ's Passover, and it is made present the sacrifice Christ offered once for all on the cross remains ever present.[59] "As often as the sacrifice of the Cross by which 'Christ our Pasch has been sacrificed' is celebrated on the altar, the work of our redemption is carried out."[60] CCC Section 1364.

Because it is the memorial of Christ's Passover, the Eucharist is also a sacrifice. The sacrificial character of the Eucharist is manifested in the very words of institution: "This is my body which is given for you"

---

[58] CCC Section 1363. In the sense of Sacred Scripture the memorial is not merely the recollection of past events but the proclamation of the mighty works wrought by God for men. (Cf. Exodus 13:3.) In the liturgical celebration of these events, they become in a certain way present and real. This is how Israel understands its liberation from Egypt: every time Passover is celebrated, the Exodus events are made present to the memory of believers so that they may conform their lives to them. [My underline.]

[59] Cf. Hebrews 7:25-27.

[60] LG 3; cf. 1 Corinthians 5:7.

and "This cup which is poured out for you is the New Covenant in my blood."[61] In the Eucharist Christ gives us the very body which he gave up for us on the cross, the very blood which he "poured out for many for the forgiveness of sins."[62] CCC Section 1365.

The Eucharist is thus a sacrifice because it *re-presents* (makes present) the sacrifice of the cross, because it is its *memorial* and because it *applies* its fruit:

> [Christ], our Lord and God, was once and for all to offer himself to God the Father by his death on the altar of the cross, to accomplish there an everlasting redemption. But because his priesthood was not to end with his death, at the Last Supper "on the night when he was betrayed," [he wanted] to leave to his beloved spouse the Church a visible sacrifice (as the nature of man demands) by which the bloody sacrifice which he was to accomplish once for all on the cross would be re-presented, its memory perpetuated until the end of the world, and its salutary power be applied to the forgiveness of the sins we daily commit.[63] CCC Section 1366

> The sacrifice of Christ and the sacrifice of the Eucharist are *one single sacrifice*: "The victim is one and the same: the same now offers through the ministry of priests, who then offered himself on the cross; only the manner of offering is different." "And since in this divine sacrifice which is celebrated in the Mass, the same Christ who offered himself once in a bloody manner on the altar of the cross is contained and is offered in an unbloody manner ... this sacrifice is truly propitiatory."[64] CCC Section 1367

---

[61] Luke 22:19–20.
[62] Matthew 26:28.
[63] Council of Trent (1562): DS 1740; cf. 1 Corinthians 11:23; Hebrews 7:24, 27.
[64] Council of Trent (1562) Doctrina de ss. Missae sacrificio, c. 2: DS 1743; cf. Hebrews 9:14,27.

So Catholics use a special priesthood to recreate the sacrifice Christ offered on the Cross. Although it is unbloody and in a different manner, still the "sacrifice of Christ and the sacrifice of the Eucharist are *one single sacrifice*: ... 'The same Christ who offered himself once in a bloody manner on the altar of the cross is contained and is offered in an unbloody manner.'"[65]

A different concept of time gets embraced. On the one hand Jesus was crucified, dead and buried. Here the normal concept of time, as a chronological sequencing of events, is accepted. "Now once at the consummation of the ages He has been manifested to put away sin by the sacrifice of Himself" Hebrews 9:26. However the historical death, accomplished and done once, gets exploded into an eternal event that continues each time the Mass is said. This is a different concept of time.

Sacrifice carries a radically different meaning to Protestants than it does to Catholics. Protestants understand: Christ's death is a once and done historic event — never to be repeated. They symbolize this by no crucifix on the cross. The imagery of an empty cross, shows that the sacrifice (Christ's death) is finished. The **cause** of our salvation, which is Christ's death, is the definition of Protestant sacrifice. For Catholics the **effect** of Christ's death is their definition of sacrifice. Hence a Catholic "thinks of it as a sacrifice that is once and never done and therefore can never be repeated again."[66] For example Catholics uniquely say, the "sacrifice of Christ and the sacrifice of the Eucharist are *one single sacrifice*: ... 'The same Christ who offered himself once in a bloody manner on the altar of the cross is contained and is offered in an unbloody manner.'"[67] To summarize Christ's sacrifice: Protestants see the lamb as slain, Catholics see the lamb being slain. Both have full benefits of Christ applied to the believer, but the manner of getting that benefit radically differs.

Catholics use the crucifix to illustrate two primary themes. They make present (re–present) Christ's [continuing] sacrifice on the cross and they apply the fruit of Christ's work to the believer. In contrast, most Protestants use the symbol of an empty cross to memorialize Christ's

---

[65] CCC Section 1367.
[66] The Sacrifice of Christ, p.3 and 9.
[67] CCC Section 1367.

finished sacrifice at Calvary. Protestants use the communion elements to memorialize the application of Christ's redemption upon the believer. Protestants and Catholics agree on memorial aspects, application of redemptive benefits applied to the believer, and that Christ died once for all time at Calvary. Protestants and Catholics agree that Christ Jesus died and rose again — these are accomplished historical facts. But Protestants do not embrace Catholic language of sacrifice, philosophy, theology, or concept of time.

What appears and tastes like bread, becomes by the miracle of transubstantiation the real and present corporeal risen body and blood of Christ Jesus. This happens when the element is raised overhead and prayer is sent to God, calling upon Him (epiclesis) to change its substance.

> In the epiclesis, the Church asks the Father to send his Holy Spirit (or the power of his blessing[68]) on the bread and wine, so that by his power they may become the body and blood of Jesus Christ and so that those who take part in the Eucharist may be one body and one spirit (some liturgical traditions put the epiclesis after the anamnesis).
>
> In the institution narrative, the power of the words and the action of Christ, and the power of the Holy Spirit, make sacramentally present under the species of bread and wine Christ's body and blood, his sacrifice offered on the cross once for all. CCC Section 1353.

The Neoplatonist vocabulary of both "accident" and "substance" are not employed in Catholic official teaching; instead the words "species" and "substance" are employed. Nevertheless, they imply the same Neoplatonist concept and dogmatically embrace the teaching of transubstantiation.

---

[68] Cf. *Roman Missal*, EP I (Roman Canon) 90.

The signs of bread and wine become, in a way surpassing understanding, the Body and Blood of Christ; they continue also to signify the goodness of creation. CCC Section 1333

The Council of Trent summarizes the Catholic faith by declaring: "Because Christ our Redeemer said that it was truly his body that he was offering under the species of bread, it has always been the conviction of the Church of God, and this holy Council now declares again, that by the consecration of the bread and wine there takes place a change of the whole substance of the bread into the substance of the body of Christ our Lord and of the whole substance of the wine into the substance of his blood. This change the holy Catholic Church has fittingly and properly called transubstantiation."[69] CCC Section 1376

Worship of the Eucharist. In the liturgy of the Mass we express our faith in the real presence of Christ under the species of bread and wine by, among other ways, genuflecting or bowing deeply as a sign of adoration of the Lord. "The Catholic Church has always offered and still offers to the sacrament of the Eucharist the cult of adoration, not only during Mass, but also outside of it, reserving the consecrated hosts with the utmost care, exposing them to the solemn veneration of the faithful, and carrying them in procession."[70] CCC Section 1378

So the reality of the bread and wine become (transubstantiate to) the Body and Blood of Christ. In Scholastic terms, the "substance" or essence becomes Christ, whereas the signs (scholastic "accidents," or

---

[69] Council of Trent (1551): DS 1642; cf. Matthew 26:26 ff.; Mark 14:22 ff.; Luke 22:19 ff.; 1 Corinthians 11:24 ff.
[70] Paul VI, MF 56.

present language of "species") retain the appearances of the bread's smell, weight, taste. What is eaten is not bread. It is Christ.

It is highly fitting that Christ should have wanted to remain present to his Church in this unique way. Since Christ was about to take his departure from his own in his visible form, he wanted to give us his sacramental presence; since he was about to offer himself on the cross to save us, he wanted us to have the memorial of the love with which he loved us "to the end,"[71] even to the giving of his life. In his Eucharistic presence he remains mysteriously in our midst as the one who loved us and gave himself up for us,[72] and he remains under signs that express and communicate this love.

The Church and the world have a great need for Eucharistic worship. Jesus awaits us in this sacrament of love. Let us not refuse the time to go to meet him in adoration, in contemplation full of faith, and open to making amends for the serious offenses and crimes of the world. Let our adoration never cease.[73] CCC Section 1380

The Lord addresses an invitation to us, urging us to receive him in the sacrament of the Eucharist: "Truly, I say to you, unless you eat the flesh of the Son of man and drink his blood, you have no life in you."[74] CCC Section 1384

What material food produces in our bodily life; Holy Communion wonderfully achieves in our spiritual life. Communion with the flesh of the risen Christ, a flesh

---

[71] John 13:1.
[72] Cf. Galatians 2:20.
[73] John Paul II, Dominicae cenae, 3.
[74] John 6:53.

"given life and giving life through the Holy Spirit,"[75] preserves, increases, and renews the life of grace received at Baptism. This growth in Christian life needs the nourishment of Eucharistic Communion, the bread for our pilgrimage until the moment of death, when it will be given to us as viaticum. CCC Section 1392.

Further Grammatical Analysis

The parables are full of substituted identities where "this is" means substitute one meaning into the other imagery. For instance, in the parable of the sower who sowed some seed on the good soil — "*This is* the man who hears the word, and understands it; who indeed bears fruit" Matthew 13:22. [My italics.] When the scriptural author of a parable intends the substitution, the scripture makes it plain.

From a layman's perspective, whenever the priest presents the bread with the words, "This is my body which is broken for you, do this in remembrance of me." The faithful Catholic thinks, "This [truly] is Christ." The accident of bread serves as an image to trigger faith in the substance of Christ. Catholics do not think they idolize bread; they are taught that they worship and adore the real presence of Christ because that which was once bread now is transubstantiated into the real presence of Christ.

> Because Christ himself is present in the sacrament of the altar, he is to be honored with the worship of adoration. "To visit the Blessed Sacrament is ... a proof of gratitude, an expression of love, and a duty of adoration toward Christ our Lord" (Paul VI, MF 66). CCC Section 1418.

The phrase Christ spoke to the disciples, "This [bread] is my body" gets allegorized to mean "This is Christ" [His human body, blood, spirit, soul and His divinity.]

> "The signs of bread and wine become, in a way surpassing understanding, the Body and Blood of

---

[75] PO 5.

Christ; they continue also to signify the goodness of creation." CCC part of Section 1333

Bread's species (or accident in Scholastic terminology) signify the created aspects but by mysterious miracle beyond reason its *substance* becomes (or transubstantiates to) the body and blood of Christ. Yet the historical context of Christ's words, signify that "This" refers to the bread that Christ had blessed, broken and commanded his disciples to take and eat. Christ had not yet had his body broken upon the cross. His glorified resurrected human body was not present for the disciples to eat at the last supper which Christ Jesus presided at.

Catholic Position Critiqued

Four problems exist. A) Philosophy, B) Allegorization, C) Time Warping, and D) Manducation

A) Philosophy.

According to Catholic doctrine the substance that you feed upon is Christ, not bread. But according to Saint Paul, you eat bread

> The Council of Trent summarizes the Catholic faith by declaring: "Because Christ our Redeemer said that it was truly his body that he was offering under the species of bread, it has always been the conviction of the Church of God, and this holy Council now declares again, that by the consecration of the bread and wine there takes place a change of the whole substance of the bread into the substance of the body of Christ our Lord and of the whole substance of the wine into the substance of his blood. This change the holy Catholic Church has fittingly and properly called transubstantiation."[76] CCC Section 1376.

---

[76] Council of Trent (1551): DS 1642; cf. Matthew 26:26 ff.; Mark 14:22 ff.; Luke 22:19 ff.; 1 Corinthians 11:24 ff.

> The Lord Jesus … took bread; and when He had given thanks, He broke it, and said, "This is My body, which is for you; do this in remembrance of Me." … For as often as you eat this <u>bread</u> … whoever eats the <u>bread</u> … so let him eat of the <u>bread</u>.

1 Corinthians 11:23–24, 26, 27, 28. My underlines.

Underlying the bread substance is a whole realm of philosophy foreign to the Scriptures. In Platonism and Neoplatonism the essence (the ideal or the substance) of something is its reality. Catholicism utilizes Platonism, so that the transubstantiated bread looks like bread (particular sense perception), but in reality the substance is now Christ. Scholastics spoke of the bread–ness as the substance and the accidents of bread as the particular qualities. Essentially in Catholic transubstantiation, bread still looks like bread, but Christ-ness had replaced the bread–ness. But Paul does not say "whoever eats the accidents of the bread." Paul says, "whoever eats of the bread." Gold alchemists believed they could get to the essence of gold through non-gold accidents. All alchemist attempts to derive gold from that which is not gold are futile. That is why today, the usual understanding is that the accidents and essence are inseparable.[77] Put another way, the substance cannot be present without the species.[78]

Catholics think outward particulars (the accident) can be separated from essence or substance; yet everyone else knows the essence and accidents are inseparably linked. Should someone offer to sell you a set of invisible clothes, decline the offer. Yet when you see bread, the Catholics want you to see the invisible body and blood of Christ and worship Him. By all means find God by faith and find Him spiritually

---

[77] John Hooper's 1st chapter is exclusively dedicated to the topic that "the substance of bread and wine in the Lord's Supper remains no less after the utterance and sanctification of the words than before", John Hooper, *A Defense of the True Doctrine and Use of the Lord's Supper.* The English form of this document is translated from the Latin by Elio Cuccaro, *Monument to Memorialism John Hooper's Defense of the Lord's Supper a Translation and Analysis,* a Ph. D. thesis presented to Drew University 1987, pages 6–81.

[78] *Zwingli and Bullinger,* Bromiley's footnote 19, p.342.

present in the ceremony. But when you see bread, see bread. Paul warns us, "See to it that no one takes you captive through philosophy and empty deception, according to the tradition of men, according to the elementary principle of the world, rather than according to Christ." Colossians 3:8.

B) Interpretive Allegorization occurs during the Mass.

For simplicity, I shed the technical details. So bear with me.

Initially:	This bread is bread.
With the epiclesis:	This bread *becomes* Christ's body
Participant eats Christ:	This is My body.

In interpretive allegorization substitution occurs.
> This [bread] is bread
> Allegorize (substitute) Christ for bread (in both sides)
> This [Christ] is Christ.
> This is My body

Catholics employ the hermeneutic of allegorical interpretation to accomplish the "change" of the substance of bread with the body of Christ. (See Appendix B.3 to understand why interpretive allegorization is **not** a legitimate biblically sanctioned method of interpretation. Furthermore, interpretative allegorization substitutes one object for another and in the process annihilates the reality of one of the entities. In this case, the "body of Christ" gets substituted for "this bread.").

The more difficult but proper method uses typology (analogous correlation.) Typology maintains the full identity of both objects while paradoxically sustaining relationship and differences between the two objects. (See Appendix B.2. Typological Interpretation.) Bread is like Christ's body for both were broken, but paradoxically bread is not Christ's body. When the Eucharistic elements are fully retained in accident and substance, then veneration (idolization) of the consecrated elements will cease. Then the elements can be viewed as a means of connecting to Christ by faith. As we see bread, we remember what Christ

Jesus has done for us, our spirit opens to the Holy Spirit who draws us into communion with Christ and He draws us into communion with our fellow saints. Then we will move from the symbol (bread) to God and His blessings for us. When we substitute the symbol (bread) for God, we get caught in idolatry.[79]

C) Time Warping.

A third problem involves the warping of time. The historic event of Christ's death gets expanded into an eternal event — for Catholics teach that the Mass is a re-presentation (a making present) of Christ's selfsame sacrifice at Calvary. In contrast, Christ's death at Calvary is a sin offering accomplished once for all time. The finished sacrifice has been presented to the Father in heaven. "He, having offered one sacrifice

---

[79] Exodus 20 contains more than ten imperative statements, totaling 14 or 15 in all. Various groups parse the commandments differently.

Ten Commandments

Groups using the same ten commandments				
Modern Jews, Talmudic Division	A			
Anglican, Reformed, Philo, Josephus, first century Jews		B		
Orthodox			C	
Roman Catholic, Lutheran				D
Commandment	A	B	C	D*
I am the Lord your God	1	preface	1	1
You shall have no other gods before me	2	1	1	1
You shall not make for yourself an idol	2	2	2	1
You shall not make wrongful use of your God's name	3	3	3	2
Remember the Sabbath and keep it holy	4	4	4	3
Honor your father and mother	5	5	5	4
You shall not murder [or kill]	6	6	6	5
You shall not commit adultery	7	7	7	6
You shall not steal	8	8	8	7
Bear no false witness against neighbor	9	9	9	8
Do not covet [or take] neighbor's wife	10	10	10	9
Do not covet anything that belongs to your neighbor	10	10	10	10

*Some Lutheran churches swap house for wife in 9 and in 10 swap wife for house.

for sins for all time, sat down at the right hand of God," Hebrews 10:12. In the Eucharist, all Christendom agrees the *effects* of Christ's death are offered anew. Catholics uniquely add their view that Christ's *death is being offered anew.*

D) Manducation.

A fourth problem is even more serious. Catholics teach that believers must physically eat Christ's sacrifice by faith for the forgiveness of sin. They use analogy to justify this. Just as Israelites ate the Passover, so Christians must eat Christ. The problem is this: Christ's sacrifice at Calvary is *not* a Passover peace offering. It is a Day of Atonement sin offering — where blood enters into the tabernacle and no one eats of this sacrifice. (Leviticus 6:30; 16:27; and Hebrews 13:10–12).[80] Hence from Tabernacle typology, we learn that Christians do not physically eat of that sin sacrifice Christ made at Calvary. Christians *spiritually partake of the benefits* that Christ won for them when he made that sin sacrifice. Just as the San Andreas earthquake fault has the potential of leveling San Francisco, so this problem's fault has potential to topple two Catholic doctrines: Papal infallibility and the necessity of a special priesthood who make epiclesis. I am personally most troubled by idolatry — the veneration of the bread as if it is God.

> For though we walk in the flesh, we do not war according to the flesh, for the weapons of our warfare are not of the flesh, but divinely powerful for the destruction of fortresses. We are destroying speculations and every lofty thing raised up against the knowledge of God, and we are taking every thought captive to the obedience of Christ. 2 Corinthians 10:3–5.

---

[80] See Hilary Arthur Nixon, *The Mystery of Ezekiel's Temple Liturgy. Why Ezekiel's Temple Practices Differ From Levitical Law*, (Bloomington, Indiana: WestBow Press, 2018 [rev(ision) date 05/08/2019]), p. 62–68; 85–88.

D. Martin Luther

In the sacrament of Holy Communion, Luther saw the believer letterally eating both physical bread and with that bread the body and blood of Christ (the God-man). In, with, through over the cup, he also drinks Christ's body and blood. The believer exercises God–given faith, which unleashes the power not only to see Christ, but also to find the means of grace to forgive sin. God ordained His Word to work through this channel of grace. When an unbeliever eats bread, he still eats bread and Christ, but lacking faith, he eats damnation — by not discerning the body and blood of Christ. For Luther no amount of reasoning could fathom this experiential mysticism of faith. So, no attempt is made. Luther carefully avoided use of the word "substance" — a scholastic (not a biblical) concept[81], but today the Lutheran position is commonly called consubstantiation. "Con" in Latin means "with." "This is my body" Luther understood to mean, "This [bread] is (with) my body."

For Luther the Word was all important; Logos theology stems from the scripture. (The Greek word "Logos" gets translated as the Word.)

> In the beginning was the Word, and the Word was with God, and the Word was God. He was in the beginning with God. 3All things came into being through Him, and apart from Him not even one thing came into being that has come into being. In Him was life, and the life was the Light of mankind. And the Light shines in the darkness, and the darkness did not grasp it. John 1:1–5 NASB

> This was the true Light that, coming into the world, enlightens every person. He was in the world, and the world came into being through Him, and yet the world did not know Him. He came to His own, and His own people did not accept Him. But as many as received Him, to them He gave the right to become children of God, to those who

---

[81] Luther was loath to use the idea of "substance". It was not a scriptural term, rather it was a scholastic sophistication as Erasmus and Melancthon had previously pointed out. See Roland H. Bainton, *Here I stand. A Life of Martin Luther*, Abingdon–Cokesbury Press, New York, 1950, p. 139.

believe in His name, who were born, not of blood, nor of the will of the flesh, nor of the will of a man, but of God. John 1:9–13 NASB

The sacrament for him (Luther) was not a chunk of God fallen like a meteorite from heaven. God does not need to fall from heaven because he is everywhere present throughout his creation as a sustaining and animating force, and Christ as God is likewise universal, but his presence is hidden from human eyes. For that reason God has chosen to declare himself unto mankind at three loci of revelation. The first is Christ, in whom the Word was made flesh, The second is Scripture, where the Word uttered is recorded. The third is that sacrament, in which the Word is manifest in food and drink. The sacrament does not conjure up God as the witch of Endor but reveals him where he is.[82]

The revelation of the real presence of Christ in the sacrament, the faith–experience of Christ, the Augustinian mysticism, is extremely hard to understand because it is rooted in a motif quite foreign to most. In the early church, before the concept of the Trinity (One God yet three persons: Father, Son, Holy Spirit) became clear, the basic motif was that of God (the Father) who spoke His Word (the Logos: the Son and the Scripture) and the creativity/empowerment backing up the Word was the spirit (the Holy Ghost.) Therefore, Genesis 1:1 "In the beginning God created the heavens and the earth" meant God (the Father) said (spoke the Word) "let there be light" and there was light (both the true light which is Christ and the echoes of that light which the Holy Spirit makes into physical manifestations of that light). This is very hard to comprehend from our Aristotelian world view — where reality is the stuff of the universe, and ideas are but secondary guesses at the nature of the stuff. In contrast, Plato (Platonism, Neo–Platonism) and the Augustinian understands the reality as spiritual. Here the spiritual is the ideal, the essence and the reality. All subsequent manifestations

---

[82] Bainton, p. 140.

(material things) are approximations. In the creation example: the Light (lightness) is the spoken Word (Christ), whereas any light in creation is only an approximation of that light. Hence the sun, lightning, candle light, the light of inner human thought — they all have aspects of that real (spiritual) light but do not come close to fully embracing, comprehending, or being what the true real light is.

Martin Luther began his religious life as an Augustinian monk. It was here he by faith experienced through the sacrament Christ (who is always here), reveals himself to the believer and empowers him to obtain the forgiveness of sin. It is not because the Priest can magically "make God." The Priest cannot make the "sacrifice of Christ" That sacrifice was made once and for all time at the Cross. For Luther, Christ is present in the elements because Christ *declared the Word*, "This is my body." The Word declared — that is reality. Thus faith sees the sacrament as a channel to see Christ and receive his Grace. In the sacrament, Luther insisted on Christ's real presence and held that the Words of Christ empower forgiveness of sin. These two keys (real presence, empowerment by the Word) are clearly seen in Luther's shorter Catechism.

> Only scripture, *Sola Scriptura*, is Luther's basis for doctrine and teaching. Using the tools of exegesis Luther heavily employed reason (logical deduction from known premises). But all reason (common sense) gets dropped when the believer's faith must see the God-man through the sacrament. What God's Word says must be comprehended, even if it is incomprehensible. Therefore, faith takes it in and reason (man's common sense) gets overridden. With the Tri–unity there is but one God, yet three persons are seen in that God. Faith holds to it, even if it is unreasonable. Likewise, faith holds fast to Christ's word, "This is my body." This cannot be explained by reason or grammar. It is a matter of God–given faith to see this. "Faith is given to those who avail themselves of those outward rites which again God has ordained as organs of revelation, the sacraments."[83]

---

[83] Bainton, p. 224.

For although he is everywhere and in all creatures and I may find him in stone, fire, water, or rope, since he is assuredly there, yet he does not wish me to seek him apart from the Word, that I should throw myself into fire or water or hang myself with a rope. He is everywhere, but he does not desire that you should seek everywhere but only where the Word is. There if you seek him you will truly find, namely in the Word. These people do not know and see who say that it does not make sense that Christ should be in bread and wine. Of course Christ is with me in prison and the martyr's death, elsewhere should I be? He is truly present there with the Word, yet not in the same sense as in sacrament, because he has attached his body and blood to the Word and in the bread and wine is bodily to be received.[84]

Subsequent followers of Martin Luther view the risen human body of Christ Jesus as having a divine attribute of omnipresence. Technically this is called the communication of attributes, where the divine nature (i.e. ubiquity) gets imparted to the human finite body.[85] Hence they have

[84] Bainton, p.224.

[85] These insights into the development of Lutheran theology are paraphrased from Louis Berkhof, *The History of Christian Doctrines*, (Banner of Truth Trust, Carlisle, Pa, 1975), p. 115–116.

Communicatio idiomatum is the Lutheran doctrine that "each of Christ's natures permeates the other (*peridhoresis*), and that His humanity participates in the attributes of His divinity." (Neve, *Lutheran Symbolics*, p. 132). Divine attributes of omniscience, omnipresence, and omnipotence are ascribed to the human nature. There was hesitancy to ascribe human attributes to the divine nature. Eventually Lutherans fully dropped the idea of the divine participation in the human attributes.

Eventually Lutheran realized that logic required a communication of attributes at the time of the union of the two natures. But how then can they explain the humiliation of Jesus? Two schools diverged. The Giessen (primarily Chemnitz) taught that Christ had divine attributes received in the incarnation, but that He laid them aside or used them only occasionally. The other school Tuebingen (Brenz) taught that Christ always possessed the divine attributes, but concealed them, or used them only secretly. The Formula of Concord favored the Giessen view which ultimately became dominant. Quenstedt fashioned its most complete form; he views the divine powers in Christ's manhood as mere potentiality.[Berkof

both the corporeal human and divine body of Jesus over, in, around and through the bread. In Lutheran Theology, once the pastor speaks the Word, the Holy Spirit links the bread with Christ's body. Then the participant eats *both* bread and the body and blood of Jesus (who is over, in, through and around the bread). Rationally I see a type of impanation happening, so the human body of the risen Lord Jesus is not confined to a particular finite space. (It is as if the human nature took on the divine attribute of omnipresence). This is NOT just my rational explanation — Luther and others do it.[86] But I have found none who go so far as to logically say the risen human nature becomes infinite and

---

notes::] Beginning in the twenty-first century, Lutherans were discarding their view conforming to the Reformed view.

[86] The following expression of Lutheran theology is from an eight page monograph by Jonathan Leach. Who do You Say that I Am? A Study of Zwingli's Alloeosis and the Damage It does to the Doctrine of Christology. (This is no longer found on the internet.) Both Zwingli and Luther hold that Christ is both God and man in one person. When approaching difficult topics, Zwingli emphasized the individual roles of the two natures (divine and human) and Luther emphasizes the union of the God-man. In the following formal statement of Lutheran Christology, you will see this Lutheran emphasis on the union.

Lutherans understand that the Word became flesh (John 1:10). When God became man, Jesus, the Son of God assumed a non–personal (not an existing person) human nature and was united with it in the one person, Jesus Christ. Chemnitz explains the result of this union...

"These two natures in Christ do not subsist individually, by themselves, or separately, so that there is one Christ the God and another person who is Christ the man; but they are united into one hypostasis or person, so that there is one Christ who is at the same time God and man...[for] as Luther rightly says, the hypostatic union does not permit the kind of division whereby I can properly say that the divine nature of Christ does this or the human nature does that." [Martin Chemnitz, *The Two Natures of Christ*, trans. By J. A. O. Preus. (St Louis: Concordia Publishing House, 1971), p.162–163].

Because of this union, there is a communication of attributes which takes place within the person.

The Lutheran dogmaticians break down the communication of attributes into three classes: *genus idiomaticum*, *genus maiestaticum*, and *genus apotelesmaticum*. The *genus idiomaticum* states that "attributes belonging essentially only to one nature (divine: omnipotence, omniscience. Human: being born, dying) are always ascribed to the whole person of the God-man. (John Jeske, "The Communication of Attributes in the God-man Christ Jesus," 1974, p. 3).

The union of the two natures is not such that the two natures mix or become something entirely different (cf. Eutychianism). Rather, the individual natures retain their essence and at the same time communicate their attributes to the God-man....

The *genus maestaticum* states that the "human nature shares in the divine power, knowledge, and glory of the Son of God." [Jeske, p.4]...

The implications of the *genus maiestaticum* are far reaching. Jesus Christ the God-man, is omnipotent (has power to take his life up again) [John 10:9–10], omniscient (he knew their thoughts), omnipresent ('I will be with you always' Matthew 9:4), and deserving of the divine honor of God [John 5:23].

The applications of this teaching extend beyond the brief scope of this paper; allow one example to suffice; The sacrament of the Eucharist. If an individual holds a view in line with Zwingli's alloeosis, they (usually) will teach that Christ's human body was separated at the time of his death and was seated at God's right hand where it remains to this day. This is also in keeping with their view that God is omnipresent only according to his divine nature. Guided by this misunderstanding, they are horrified at the Lutheran doctrine of Real Presence.

[we skip the quote of a Reformed theologian to prove his point. — My insertion]

"If we take 'This is my body' and 'This is my blood' literally [letterally], an absurdity results. If Jesus meant that the bread and wine were at that moment in the upper room actually his body and his blood, he was asserting that his flesh and blood were in two places simultaneously, since his corporeal form was right there beside the elements. To believe that Jesus was in two places at once is something of a denial of the incarnation, which limited his physical human nature to one location." [Millard J. Erickson, *The Word Became Flesh*, (Grand Rapids, Michigan: Baker Book House, 1985), vol 3, p. 1121.

In spite of this, Lutherans boldly cling to the Real Presence. Why? *Sola Scriptura*. It goes back to the Marburg colloquy. Zwingli's reason needed to deny that 'is' means 'is' because according to his human nature, Christ's body was in heaven and ... could not be everywhere on earth in a sacramental presence.... Luther, however, had no need to change the words from their intended meaning. Luther understood that the union of the two natures in Christ was inseparable. He recognized that the human nature received gifts from the divine nature, such as omnipresence [This is not intended to suggest ubiquity. See his endnote.] He understood that while his Christology required faith (as also the doctrine of the Holy Trinity), Scripture was the only authoritative source for teaching. He must hold his reason captive to Scripture. 'Is' must mean 'is.'

Finally, the *genus apotelesmaticum* emphasizes that "Christ performs all his official acts according to both natures, each nature contributing its proper share to the act in intimate communion with the other." [Jeske, p.5]. This emphasizes that when Christ does an official act, such as Prophet, Priest, or King, he does it as the God-man. For example, Paul wrote to Timothy about Christ's act as mediator and both the divine and human natures are emphasized in the verse. "For there is One *God* and one mediator between God and men, the *man* Christ Jesus," 1 Timothy 2:5.

hence is no longer fully human. Why do not they admit it? Because the Creeds declare unorthodox anyone who separates or mixes the fully human and fully divine natures of Christ.[87] Berkhof notes, beginning

---

"Who do you say that I am?" Do you join in with Peter's confession?: "You are the Christ, the Son of the living God!" [Matthew 16:16]. Or do you hold to Ulrich Zwingli's view, who could rightly agree with any statement of/about Christ, but only by means of *alloeosis*?

Zwingli cannot say that God died, because that is irrational. Lutherans agree that God by his very essence cannot die, thus we do not claim that the 'Godhead' died. And yet, in Christ, God and man are inseparably united together so that the God-man died, that is, God died. That is why Peter can say that the Jews "killed the author of life," [Acts 3:15]. Paul reinforces God's death (and our redemption) when he states that God's own blood paid our ransom. "Be shepherds of the church of God, which he bought with his own blood." [Acts 20:28].

If you carry out Zwingli's view to its conclusion, that God did not die and Christ only died according to the human nature, then only a man died. And if only a man died, then our faith is futile and we are still in our sins, [1 Corinthians 15:17]. It is only because of the unique union of both natures in Christ that we are reconciled to God. By virtue of his human nature, he endured the temptation and suffering in our place and yet lived a perfect life. By virtue of his divine nature, his life, death and resurrection are for all people.... [End of quoting Leach]

In summary, the above work clearly shows that Lutheran emphasis on the hypostatic union. The Reformed and Zwingian emphasis is on the two distinct natures.

[87] The most complete Reformed statement on the one person, but two natures of Christ is found in Heinrich Bullinger, **The Second Helvetic Confession,** 1566, chapter XI. Jesus Christ true God and Man, and the only Savior of the World. I quote a few lines. This translation is from Philip Schaff, *Creeds of Christendom* 3 volumes, 6th edition. (New York, Harper and Row, 1931) vol 1. p. 402–404. (The entire volume is on the internet at: https://ccel.org/ccel/schaff/creeds1 and is well worth a careful study.)

> "Therefore the Son, according to his Divinity, is coequal and consubstantial with the Father; true God, not merely by name or adoption or by conferring of a dignity, but in essence and nature. …

Hence we acknowledge in one and the same Lord Jesus Christ two natures, a divine and a human, which are conjoined and united in one person without absorption or confusion and mixture. …

We worship one Lord Christ, not two; one true God-Man, coequal (or of one substance, consubstantialis, ὁμοούσιος) with the Father as regards his divine nature, and coequal with us men, sin only excepted (Heb. iv. 15), as regards his human nature."

The Second Helvetic Confession, chapter 11 Unorthodox Advocates Named

in the twenty-first century, Lutheran theologians trended away from omnipresence of Christ's body conforming to the Reformed view of Holy Communion.[88]

Martin Luther Critiqued

At the Diet of Worms in 1521, Luther famously said, "Unless I am convinced from Scripture and plain reason … Here I stand. I cannot do otherwise. God help me. Amen."[89] Luther needed the tools of exegesis and the reasoning behind them to get to rightly understand God's written word. Luther reasoned enough to form his theology of the Eucharist, but Luther would not let Zwingli logically push him to the grammar or rational consequences of his "faith" position. Martin Luther's view of the sacrament is a theology of the Word and individual faith, not of reason or logic. For Luther, true faith holds to what the

Unorthodox by Denying	Advocate
Full deity of the Son of God	Arius, Servetus
Virgin conception by the Holy Spirit	Ebionites (taught Jesus was natural son of Joseph & Mary)
Faith in Christ as Savior from sin	Gnostic (taught knowledge saves)
God of OT is God of Jesus	Valentinus, Marcion (taught OT god is a lesser diety)
True humanity (His soul had reason)	Apollinaris (Jesus had human body & soul, but divine mind)
His flesh had a soul & could suffer	Eunomius
One person. Unity of the God–man	Nestorius (stressed the two natures, not hypostatic union.)
Jesus:1 person, 2 true natures	Eutychianism, Monothellitism, Monophysitism (hybrid mix)

[88] Berkhof, p. 116.
[89] At the Diet of Worms, January 27 to May 25, 1521 Luther stood on reason and of course the Scriptures. "Unless I am convicted by the Scripture and plain reason I do not accept the authority of popes and councils, for they have contradicted each other — my conscience is captive to the Word of God. I cannot and I will not recant anything, for to go against conscience is neither right nor safe. God help me. Amen."
The first printed version added the words, "Here I stand I cannot do otherwise." The words, though not recorded on the spot, may nevertheless be genuine, because the listeners at the moment may have been too moved to write. Roland Bainton, *Here I Stand. A Life of Martin Luther*, Abingdon–Cokesbury Press, NY, 1950, p.185.

Word has declared, even if it does not make rational sense. When our experience and the Scriptural explanation of the experience match, then there is authentication that the experience is understood correctly. Luther's experience of God in the sacrament, and his matching of "this is my body" with that experience precluded him from accepting any other view.[90]

He also knew enough church history, to step carefully so none would charge him with doctrinal heresy claiming he mixed the divine and human nature of Christ. All orthodoxy has divine presence of Christ in/with/through the Eucharist. They agree on the spiritual benefits the human Jesus accomplished as sin–bearer at Calvary. They differ as to their understanding of Jesus's presence in the ceremony of the Eucharist.

Luther sought to avoid non–biblical philosophies. Luther's emphasis on the words spoken to trigger an individual's faith and his exegesis elucidating Scriptural insights on the Eucharist are superb. His Word theology (God said it, that settles it) lends itself to a dogmatic interpretation that is frustrating to rationally and analytically handle. Studying his mystical roots in Augustinian Platonism are mind boggling. Luther is right to hold to what Scripture clearly says.

I do not like Luther's or subsequent Lutheran expansion of the finiteness of the humanity of the risen Lord Jesus into near ubiquity. For how can a human body, defined as visible with flesh and bone, be redefined as almost ubiquitous and invisible? They make a spirit out of Christ's flesh. To me, he mixed the divine and human natures of Christ. From his perspective, he was understanding things the way he saw them — stressing the unity of Christ the God-man and maintaining Christ's body was with the bread in the Lord's Supper. As Calvin says of a Lutheran, "removing the distinction between the natures and urging the unity of the person, he made man out of God and God out of man."[91]

---

[90] H. Boehmer, *Luther in the Light of Modern Research* (Tr. E. S.G. Potter, New York: Dial Press, 1930), p. 241 writes, "Luther felt the inward need not only to think the personal communion with his Lord and Master but actually to experience it through communion. Zwingli did not understand this need at all. Calvin, as Luther realized at once, not only understood it but felt it himself."

[91] John Calvin, *Institutes of the Christian Religion*, ed. John T. McNeill, (Philadelphia: Westminster Press), 1960, p. 4.17.30. Hereafter referred to as *Institutes*.

"This is my body" is not taken as letterally as Luther claimed. He correctly retained bread throughout the ceremony, but he added words and his reasoning to get his theology with those words. "This [bread] is [with] my body." Like Calvin, Luther should say, a synecdoche or metonymy is at work. For although the bread is a symbol of the body of Christ, their association is so strong and close that it is an easy transition to speak of one for the other. Paul does this in 1 Corinthians 10:16–17, "is not the bread that we break a participation in the body of Christ? Because there is one loaf, we, who are many, are one body, for we all share the one loaf" (NIV).

Still, Luther is a member of the orthodox house of faith, as I judge. Yet Luther drew the orthodox line differently. Consider the Marburg Colloquy (Oct. 1–3, 1529) where Landgrave Philip of Hesse sought to unite the Protestants[92] against the growing intolerance of the Catholics. Notables[93] came. All earnestly desired union. Luther and Zwingli agreed on 14 points of doctrine. But when it came to the 15th point (on the Eucharist), they agreed only on 1/3 of that point.[94] Luther took a piece of

---

[92] At the first Diet of Speyer (also spelled Speier and Spire) the 1526 decision was to allow each Prince to order ecclesiastical affairs in his own state in accord with his own conscience. decision. Tacit toleration (or liberty) was extended to those not of that fiefdom. The second Diet of Speyer convened on February 21,1529. It was controlled by a well organized Catholic majority. They legislated the end of all toleration of Lutherans in Catholic districts; yet toleration and liberty must be extended to Catholics in Lutheran districts.

On April 16,1529 six princes and fourteen cities made a formal protest to Archduke Ferdinand. From this point on Evangelicals became known as Protestants because they *testified* to the unfair arrangement; they *testified* correctly that the majority of one diet could not rescind the unanimous action of the previous assembly. Thus they appealed to the emperor not so much in protest, but as bearing witness of the injustice of the second Diet of Speyer.

[93] Luther and Melanchthon represented Saxony, Zwingli came from Zurich, Oekolampadius from Basel, Bucer from Strassburg. Other Lutherans were Jonas, Brenz, Cruciger and Osiander; other Reformers were Capito and John Sturm.

[94] Paraphrasing Bainton, p. 319–320. Luther almost went along with the accord according to Bucer. Oekolampadius held the body of Christ has ascended into heaven, the flesh profits nothing, the words had to be taken metaphorically. Luther retorted then why not take the ascension of Christ metaphorically. Zwingli went to the problem by affirming that flesh and spirit are incompatible. Therefore the presence of Christ can only be spiritual. Luther replies that flesh and spirit can be conjoined and the spiritual, which no one denied, does not exclude the physical.

chalk and drew a circle on the table. He wrote inside that circle, "This is

---

Although deadlocked, huge gains had been made. Zwingli advanced from the Lord's Supper as only a memorial to the position that Christ is spiritually present. Luther conceded that whatever the nature of the physical presence, it is of no benefit without faith — thus excluding magical views. Hence they agreed that transubstantiation was not correct. The Lutherans then proposed a formula of concord. They acknowledged that they had not properly understood the Swiss view. For themselves, they declared that "Christ is truly present, that is substantively, essentially," even though it is not "quantitatively, qualitatively, or locally" present. The Swiss rejected this for two reasons. It did not protect the spiritual character of the Lord's Supper. It did not make sense that something could be present but not locally present. Luther resorted to a faith response saying that geometrical conceptions cannot be used to describe the presence of God. The hope for a common confession was dead.

Still the Swiss offered intercommunion in spite of the differences. According to Bucer, Luther momentarily agreed — "until Melancthon interposed out of regard for Ferdinand and the emperor." Evidently Melancthon still hoped that the Catholics and the Lutherans could be reconciled, but knew that was impossible if Luther united with the Swiss Reformers. Still it is noteworthy that Luther at first was willing to enter into agreement to have a consolidated Protestantism.

Eventually Melancthon's approach to reconcile with the Catholics failed, and union of the Protestants was resumed at the Wittenberg Concord (1536). There Melanchthon and Luther stated essentially the Lutheran position but without insistence of the ubiquity of Christ's body. That removed one of the Swiss objections. Still this concord failed because the Swiss Zwinglians still felt the spiritual nature of the Lord's Supper was not preserved.

However the account by Schaff. p. 620–650, has Luther always opposed to union at Marburg. When forced, Luther wrote this summary on the Supper:

We all believe, with regard to the Supper of our blessed Lord Jesus "Christ, that it ought to be celebrated in both kinds, according to the institution of Christ; that the Mass is not a work by which a Christian obtains pardon for another man, whether dead or alive; that the sacrament of the altar is the sacrament of the very body and very blood of Jesus Christ; and that the spiritual manducation of this body and blood is especially necessary to every true Christian. In like manner, as to the use of the sacrament, we are agreed that, like the word, it was ordained of Almighty God, in order that weak consciences might be excited by the Holy Ghost to faith and charity.

And although at the present we are not agreed on the question whether the real body and blood of Christ are corporally present in the bread and wine, yet both parties shall cherish Christian charity for one another, so far as the conscience of each will permit, and both parties will earnestly implore Almighty God to strengthen us by his Spirit in the true understanding. Amen.

The two unresolved issues were the physical human presence of Christ and whether the eating of the elements involved chewing (manducation) on that physical body.

my body." Luther insisted his understanding was neither metaphorical nor a synecdoche. Luther held to this by faith and experience. By faith you ate bread and you ate the God-man (both the deity and the humanity because they are inseparably combined.)

Zwingli maintained 1) communion is a sign or seal of divine grace already available to the believer and 2) the bread and wine were symbols of the body and blood of Christ, who was locally present in His own human body in heaven and not on earth. With or without the elements, as the believer exercises his faith (by remembering what Christ has done for him), the Holy Spirit administers spiritual union with the Father and the Son, — and the Holy Spirit spiritually brings the benefits of Christ's death to the believer. This is a spiritual feast. The risen human body of Christ Jesus was only at the right hand of the Father in heaven and by reason was therefore NOT in the Eucharist.[95] Zwingli saw Christ's spiritual presence, but not Christ's humanity in the sacrament, so Luther judged Zwingli as having a different spirit [non-Christian]. This set the stage for church splits which have continued into the twentieth century. Ironically Marburg also initiated attempts to get confessional and consensus on theological issues.

On October 16, 1529, Luther modified the 15 Marburg articles into the 17 Articles of Schwabach which became the basis for membership in the Lutheran League of the Northern German States. These articles became the basis for the Augsburg Confession (1530).

Martin Luther: On the Sacrament of the Altar[96]

What is the Sacrament of the Altar?
>It is the true body and blood of our Lord Jesus Christ under the bread and wine, for us Christians to eat and to drink, instituted by Christ Himself.

---

[95] The angel said to Mary, "He is risen, he is not here" (Mark 16:6). Implying that the human risen body of Jesus is not everywhere, but it finitely localized.

[96] *Dr. Martin Luther's Small Catechism* with an American Translation text, (New Haven, Missouri: Leader Publishing Co., 1971), p. 20–21.

Where is this written?

> The holy Evangelists Matthew, Mark, Luke, and St. Paul [the Apostle] write: Our Lord Jesus Christ, the same night He was betrayed, took bread. He gave thanks, broke it, and gave it to His disciples, saying, "Take, eat; this is My body, which is given for you. Do this to remember Me."
>
> He did the same with the cup after the supper. He took it, gave thanks, and gave it to them, saying, "Drink of it, all of you. This cup is the new covenant in My blood, poured out for you to forgive sins. Every time you drink it, do it to remember Me."

What is the benefit of such eating and drinking?

> That is shown us by these words, "Poured out for you to forgive sins"; namely, that in the Sacrament forgiveness of sins, life, and salvation are given us through these words. For where there is forgiveness of sins, there is also life and salvation.

How can bodily eating and drinking do such great things?

> It is not the eating drinking indeed that does them, but the words here written, "Poured out for you to forgive sins"; which words, besides the bodily eating and drinking, are the chief thing in the Sacrament; and he that believes these words has what they say and express, namely, the forgiveness sins.

Who, then, receives such Sacrament worthily?

> Fasting and bodily preparation are indeed a fine outward training; but he is truly worthy and well prepared who has faith in these words, "Poured out for you to forgive sins."
>
> But he that does not believe these words, or doubts, is unworthy and unprepared; for the words "for you" require all hearts to believe.
>
> > [End of Martin Luther: Words on the Sacrament of the Lord's Supper.]

Martin Luther: Christian Questions with Their Answers[97]

for those who intend to go to the Sacrament

1. Do you believe that you are a sinner?
   Yes, I believe it; I am a sinner.

2. How do you know this?
   From the Ten Commandments' these I have not kept.

3. Are you also sorry for your sins?
   Yes, I am sorry that I have sinned against God.

4. What have you deserved of God by your sins?
   His wrath and displeasure, temporal death, and eternal
   damnation. Rom. 6:21,23

5. Do you also hope to be saved?
   Yes, such is my hope.

6. In whom, then, do you trust?
   In my dear Lord Jesus Christ.

7. Who is Christ?
   The Son of God, true God and man.

8. How many Gods are there?
   Only one; but there are three Persons: Father, Son, and
   Holy Ghost.

9. What, then, has Christ done for you that you trust in Him?
   He died for me and shed His blood for me on the cross
   for the forgiveness of sins.

---

[97] *Dr. Martin Luther's Small Catechism*, p. 31–36.

10. Did the Father also die for you?

> He did not; for the Father is God only, the Holy Ghost likewise; but the Son is true God and true man; He died for me and shed His blood for me.

11. How do you know this?

> From the holy Gospel and from the words of the Sacrament, and by His body and blood given me as a pledge in the Sacrament.

12. How do those words read?

> Our Lord Jesus Christ, the same night He was betrayed, took bread. He gave thanks, broke it, and gave it to His disciples, saying, "Take, eat; this is My body, which is given for you. Do this to remember Me."

> He did the same with the cup after the supper. He took it, gave thanks, and gave it to them, saying, "Drink of it, all of you. This cup is the new covenant in My blood, poured out for you to forgive sins. Every time you drink it, do it to remember Me."

13. You believe, then, that the true body and blood of Christ are in the Sacrament?

> Yes, I believe it.

14. What induces you to believe this?

> The word of Christ, "Take, eat' this is my body"; "Drink of it, all of you. This is My blood."

15. What ought we to do when we eat His body and drink His blood, and thus receive the pledge?

> We ought to remember and proclaim His death and the shedding of His blood, as He taught us: "Every time you drink it, do it to remember Me."

16. Why should we remember and proclaim His death?

That we may learn to believe that no creature could make satisfaction for our sins but Christ, true God and man; and that we may learn to look with terror at our sins, and to regard them as great indeed, and to find joy and comfort in Him alone, and thus be saved through such faith.

17. What was it that moved Him to die and make satisfaction for your sins?

His great love to His Father and to me and other sinners, as it is written in John 14; Rom. 5; Gal. 2; Eph. 5.

18.Finally, why do you wish to go to the Sacrament?

That I may learn to believe that Christ died for my sin out of great love, as before said; and that I may also learn of Him to love God and my neighbor.

19. What should admonish and incite a Christian to receive the Sacrament frequently?

In respect to God, both the command and the promise of Christ the Lord should move him, and in respect to himself, the trouble that lies heavy on him, on account of which such command, encouragement, and promise are given.

20. But what shall a person do if he be not sensible of such trouble and feel no hunger and thirst for the Sacrament?

To such a person no better advice can be given than that, in the first place, he put his hand into his bosom, and feel whether he still have flesh and blood, and that he by all means believe what the ? Scriptures say of it in Gal. 5 and Rom 7.

Secondly, that he look around to see whether he is still in the world, and keep in mind that there will be no lack of sin and trouble, as the Scriptures say in John 15 and 16; 1 John 2 and 5.

Thirdly, he will certainly have the devil also about him, who with his lying and murdering, day and night, will let him have no peace within or without, as the Scriptures picture him in John 8 and 16; 1 Peter 5; Eph. 6; 2 Tim. 2.

NOTE

These questions and answers are no child's play, but are drawn up with great earnestness of purpose by the venerable and pious Dr. Luther for both young and old. Let each one take heed and likewise consider it a serious matter; for St. Paul writes to the Galatians 6 "Don't make a mistake; you can't fool God." [End of Martin Luther: Christian Questions with Their Answers.]

Missouri Synod Lutheran Catechism

They name their catechism *Dr. Martin Luther's Small Catechism*.[98] I quote sections 242-243 and 296-328.

Note: Lutherans speak only of "Christ" stressing the unity of the God-man. They emphasize the real presence of Christ. While they eat bread and wine naturally (306); they supernaturally receive in faith Christ's body and blood which is eaten by mouth (307, 308). They stress forgiveness of sin because the Word has spoken it and faith partakes of it. [All **bold**, *italic* and NOTE in this section are markings made by the Missouri Synod Lutherans.].

The Sacraments

242. What do we mean by the Sacrament?

By a Sacrament we mean a *sacred act* —

A. Instituted *by God Himself*;

---

[98] *Dr. Martin Luther's Small Catechism* with an American Translation text, (New Haven, Missouri: Leader Publishing Co., 1971).The translation by William F. Beck is An American Translation (AAT). The questions and answers are from Dr. Heinrich C. Schwan and other official revisers and Christian innovators.

B. In which there are *certain visible means connected with His Word*; and

C. By which God *offers, gives,* and *seals* unto us *the forgiveness of sins* which Christ has earned for us.

243. How many such Sacraments are. there?

There are *only two* such Sacraments, Holy Baptism and the Lord's Supper.

The Sacrament of the Altar

296. By what other means is the Sacrament of the Altar know?

The Sacrament of the Altar is known also as the *Lord's Supper,* the *Lord's Table, Holy Communion,* the *Breaking of Bread,* and the *Eucharist.*

> 673　When you meet, you can't be eating the Lord's Supper 1 Cor.11:20
>
> 674　You can't share the Lord's table and the table of devils. 1 Cor 10:21.
>
> 675　All of us are one body, because there is one bread and all of us share that one bread. 1 Cor 10:17 (communion).
>
> NOTE.—See 1 Cor.10:16
>
> 676　They were loyal to what the apostles taught in their fellowship, in breaking bread, and in praying. Acts 2:42
>
> 677　He gave thanks, broke it. 1 Cor 11:24. (Eucharist.)
>
> NOTE.—Matt. 26:26–28. Mark 14:22–24. Luke 22:19–20. 1 Cor. 11:23–25

297. Who instituted this Sacrament?

Our Lord Jesus Christ, the *truthful, all-wise,* and *almighty God-man,* has instituted this Sacrament.

> 678　The LORD is right in what He says, and you can trust everything He does. Ps 33:4.
>
> 679　Now to Him who by the power working in us can do far, far more than anything we ask or imagine, to Him be glory in the Church. Amen. Eph. 3:20–21.

298. What are the visible means (elements) in this Sacrament?

The visible means are *bread*, prepared of flour, and *wine*, the fruit of the vine.

299. What does Christ give us in, with, and under these visible means in the Lord's Supper?

In, with, and under the *bread* Christ gives us His *true body*; in, with, and under the *wine* He gives us His *true blood*. (Real Presence).

300. Why do you believe in the real presence of Christ's body and blood in the Lord's Supper?

I believe in the real presence —

A. Because Jesus says, "This is My body, which is given for you; This cup is the new covenant in My blood, poured out for you to forgive sins" (Matt. 26:26–28; Mark 14:22–24; Luke 22:19–20; 1 Cor. 11:24–25);

B. Because the Bible states that the cup is the *communion* of the blood of Christ and that the bread is the *communion* of the body of Christ;

680   Is the cup of blessing which we bless not a communion of the blood of Christ? Is he bread not a communion of the body of Christ? 1 Cor. 10:16

C. Because the Bible states that *unworthy communicants are guilty*, not of the bread and wine, but *of the body and blood of Christ.*

681   Then anyone who eats the bread or drinks the Lord's cup in an unworthy way is sinning against the Lord's body and blood 1 Cor. 11:27

D. Because no man has the right to change the meaning of a *divine institution and testament.*

682   This is My blood of the covenant. Mark 14:24.

683   Once a will is ratified, even if it's only a man's will, nobody sets it aside or adds to it. Gal. 3:15.

301. Are bread and wine changed into the body and blood of Christ?

Bread and wine are *not changed* into the body and blood of Christ; for the Bible expressly declares that *bread and wine are still present in the Sacrament.*

> 684 Every time you eat this bread and drink the cup, you are telling how the Lord died, till He comes. Then anyone who eats the bread or drinks the Lord's cup in an unworthy way is sinning against the Lord's body and blood. Examine yourself and then eat some of the bread and drink from the cup. 1 Cor. 11:26–28.

> 685 Is the cup of blessing which we bless not a communion of the blood of Christ? Is the bread which we break not a communion of the body of Christ? 1 Cor. 10:16;

302. For what use does Christ, our Lord, in with, and under the bread and wine give us Christians His body and His blood?

Christ gives us Christians His body and His blood *to eat and to drink.*

303. Should all communicants receive also the wine ?

All communicants should *receive the wine* as well as the bread, because the Lord said, "Drink of it, all of you." Matt. 26:27

> 686 They all drank of it. Mark 14:23.

NOTE—See 684.

304. Are we to adore the bread and the wine in the Sacrament?

We are *not to adore* the bread and the wine; for the Lord has declared that we should *eat* the bread and *drink* the wine.

305. Is the Sacrament to be regarded as an unbloody sacrifice for the wins of the living and the dead?

The idea that the Sacrament is a real, though unbloody, sacrifice for the sins of the living and the dead is *contrary to the Word of God*, which teaches that Christ's *one sacrifice* made full atonement for *all sins.*

> 687 By one sacrifice He forever made perfect those who are made holy ... Now where sins are forgiven, there is no more sacrificing for sin. Heb. 10:14, 18.

306. In what manner are bread and wine received by the communicant?
    Bread and wine are received by the communicant *like any other food, in a natural manner.*

307. How are Christ's body and blood received by the communicant?
    Like bread and wine, Christ's body and blood are received by the communicant *with his mouth*, but in a *supernatural manner.*

308. What do we call the eating and drinking of Christ's body and blood in, with, and under the bread and wine?
    We call this eating and drinking a *sacramental eating and drinking* because it takes place only *in the Sacrament of the Altar.*

309. What does Christ, our Lord, require when He says, "Do this to remember Me"?
    When the Lord says, "Do this to remember Me." He requires that this *Sacrament should forever be administered* in His Church and that we should *especially remember* and *proclaim His death* when we partake of the Lord's Supper.

    688   Every time you eat this bread and drink the cup, you are
            telling how the Lord died, till He comes. 1 Cor.11:26.

310. When only have we the true Lord's Supper?
    We have the true Lord's Supper *only* when we administer it *according to Christ's institution*; for He said, "Do this."

311. Are we to receive the Lord's Supper once in our life, as we do Baptism?
    We should receive the Lord's Supper *frequently*; for St. Paul says, "*Every time* you eat this bread and drink the cup."

312. Why should we receive the Lord's Supper frequently?
    We should receive the Lord's Supper frequently because—

A. Christ *commands*, or urgently invites us saying, "Do this in remembrance of Me";

689   Every time you drink it, do it to remember Me. Every time you eat this bread and drink the cup, you are telling how the Lord died till He comes. 1 Cor. 11:25–26.

690   They were loyal to what the apostles taught in their fellowship, in breaking of bread, and in praying. Acts 2:42.

B. Christ *promises* to bestow upon us His blessings, "Poured out for you to forgive sins";

691   Come to me, all you who are working hard and carrying a heavy load, and I will give you rest. Matt. 11:28.

C. *We need* the forgiveness of sins and the strength to resist the devil, the world, and our flesh.
1NOTE —See No. 20 under [Luther's] Christian Questions [with Their Answers.]

313. What do these words, "Poured out for you to forgive sins," tell us?
    These words tell us that in the Sacrament Christ gives to *every* communicant as a *pledge* of the remission of sins that *same body and blood* with which *He earned for us* the forgiveness of sins.

314. What do we receive together with the forgiveness of sins?
    "Where there is forgiveness of sins, there is *also life and salvation*."

315. For what purpose, then, do we approach the Lord's Table?
    We approach the Lord's Table —
    A. Chiefly to receive forgiveness of our sins and thus to be *strengthened in our faith* in our Lord Jesus Christ.

692   This is My body, which is given for you. Do this to remember Me ... This cup is the new covenant in My blood, poured out for you. Luke 22:19–20

B. To *obtain strength for a holier life*

693   He died for all that those who live should no longer
      live for themselves but for Him who died and rose for
      them … So if anyone is in Christ, he is a new being. 2
      Corinthians 5:15–17

C. To bear testimony that we are of one faith with those
who commune with us.
NOTE—See 1 Cor. 10:17; Acts 2:42.

316. Has eating and drinking the power to impart the forgiveness of
sins?

It is not the eating and drinking indeed that imparts the
forgiveness of sins.

317. How, then, does the Sacrament impart such forgiveness of sins?

By His words "Poured out for you to forgive sins" Christ
has placed the forgiveness of sins into the Sacrament, and
there *He offers, gives, and seals* it to all communicants.
These words, therefore, are the *chief thing* in the
Sacrament.

318. How do we receive this benefit?

We receive this benefit *only by believing these words*,
"poured out for you to forgive sins."

319. Why should we consider the true worthiness of a communicant?

We should consider this because St. Paul expressly
instructs us: "Examine yourself and then eat some
of the bread and drink from the cup. Anyone who
eats and drinks without seeing that the body is there
is condemned for his eating and drinking" (1 Cor.
11:28–29).

320. Is it necessary to fast before partaking of the Sacrament?

Christ *nowhere commands nor forbids* us to fast.

321. Is any other bodily preparation commanded for true worthiness?

No other bodily preparation is commanded for true worthiness; but a proper regard for the Lord's Supper should induce us to appear at the Lord's Table with *modesty* and *reverence*.

322. In what does true worthiness consist?

True worthiness consists *in faith* in these words, "Poured out for you to forgive sins."

323. Who is unworthy and unprepared?

A person who *does not believe* these words, "Poured out for you to forgive sins," or *who doubts* these words, is unworthy and unprepared. For the words "for you" require all hearts to believe.

324. How should we examine ourselves before partaking of Communion?

We should examine ourselves to see —

A. Whether we *truly repent* of our sins;

B. Whether we *believe* in Jesus Christ as our Savior;

C. Whether we have the good and earnest purpose with the aid of God the Holy Spirit henceforth to *amend* our sinful lives.

NOTE.— As a preparation for Holy Communion use [Luther's] Christian Questions [with Their answers].

325. May believers whose faith is weak approach the Lord's Table?

Believers whose faith is weak should indeed come to the Lord's Supper *that their faith may grow stronger.*

694 I believe; help my unbelief. Mark 9:24.

695 He will not break off a broken reed or put out a dimly burning wick. Isaiah 42:3.

696 Anyone who comes to me I will never turn away. John 6:37.

326. To whom must the Lord's supper be denied—

A. To those who are known to be *ungodly* and *impenitent*;

697   Anyone who eats and drinks without seeing that the body is there is condemned for his eating and drinking. 1 Cor. 11:29.

B. To those who have given offense and have not removed it;

698   So if you're bringing your gift to the altar and remember there that your brother has something against you, leave your gift there before the altar and go. First make up with your brother, and then come and offer your gift. Matt. 5:23–24.

C. To those who are not able to examine themselves, such as children and adults who have not been sufficiently instructed, and persons who are unconscious;

699   Examine yourself and then eat some of the bread and drink from the cup.

D. To those of a different, since the Lord's supper is a testimony of the *unity of faith*.

700   They were loyal to what the apostles taught in their fellowship, in breaking of bread, and in praying. Acts 2:42.

701   I urge you, fellow Christians, to watch those who cause disagreements and make people fall by going against the teaching you learned. Turn away from them. Rom. 16:17 (Close Communion.)

327. What do we ask of all those who wish to commune at our altars?
We ask that they make their intention known to the pastor, so that he may have opportunity to speak to them in the interest of their spiritual welfare.

328. Whom do we admit to the Lord's Table?
We admit to the Lord's Table those who have received sufficient instruction and have given an account of their faith.

[End of quotes from Missouri Synod Lutheran catechism]

Luther and the Reformation

Before the Reformation, the supplicant's time spent in church witnessed a show. He did not have to understand what the priest said. The ceremony was in Latin, a language he did not understand. The spectator did not have to know what the priest did. He could listen to the choir, take in the beauty surrounding the house of God, he did not have to figure out the magic of the priest changing the substance of bread to the substance of Christ. Like a circus show, he could take in what he wanted. All he had to know was what to DO. At the right time open his mouth and receive the forgiveness of sin. Christ and the cross had something to do with it. He trusted the Church and did what the Church told him to do. The Catholic theology taught that

> "The sacraments cannot be impaired by any human weakness, be it the unworthiness of the performer or the indifference of the receiver. The sacrament operates by virtue of a power within itself *ex opere operate*. In Luther's eyes such a view made the sacrament mechanical and magical. He, too, had no mind to subject it to human frailty and would not concede that he had done so by positing the necessity of faith, since faith is itself a gift of God, but this faith is given by God when, where, and to whom he will and even without the sacrament is efficacious; whereas the reverse is not true, that the sacrament is of efficacy without faith. "I may be wrong on indulgences," declared Luther, "but as to the need for faith in the sacraments I will die before I will recant." This insistence upon faith diminished the role of the priest who may place a wafer in the mouth but cannot engender faith in the heart".[99]

With Luther, the supplicant had to understand. He listened to the preaching of God's word and responded in faith. He entered into the worship and sang praise of His God. The Eucharist gave him forgiveness

---

[99] Roland H. Bainton, p. 138.

of sin, because Christ's Word put the power into the ceremony and his faith unlocked that power. Hence the reformation shifted the emphasis from spectator to participator; from watcher and taker — to experiencing that Word (Christ) by faith. Other Evangelical innovations included catechisms so families could instruct their children, congregation participation in the worship, educational emphasis so the laymen could read the Scriptures and also provide a basis for educated clergy since the monastery system had collapsed. Married clergy again became the norm, returning to the Jewish example.

"These were Luther's religious principles: that religion is paramount, that Christianity is the sole true religion to be apprehended by faith channeled through Scripture, preaching and sacrament."[100] God can only be known through Christ. Christ is only known through faith, a God given gift. The *Word* encompasses all of the God ordained channels of God's self-disclosure.

> It [the *Word*] is not to be equated with Scripture nor with the sacraments, yet it operates through them and not apart from them. The *Word* is not the Bible as a written book because "the gospel is really not that which is contained in books and composed in letters, but rather an oral preaching and a living word, a voice which resounds throughout the whole world and is publicly proclaimed." This Word must be heard. This Word must be pondered. "Not through thought, wisdom, and will does the faith of Christ arise in us, but through an incomprehensible and hidden operation of the Spirit, which is given by faith in Christ only at the hearing of the Word and without any other work of ours." More, too, than mere reading is required. "No one is taught through much reading and thinking. There is a much higher school where one learns God's Word. One must go into the wilderness. Then Christ comes and one becomes able to judge the world."[101]

---

[100] Bainton, p. 225.
[101] Bainton, p. 224 quoting Luther's Works, 17.154; 5.550; 9.610; 19.492.

E. John Calvin

Regarding the mystery of the sacrament, Calvin wrote, "I shall not be ashamed to confess that it is a secret too lofty for either my mind to comprehend or my words to declare. To speak more plainly, I rather experience than understand it." *Institutes*, 4.17.32.

> In the mystery of the Supper, Christ is truly shown to us through the symbols of bread and wine, his very body and blood, … Why? First that we may grow into one body with him; secondly, having been made partakers of his substance, that we may also feel his power in partaking of all his benefits. *Institutes* 4.17.11

Calvin's teaching on the Lord's Supper has become known as **virtualism**. Here the virtues (or benefits) of Christ's sacrifice are applied to the believer because of belief. The Holy Spirit brings spiritual union between Christ and the believers. Spiritual feasting occurs.

> Our souls are fed by the flesh and blood of Christ in the same way that bread and wine keep and sustain physical life. For the analogy of the sign applies only if souls find their nourishment in Christ — which cannot happen unless Christ truly grows into one with us, and refreshes us by the eating of his flesh and the drinking of his blood.

> Even though it seems unbelievable that Christ's flesh, separated from us by such great distance, penetrates to us, so that it becomes our food, let us remember how far the secret power of the Holy Spirit towers above all our senses, and how foolish it is to wish to measure his immeasurableness by our measure. What then, our mind does not comprehend, let faith conceive: that the spirit truly unites things separated in space.[102] Since however,

---

[102] *Institutes*, p. 4.17.10.

> this mystery of Christ's secret union with the devout
> is by nature incomprehensible, he shows its figure and
> image in visible signs best adapted to our small capacity.
> Indeed, by giving guarantees and tokens he makes it as
> certain for us as if we had seen it with our own eyes. For
> this very familiar comparison penetrated into even the
> dullest minds: just as bread and wine sustain physical
> life, so are souls fed by Christ.[103]

John Calvin also emphasized the body of Christ as the body of believers called the Church. Hence the Presbyterian usage of "communion of the saints" and the fellowship embraced in the vocabulary "Holy Communion." For Calvin, the Holy Spirit in communion spiritually raises the believer to heaven and spiritually seats the believer with Christ. Ephesians 2:4–6 states: "God ... made us alive together with Christ ... and raised us up with Him, and seated us with Him in the heavenly places, in Christ Jesus." Everyone, even Catholics,[104] hold that the church is one aspect of the body of Christ.

> Is not the cup of blessing which we bless a sharing in
> the blood of Christ? Is not the bread which we break a
> sharing in the body of Christ? Since there is one bread,
> we who are many are one body; for we all partake of the
> one bread. 1 Cor 10:16–17.

Calvin seems to stress that the believer is spiritually taken up to heaven to unite with Christ Jesus there. Zwingli seems to emphasize the spiritual union of Christ with the believer in the earthly plane. But this distinction is overly simple. Both aspects[105] are found in both advocates.

---

[103] *Institutes*, 4.17.1.

[104] Section 1331 of *CCC*. "Holy Communion, because by this sacrament we unite ourselves to Christ, who makes us sharers in his Body and Blood to form a single body [1 Corinthians 10:16–17]. We also call it: the holy things (ta hagia; sancta) — the first meaning of the phrase "communion of saints" in the Apostles' Creed — the bread of angels, bread from heaven, medicine of immortality, viaticum..."

[105] In this Sacrament we have such full witness of all these things that we must certainly consider them as if Christ *here present* were himself set before our eyes and touched by our hands. For his word cannot lie or deceive us: "Take, eat,

The nexus of Calvin's theology has the Holy Spirit transcend space to unite Christ with the believer. There is fertile ground for several doctoral dissertations in Calvin on the nature of the body of Christ, the communion of the saints, the Holy Spirit's role in sanctifying the believer — of bringing the effects of Christ's atonement into the Christian's daily life. The Eucharist is one means of grace whereby the Holy Spirit unites, spiritually feeds, excites and encourages the believer into fellowship with Christ.

Grammatically Calvin sees metonymy at work in "this is my body." The bread is a symbol of Christ's human body, but it is so similar and closely related that the bread can be spoken of in terms of the body. Paul does this in 1 Corinthians 10:16 "Is not the bread which we break a sharing [κοινωνιαν, koinonia] in the body of Christ." Calvin writes,

---

drink: this is my body, which is given for you; this is my blood, which is shed of forgiveness of sins" [Matthew 26:26–28, conflated with 1 Corinthians 11:24; cf. Mark 14:22–24, Luke 22:19–20.] By bidding us take, he indicates that it is ours; by bidding us eat, that it is made one substance with us, by declaring that his body is given for us and his blood shed for us, he teaches that both are not so much his as ours. *Institutes*, 4.17.3 [My italics.]

Christ *descends* to us both by the outward symbol and by his Spirit, that he may truly quicken our souls by the substance of his flesh and of his blood.... There is nothing more incredible than that things severed and removed from one another by the whole space between heaven and earth should not only be connected across such a great distance but also be united, so that souls may receive nourishment from Christ's flesh. *Institutes*, 4.17.24 [My italics.]

But if *we are lifted up to heaven* with our eyes and minds, to seek Christ there in the glory of his kingdom, as the symbols invite us to him in his wholeness, so under the symbol of bread we shall be fed by his body, and under the symbol of wine we shall separately drink his blood, to enjoy him at last in his wholeness. For though he has taken his flesh away from us, and in the body has ascended into heaven, yet he sits at the right hand of the Father — that is, he reigns in the Father's power and majesty and glory. This Kingdom is neither bounded by location in space nor circumscribed by any limits. Thus Christ is not prevented from exerting his power wherever he pleases, in heaven and on earth. He shows his presence in power and strength, is always among his own people, and breathes his life upon them and lives in them sustaining them, strengthening, quickening, keep them unharmed, as if he were present in the body. In short, he feeds his people with his own body, the communion of which he bestows upon them by the power of his Spirit. In this manner, the body and blood of Christ are shown to us in the Sacrament. *Institutes*, 4.17.18. [My italics.]

"the body of Christ today is called bread, inasmuch as it is the symbol by which the Lord offers us the true eating of his body."[106]

In 1536 G. Farel convinced Calvin to help him bring the Reformation to Geneva. They sought to institute a theocratic regime along the lines of the Old Testament.

> During his [Calvin's] ministry at Geneva, his reputation and influence as an ecclesiastical statesman, as a religious controversialist, educationist, and author was widespread, His theological insight, his exegetical talents, his knowledge on languages, his precision, and his clear and pithy style, made him the most influential writer among the reformers, and his *Institutes* are still of the highest authority in the non-Lutheran Protestant Churches.[107]

Calvin and H. Bullinger coauthored the 1549 work on the Lord's Supper, *Consensus Tigurinus*. The previous year, Calvin had written to the English Protector Somerset indicating the Protestant changes he would like to see in England. In 1555 Calvin sheltered English Protestant refugees. It therefore is not surprising that Calvin's influence on the Westminster Confession of Faith (1647) is strong.

The *Westminster Confession of Faith* contains both the *Shorter and Larger Catechism*. Each testifies to the effective virtualism of Calvin.

Westminster Confession of Faith: The Shorter Catechism[108]

Q. 91. *How do the sacraments become effectual means of salvation ?*
    A. The sacraments become effectual means of salvation,
    not from any virtue in them, or in him that doth

---

[106] *Institutes*, 4.17.21.

[107] *Oxford Dictionary of the Christian Church*, Ed. F. L. Cross and F.E.A. Livingstone, (London: Oxford University Press, 1974), s. v. "Calvin, John."

[108] *Westminster Confession of Faith*. The larger and shorter catechisms with scripture proofs at large. Originally convened 1643–47. Adopted 1648 by the general assembly of the church of Scotland. Issued by the publications committee of the Free Presbyterian Church of Scotland, 1967, The Shorter Catechism on the Lord's supper, p. 313–315.

administer them; but only by the blessing of Christ, and
the working of his Spirit in them that by faith receive
them.

Q. 92. *What is a sacrament?*
A. A sacrament is an holy ordinance instituted by Christ;
wherein, by sensible signs, Christ, and the benefits of the
new covenant, are represented, sealed and applied to
believers.

Q. 96. *What is the Lord's supper?*
A. The Lord's supper is a sacrament, wherein, by giving
and receiving bread and wine, according to Christ's
appointment, his death is showed forth; and the worthy
receivers are, not after a corporal and carnal manner,
but by faith, made partakers of his body and blood,
with all his benefits, to their spiritual nourishment, and
growth in grace.

Q. 97. *What is required to the worthy receiving of the Lord's supper?*
A. It is required of them that would worthily partake
of the Lord's supper, that they examine themselves of
their knowledge to discern the Lord's body, of their
faith to feed upon him, of their repentance, love, and
new obedience; lest coming unworthily, they eat and
drink judgment to themselves. [End of Westminster
Confession of Faith: The Shorter Catechism]

Westminster Confession of Faith: The Larger Catechism[109]

Q. 168. *What is the Lord's supper?*
A. The Lord's supper is a sacrament of the New
Testament, wherein, by giving and receiving bread and
wine according to the appointment of Jesus Christ,

[109] *Westminster Confession of Faith.* The Larger Catechism on the Lord's supper, p 258–268.

his death is shewed forth; and they that worthily communicate feed upon his body and blood, to their spiritual nourishment and growth in grace; have their union and communion with him confirmed; testify and renew their thankfulness, and engagement to God, and their mutual love and fellowship each with other, as members of the same mystical body.

Q. 169. *How hath Christ appointed bread and wine to be given and received in the sacrament of the Lord's supper ?*

A. Christ hath appointed the ministers of his word, in the administration of this sacrament of the Lord's supper, to set apart the bread and wine from common use, by the word of institution, thanksgiving, and prayer; to take and break the bread, and to give both the bread and the wine to the communicants: who are, by the same appointment to take and eat the bread, and to drink the wine, in thankful remembrance that the body of Christ was broken and given, and his blood shed, for them.

Q. 170. *How do they that worthily communicate in the Lord's supper feed upon the body and blood of Christ therein ?*

A. As the body and blood of Christ are not corporally or carnally present in, with, or under the bread and wine in the Lord's supper, and yet are spiritually present to the faith of the receiver, no less truly and really than the elements themselves are to the outward senses; so they that worthily communicate in the sacrament of the Lord's supper, do therein feed upon the body and blood of Christ, not after a corporal and carnal, but in a spiritual manner; yet truly and really, while by faith they receive and apply unto themselves Christ crucified, and all the benefits of his death.

Q. 171. *How are they that receive the sacrament of the Lord's supper to prepare themselves before they come unto it ?*

> A. They that receive the sacrament of the Lord's supper are, before they come, to prepare themselves thereunto, by examining themselves of their being in Christ, of their sins and wants; of the truth and measure of their knowledge, faith, repentance; love to God and the brethren, charity to all men, forgiving those that have done them wrong; of their desires after Christ, and of their new obedience; and by renewing the exercise of these graces, by serious meditation, and fervent prayer.

Q. 172. *May one who doubteth of his being in Christ, or of his due preparation, come to the Lord's supper ?*

> A. One who doubteth of his being in Christ, or of his due preparation to the sacrament of the Lord's supper, may have true interest in Christ, though he be not yet assured thereof; and in God's account hath it, if he be duly affected with the apprehension of the want of it, and unfeignedly desires to be found in Christ, and to depart from iniquity: in which case (because promises are made, and this sacrament is appointed, for the relief even of weak and doubting Christians) he is to bewail his unbelief, and labour to have his doubts resolved; and, so doing, he may and ought to come to the Lord's supper, that he may be further strengthened.

Q. 173. *May any who profess the faith, and desire to come the Lord's supper, be kept from it?*

> A. Such as are found to be ignorant or scandalous, notwithstanding their profession of the faith, and desire to come to the Lord's supper, may and ought to be kept from that sacrament, by the power which Christ hath left in his church, until they receive instruction, and manifest their reformation.

Q. 174. *What is required of them that receive the sacrament of the Lord's supper in the time of the administration of it?*

> A. It is required of them that receive the sacrament of the Lord's supper, that, during the time of the administration of it, with all holy reverence and attention they wait upon God in that ordinance, diligently observe the sacramental elements and actions, heedfully discern the Lord's body, and affectionately meditate on his death and sufferings, and thereby stir up themselves to a vigorous exercise of their graces; in judging themselves, and sorrowing for sin; in earnest hungering and thirsting after Christ, feeding on him by faith, receiving of his fulness, trusting in his merits, rejoicing in his love, giving thanks for his grace; in renewing of their covenant with God, and love to all the saints.

Q. 175. *What is the duty of Christians, after they have received the sacrament of the Lord's supper?*

> A. The duty of Christians, after they have received the sacrament of the Lord's supper, is seriously to consider how they have behaved themselves therein, and with what success; if they find quickening and comfort, to bless God for it, beg the continuance of it, watch against relapses, fulfil their vows, and encourage themselves to a frequent attendance on that ordinance: but if they find no present benefit, more exactly to review their preparation to, and carriage at, the sacrament; in both which, if they can approve themselves to God and their own consciences, they are to wait for the fruit of it in due time: but, if they see they have failed in either, they are to be humbled, and to attend upon it afterwards with more care and diligence.

[End of Westminster Confession of Faith: The Larger Catechism]

F. RENAISSANCE

Here the elements change into the resurrected risen body of Christ, not the crucified body of Christ. Erasmus advocated this idea centering attention to the mysterious changes in the body as when Christ came to his disciples through closed doors. "It is the nature and property of the resurrection body to be present at one and the same time both in heaven and also in the sacrament, and indeed everywhere."[110] In this view the resurrected body of any saint can be anywhere that the person wills it. The saints however only do the will of God and so they are only in one place at one.

Zwingli's work on the Lord's Supper interacts with this Renaissance view. If the resurrected human body is ubiquitous, then all the resurrected would be ubiquitous which is flatly contradicted by the Ascension of Christ to the right hand of the Father. If the elect only do the will of God, then Christ himself will only do the will of God. God specifically told him to "sit at his right hand, until he made his enemies his footstool" Psalm 110:1 that is until the last day. Therefore Christ "does not will to be anywhere except at the right hand of the Father."[111]

The angel spoke to Mary saying, "He is not here." (Matthew 28:6) If the resurrected body was ubiquitous, then the angel was not speaking the truth. But the angel spoke the truth, and resurrected bodies are not ubiquitous.

Christ instituted the Eucharist prior to his death and resurrection. A time problem occurs, because the disciples at the original supper would not have benefitted the way subsequent celebrants would. In truth the Lord's Supper, when instituted, carried proleptic meaning; for it looked forward to Christ's future death, burial and resurrection. The connection between the broken bread and the body of Christ carries much more significance after the crucifixion — after Christ's body was broken. The mystery becomes a bit clearer, but the spiritual bonding of Christ with his disciples happens whenever the sacrament is celebrated. Jesus however is exceptional in that he is both physically seated at the

---

[110] Zwingli's statement of the renaissance position in his work *On the Lord's Supper* in *Zwingli and [H.] Bullinger*, p. 215.

[111] Zwingli, *On the Lord's Supper*, in *Zwingli and [H.] Bullinger*, p. 218.

right hand of God and spiritually present as we partake the Eucharistic elements.

G. Receptionism and Real Presence

Consider an attempt at inclusive language. The Church of England created several statements: Ten Articles (1536), the Bishop's Book (1537), The Six Articles (1539), the King's Book (1543), and the Forty–Two Articles (1553). The Thirty–Nine Articles first appeared in 1563, but underwent several changes. These are not creeds. Rather, they seek to explain general Anglican trends in light of the then current debates. Accordingly, they are not narrow, and at times are intentionally not specific. Inclusive language seeks to embrace differing views. For instance, article 28, excludes Transubstantiation and mere symbolic views, but the wording is general enough to advocate: Real Presence and Receptionism. In Real Presence, the precise manner of Christ's body and blood are not defined, but when the sacramental elements are taken the actual human body and blood of Christ are eaten. In Receptionism, bread and wine are unchanged after consecration and are received by the communicate along with the true body and blood of Christ. Here is the American Revised 1801 statement from

Book of Common Prayer.
XXVIII Of the Lord's Supper

The Supper of the Lord is not only a sign of the love that Christians ought to have among themselves one to another; but rather it is a Sacrament of our Redemption by Christ's death: insomuch that to such as rightly, worthily, and with faith, receive the same, the Bread which we break is a partaking of the Body of Christ; and likewise the Cup of Blessing is a partaking of the Blood of Christ.

Transubstantiation (or the change of the substance of Bread and Wine) in the Supper of the Lord, cannot be proved by Holy Writ; but is repugnant to the plain words of Scripture, overthrows the nature of a Sacrament, and hath given occasion to many superstitions.

The Body of Christ is given, taken and eaten, in the Supper, only after an heavenly and spiritual manner. And the means whereby the Body of Christ is received and eaten in the Supper is Faith.

H. Practical Application and Summary

The Eucharist is a God ordained covenant renewal ceremony. Through it, God imparts His grace to believers. In remembrance, (triggered by the ceremonial words and faith), the Holy Spirit reconnects the believer (and the community of faith) to Christ. The faithful renew their allegiance to their Savior. They are renewed afresh to live as disciples of Christ because they receive the benefits Christ procured for them in His atoning death.

Luke and Paul both wrote, "for this cup is the new covenant in my blood." The cup in communion symbolizes the new covenant. This is a metaphor (an implied comparison), for the cup is not letterally the new covenant. The cup **represents** the new covenant. Using this as a *rational grammatical key*, "this [] my body," means "this *represents* my body." **Alloeosis** is this figure of speech that changes the original thought by using a later key. Calvinists, Anabaptists, and Zwinglians have no trouble seeing the bread in a figurative (or symbolic) sense. The bread, which stay bread, also represents Christ's body. The Bible also teaches that we eat bread. "The bread which we break, is it not the communion of the body of Christ?" 1 Corinthians 10:16.

Those Protestants who previously viewed the ceremony as empty (lacking the presence of God) — now have another perspective. One divine attribute is God's omnipresence. God the Father, God the Son and God the Holy Spirit are always present in their divinity even if they do not manifest or make real that presence. Have you heard of Brother Lawrence? As a simple Medieval monk, he sought to "practice the presence of God." Whether scrubbing the abbey floor or washing the pots, Brother Lawrence sought the presence and grace of God. Other common means of grace are prayer, meditation on the Scriptures and the ceremonies of baptism and the Lord's Supper. When we open our heart and mind to reflect upon Christ and all the wonders he has brought to us — the Holy Spirit spiritually unites us into the presence of Christ. The Holy Spirit also connects us with the reality of Christ's benefits. Protestants must not get so stuck on one point of doctrine that they miss the whole teaching. Yes, Jesus in his humanity is only seated at the right hand of God in heaven. All orthodox Christians say, "Amen to that truth." But now Protestants must embrace Christ's divine presence — even in the Eucharist. Calvin points out, "We are raised up with Him [Christ], and [God] seated us with Him in the heavenly places, in Christ Jesus" (Ephesians 2:6). Since we are currently spiritually seated with him, then let us see how much closer we can get to him even within the Eucharistic ceremony. We are adopted into His family. We are recipients of His Holy Spirit. As we **spiritually** draw closer to Him, he draws closer to us. God is omnipresent, yet too often Protestants forget this — especially during communion. Communion is NOT an empty ceremony. With ceremonial words and faithful belief, the Holy Spirit ushers us into the spiritual presence of Christ! The symbols are used by God as a means of grace: for as we **remember** and **believe** what Christ has done, we draw closer to him and open ourselves to be recipients of His blessings. Through this, we find forgiveness of sin, get excited about our walk with Christ. We "pursue … sanctification without which no one will see the Lord" Hebrews 12:14.

God is omnipresent. He is present everywhere. Rarely does He manifest that presence. (To help us visualize what a manifestation of God's normally un-manifested presence might be like, look at the image on last page of this section.) Whether manifested or not, we need to put into practice the presence of God. In His deity Jesus, the Christ, is "with us always" (Matthew 28:20.) In Him we live and move and exist (Acts 17:28). Believe this, not only in your daily life, but most especially in the Lord's Supper!

God is omniscient. He knows all. He sees all. Therefore, we fear God and keep His commandments. If we partake of communion unworthily, we enable His curse. "Judging the body rightly" means we have a job to do; we examine ourselves in order to partake the Lord's Supper worthily. Do not dismiss this point. God still makes some weak, sick and puts to death others for not discerning what Communion bread, wine and cup signify. God is omniscient and present in His deity in the ceremony.

> Whoever eats the bread or drinks the cup of the Lord in an unworthy manner, shall be guilty of the body and the blood of the Lord. But let a man examine himself, and so let him eat of the bread and drink of the cup. For he who eats and drinks, eats and drinks judgment to himself, if he does not judge the body rightly. For this reason many among you are weak and sick, and a number sleep. 1 Corinthians 11:27–30B

Additionally, we are careful to follow the creeds regarding the nature of Christ.

> Chalcedon Council (451 AD) We apprehend this one and only Christ–Son, Lord, only–begotten — in two natures; without confusing the two natures, without transmuting one nature into the other, without dividing them into two separate categories, without contrasting them according to area or function. The distinctiveness of each nature is not nullified by the union. Instead, the "properties" of each nature are conserved and both natures concur in one "person" and in one hypostasis. They are not divided or cut into two persons, but are together the one and only and only–begotten Logos of God, the Lord Jesus Christ.

Historically Lutherans and Catholics prioritize the unity of the God-man. Accordingly, their view of the Eucharist reflects that teaching. Both views can be criticized for not "conserving the human nature of Christ." The Bible teaches that Jesus is seated at the right hand of God in heaven. Catholics maintain a finite humanity of Christ: seated at the right hand of God in heaven *and* also in the consecrated Eucharist. Lutherans expand the humanity to be nearly ubiquitous, to be as present as his deity is. Ironically Lutherans stray farther than the Catholics. But, both stray from the truth from my perspective. Calvin and Zwingli view Christ's human body as only seated in heaven. All groups however insist on the divine presence of the Father, Son and Holy Spirit — even in the ceremony of the Eucharist!

Zwingli begins with the obvious figure of speech "this (cup) is My blood of the covenant." All universally understand the cup **represents** the New Covenant. When Zwingli sought to apply the same logic and reason to the first set of words ("This is my body"), he ran into dogmatic opposition from Luther and the Catholics. Rationally the cup, bread and wine *represent* (as symbols) the New Covenant, the body and the blood of Christ.

I have sought to share more light on the truth and minimize the emotional heat of argument. In doing so I have presented two new perspectives. 1) Allegorical interpretation is not biblically sanctioned. The allegorical hermeneutic is employed by those teaching: "This [bread] (transubstantiates to) my body." (See Appendix B.3.) 2) In the Old Testament, sin offerings whose blood is presented inside the tabernacle are NOT to be eaten by anyone. Christ's sin offering at Calvary is the fulfilment of that tabernacle type. His blood was presented in the heavenly equivalent of the tabernacle. Hence no one letterally eats of the sacrifice at Calvary. In Holy Communion there is spiritual feasting, but NO ONE letterally physically eats of Christ's sacrifice.[112]

> But no sin offering of which any of the blood is brought into the tent of meeting to make atonement in the holy place shall be eaten; it shall be burned with fire. Leviticus 6:30.

> But the bull of the sin offering and the goat of the sin offering, whose blood was brought in to make atonement in the holy place, shall be taken outside the camp, and

---

[112] I have seen Catholic teaching that differentiates **animal** sacrifice for Christ's **spiritual** sacrifice, but it misses the commonality of the type —when blood of sacrifice is presented inside the tabernacle (earthly or heavenly), nothing of that sin offering is eaten.

they shall burn their hides, their flesh, and their refuse
in the fire. Leviticus 16:27.

We have an altar from which those who serve the
tabernacle have no right to eat. For the bodies of those
animals whose blood is brought into the holy place by
the high priest as an offering for sin, are burned outside
the camp. Therefore Jesus also, that He might sanctify
the people through His own blood, suffered outside the
gate. So, let us go out to Him outside the camp. Hebrews
13:10–13.

No one letterally eats blood. Both Old and New Testaments prohibit
eating blood!

You shall not eat any blood, Leviticus 7:26.
Abstain from … blood, Acts 15:20.

In appendix A and B we learn that interpretive allegorization ought
not to be used, and is condemned by Paul. Furthermore the use and
triumph of typology is explained.

Figure 1
Perspectives on the Eucharist

	Physically eat bread and drink wine	How does communicant receive benefits of Christ	How is Christ present	Vocabulary	Where is the human body of Jesus, the Christ	Covenant Renewal Ceremony called
Catholic	no	physical manducation: eating His body and blood	At epiclesis (priest's prayer) bread and wine transubstantiate into the God-man	transubstantiation: substance of bread and wine become the body and blood of Christ (by re-creating the eternal event in an unbloody manner)	1. Seated in heaven at the right hand of God and 2. In the consecrated elements of the Mass	Mass (meaning the sending of Christ)
Luther	yes	spiritual manducation: by faith in mouth spiritually eating His body and blood	Christ's humanity acquires divine attribute of ubiquity. So God-man always present	consubstantiation: God-man coexists with (in, under, through) the bread and wine.	1. Seated in heaven at the right hand of God and 2. Omnipresent	Lord's Supper and Sacrament of the Altar.
Zwingli	yes	by faith remember His broken body and blood shed	Deity (on earth and in heaven). Humanity seated only on God's heavenly throne	Memorialism: in faith remember what Christ has done, Holy Spirit connects you to Christ and His benefits Also called Virtualism.	1. Seated in heaven at right hand of God	Lord's Supper

Calvin	yes	By faith remember. Church partakes in unity of faith	Deity (on earth and in heaven). Humanity seated only on God's heavenly throne	Memorialism (as above). Corporate participation in the church (the body of Christ.) Also called Virtualism.	1. Seated in heaven at right hand of God	Communion

Note: Manducation means chewing. John 6:63, "It is the Spirit who gives life; the flesh provides no benefit." Christ fulfilled two Day of Atonement sin offerings but because that sacrificial blood was put on the mercy seat, no one ate of that sacrifice. Leviticus 6:30, "But no sin offering of which any of the blood is brought into the tent of meeting to make atonement in the Holy Place shall be eaten; it shall be burned with fire."

Note: Christ's humanity is neither ubiquitous nor omnipresent: the angel said, "He is not here, for He has risen" (Matthew 28:6)

Figure 2
Practice the Presence of God even if He
does not manifest His Presence.

I. A PRAYER

Working God, open our eyes and ears,
      For too often when we see Your hand,
      We stop there amazed at Your present acts.
      Yet those miracles are meant to move us
      To respond to You and Your Message.

Loving Father, embrace us,
      For too often we indulge minds in the Bible,
      And stop satisfied with Your truth.
      Yet through that truth,
      We are meant to marvel at and love You.

Invisible God, open our hearts and minds,
      For too often even in Holy Communion,
      We find You not or we idolize what You are not.
      Yet through the grammar and Your Word,
      Draw us closer to You.
      Re-unite us with Christ and renew us in Him.

Gracious God, empower us,
      For too often when we find Your grace,
      We stop there with soul satisfied.
      Yet Your sanctifying grace moves us
      to love You, our neighbors and ourselves.

As Moses prayed, we pray,   (Exodus 33:13)
      "Let us know Your ways,
      That we may know You,
      So that we may find favor in Your sight."

But in addition to wisdom we need Your Holy Spirit
      to write your law into our hearts and lives
      so that, living by faith in Christ, we might show and share
      your glory both now and forever more.

      In the name of Jesus, our Savior, our Lord
      and our returning King we pray. Make it so. (Amen.)

Appendix

A. Definitions: Letteral, Literal, Typological and Allegorical

In recent times, the development of dictionaries focused primarily on the basic meaning of words. From a recent grammatical perspective, literal implies no figures of speech, while figurative language (or tropes) meant embellishments beyond plain language or a "deviation from the ordinary meaning." That is how George Puttenham in 1589 defined the terms in his book, *The Arte of Prosie*. But Hugh Blair (in his *Lectures on Rhetoric and Belles Letters*, 1783) said, "Though figures imply a deviation from what may be reckoned the most simple speech, we are not thence to conclude, that they imply anything uncommon or unnatural." In fact figures of speech pervade the Indo–European languages and are a natural part of them. Semitic and oriental languages emphasize linguistic formats or constructs, like parallelism or acrostic, which adds depth of understanding. When the original author is using those formats, our understanding is heightened when we perceive the formats used. Idioms are almost impossible to put into another language on a word-by-word basis. Below are my definitions which drastically alter definitions from the near past. I take a hermeneutical (or interpretative) approach to understand the author's intent.

> **Letteral interpretation** takes words at their basic meaning. It may allow the substitution of a name's meaning.[113] It allows decoding of code-words.[114] It

---

[113] Example of name's meaning substituted for name: David in Hebrew means Beloved. "My servant David will be king" (Ezekiel 37:24) letterally can mean: "My servant Beloved will be king."

[114] Example of decoding code word(s): "My servant Beloved will be king" means "My servant Beloved [Jesus, the Messiah] will be king." How one knows "My

disallows reasoning to expand understanding of those words with figures of speech and idioms. This is NOT the usual way an author intends to be understood. Context ought to determine intended meaning.

Literal interpretation understands the original author's intent. Visible meanings and hidden meanings explained within the text are aspects of an author's intent. Hence literal interpretation includes: letteral interpretation, figures of speech, idioms, and linguistic formats **when used by the original author**.

Typological interpretation seeks to draw out moral principles intrinsic in past and current events. It seeks to make proportionate analogies. The value or acceptance of the derived analogy can be evaluated by tests of correspondence, correlation, and coherence. Constitutional jurists attempt to use the mindset of the original writers of the constitution to draw principles to apply to their decisions today.

Allegorical interpretation adds ideas or formats[115] the original author did NOT have in mind. The method is

---

servant Beloved" refers to "Jesus, the Messiah" is based on God the Father's frequent identification of "My Beloved" as Jesus, the Messiah. God, the Father audibly called Jesus "My beloved Son" at the baptism of Jesus (Mt 3:17), and at the transfiguration of Jesus (Mt 17:5). Scripture also calls Messiah "My Beloved" Isaiah 42:1–4 which is quoted by Mt 12:18–21. Isaiah often uses the phrase "My servant" which can refer to the nation of Israel or the Messiah. Note: this determination is based: a) Identification of "My" as God the Father speaking and studying the usage of the Father's words (My, Servant, Beloved). This is not allegorical (substitution) or gnostic (hidden knowledge) decoding where Messiah is (substituted for) "My servant Beloved."

[115] Note: often formats are forced into the text. This is allegorizing interpretation. It may a good intentioned editor, but inspiration applies only to the original authors. For example periods and paragraphs are NOT in the original biblical texts, but they show up in prose and poetry in our English Bibles. Chapter divisions began in the early thirteenth century with Hugo de Sancto Caro and Stephen Langton. Stephen's system is the one we use today. While these chapter divisions are editor

to substitute one thing for another. I will show this is
NOT an acceptable method of hermeneutics although
historically it has been widely used.

Context becomes the key to determine what an original author
intends. For example, regarding Herod, "Tell that fox" (Luke 13:32).
Understood within the original context means Herod represents a fox.
That is literally what the author intended to communicate. Letterally,
without using the metaphor, the sentence becomes wooden — indicating
the "Fox's name is Herod."

Should we allow letteral interpretation to alter our theological
systems? Yes! "For truly I say to you, until heaven and earth pass away,
not the smallest letter or stroke shall pass from the Law until all is
accomplished," Matthew 5:18. God's word did not come to us as a
system. It came to us in the forms God gave it to us. We do well if we hold
to God's word rightly understood, even when it alters our theological
understanding. E.g., Messiah "will reign on David's throne" Isaiah 9:7.
Do we allegorize this in order to make it say, Messiah reigns from
God's heavenly throne? We certainly can use typology to make a valid
analogy (or type). Just as God predicted Messiah will rule from a throne
in the future, so we see today that Jesus, the Christ, rules the Church
from the Father's throne in heaven. But is the current arrangement the
final picture before the eternal estate? Psalm 110:1 "The LORD said to
my Lord: "Sit at My right hand until I make Your enemies a footstool
for Your feet." Christ leaves that throne when He Comes back to earth

---

additions (with good intentions), they are not part of the original inspired text.
For example I think Genesis chapter 1 (the macro view of creation) should end
at Genesis 2:3. And Chapter 2 (the specific details about mankind's creation)
begins at Genesis 2:4. OT verse divisions mostly arose with Masoretic additions
of the sof passuq ("full stop" in English the equivalent is the colon ':'). The 916
AD Tanakh manuscript contains these. But most attribute OT verses with Rabbi
Isaac Nathan ben Kalonymus who made the first Hebrew Bible concordance
(1440's). New Testament verses began with Santes Pagnino (1470–1541) but his
system had much longer lines than we use today. Today's verse divisions began
with Robert Estienne with his numbering of his 1551 edition of the Greek NT.
So chapter and verse divisions are editor inspired, not God inspired. Editors also
push their well intentioned stanza in the psalms, but this does not establish a
strophic arrangement by the original author.

to pick up His rule on David's throne. He sits on the heavenly throne "until" he does not rule from that throne!

Lately "literal" has mostly been used to designate what I call "letteral." That perspective is grammatical, examining a phrase out of its context. These confusing definitions are not new! Philo and the school of Alexandria (Clement of Alexandria and Origen) insisted "literal" excluded metaphor. The school of Antioch (Theophilus of Antioch, Diodorus of Tarsus, Theodor of Mopsuestia, Chrysostom and Theodoret) insisted that the literal meaning cannot exclude metaphor. For Antioch and me "' literal' means the customarily acknowledged meaning of an expression in its particular context."[116] In modern literary criticism those who seek the author's "true motive or intention" are classified as "expressive criticism."[117]

Be extremely careful to understand what definitions an author is using. Original authors legitimately make allegories and interpret them. When we understand what the original author intends with the allegory, we are within the realm of literal interpretation. When we impose an idea, not intended by the author, allegorical interpretation is at work. In contrast, the hermeneutic of typology legitimately draws out a truth, a proverb, or makes applications to similarities today. Typology embraces both the similarities and paradoxical differences of analogy, correspondence, and jurisprudence.

In modern analysis the following terms are applied to the phrase the "road of life."

"Life" is the *tenor* or primary literary term. "Road" is the *4:22* or secondary figurative term. I. A. Richards in *The Philosophy of Rhetoric*

---

[116] Mickelsen, p. 33. Cf. R. Grant, *The Interpreter's Bible*, I,111.

[117] From Baldick, s.v. criticism, p. 48, "the various kinds of criticism fall into several overlapping categories: theoretical, practical, impressionistic, affective, prescriptive, or descriptive. Criticism concerned with revealing the author's true motive or intention (sometimes called 'expressive' criticism emerged from Romanticism to dominate much nineteenth and twentieth century critical writing, but has tended to give way to 'objective' criticism, focusing on the work itself (as in New Criticism and structuralism), and to a shift of attention to the reader in reader– response criticism. Particular schools of criticism also seek to understand literature in terms of its relations to history, politics, gender, social class, mythology, linguistic theory, or psychology."

(1936) argues the total meaning of the figure is a complex interaction between the tenor and the vehicle. [118]

B. METHODS OF INTERPRETATION

Medieval interpretation focused in 4 directions.

History was literally what the forefathers did.
Doctrine allegorically fashioned faith.
Morals derived from types.
Anagogy (eschatology) envisioned our future.

By the thirteenth century, an elaborate system of "Senses" had been constructed, dividing the sense of anything in the Old Testament into four levels of meaning: the literal, the allegorical (referring to the New Testament or the Christian Church), the moral or topological (referring to the fate of the individual soul), and the anagogical (referring to universal history and eschatology). In the standard illustration of this scheme:: Jerusalem is literally a city, allegorically the Church, topologically the soul of the believer, and anagogically the heavenly City of God.[119]

The anagogical sense was seen as the highest [level of meaning], relating to the ultimate destiny of humanity according to the Christian scheme of universal history. ... Anagogy or anagoge is thus a specialized form of allegorical interpretation, which reads texts in terms of eschatology.[120]

Although four senses could be worked from a text, there were only three methods used.

1. Literal grammatical historical method — to interpret the author's evident meaning.
2. Allegorical interpretation — to further the philosophy, doctrine and future hope.
3. Typological interpretation — to apply analogies between then and now. Thus, derive a moral sense of how a disciple ought to live.

---

[118] Chris Baldick, s.v. tenor, p. 223.
[119] Chris Baldick, s.v. typology, p. 232.
[120] Baldick, s.v. anagogical, p. 9.

But before we go into these three methods, a word of caution is needed about the four–fold senses historically sought for.

> This does not mean that interpreters always tried to find all four senses. Sometimes two or three senses were sufficient to the task at hand. Unfortunately, however, this pursuit of multiple meanings is really a magical approach to language. It removes any certainty of meaning. It is true that a passage may have teaching that simultaneously applies to a man's conduct, to his belief, and to his hope. But not all these ideas are expressed by the original writer in the same word or phrase. Certain sections of a chapter may deal with conduct, or doctrine, or the consummation. But one particular expression like "Jerusalem" in any one passage has only one sense. Where it means the literal, earthly city, it does not refer to the heavenly city. One basic meaning may have a higher application of that meaning … but in each context the train of thought determines the meaning it has in that particular place.[121]

Basically, there is one interpretation the author intends for us to get. We use the literal historical grammatical method to get at this original intent. We may find many applications to our daily life, to doctrine or even our future hope. I will show that these other three senses may legitimately be derived using the typological method. Admittedly typology is more cumbersome than interpretive allegory. But interpretive allegorical is not a biblically sanctioned method of exegesis; typology is the biblically sanctioned method!

It is significant that reformation began when men questioned the allegorical and mystical approach to Scripture. The Middle Ages reveal the tragic results of close alignment between allegorizing and ecclesiastical tradition.[122]

---

[121] Mickelsen, p. 35–36.
[122] Mickelsen, p. 38.

B.1. Literal Historical Grammatical Interpretation

The task of interpreters of the Bible, is to *"find out the meaning of a statement (command, question) for the author and for the first hearers or readers, and thereupon to transmit that meaning to modern readers.* [His italics.][123] Hence there are two tasks. Ferret out the original author's intent. Then figure out if contemporary mindset attaches different meanings to those words. For instance, the word Paul used in Galatians 4:24 "allegorically speaking" did not mean to Paul what we think it means today. Since the time of Augustine[124] (fourth century AD) this text has been thought to be the only biblical sanction of allegorical interpretation (attaching meanings the original author did not intend — using substitution). But in fact, Paul is using correspondence (typology) to draw out applications. Paul quite letterally used a newly coined word which Philo had begun to circulate in 40 A.D. For Paul this word letterally means, "Saying other [things]."

> For it is written that Abraham had two sons, one by the bondwoman and one by the free woman. But the son by the bondwoman was born according to the flesh, and the son by the freewoman through the promise. This is **allegorically speaking** [αλληγορουμενα]: for these women are two covenants, one proceeding from Mount Sinai bearing children who are to be slaves; she is Hagar. Now this Hagar is Mount Sinai in Arabia, and **corresponds** to the present Jerusalem, for she is in slavery with her children. But the Jerusalem above is free; she is our mother. Galatians 4:22–26. [My bold emphasis.]

Note carefully that Paul is not using the allegorical method for he does not intend the reader to substitute the Old Covenant for Hagar, nor Mount Sinai for Hagar, nor the present Jerusalem for Hagar. Instead he is linking (grouping) them all together because they all have a common

---

[123] Mickelsen, p. 5.
[124] Augustine, *De Trinitas*, xv.15 {*On the Trinity*, Chapter 9. — Of the term "Enigma"}.

characteristic: bondage. Hence Hagar "**corresponds** to the present Jerusalem."

Since the time of Saint Augustine, the church has transliterated the Greek Word, αλληγορεω, into "allegorical" — hence the normal translation of "This is allegorically speaking" Galatians 4:24. Consequently almost all think Paul was legalizing interpretive allegorization. But this is **not** the case. Paul did not use the traditional word for allegorization (ὑπονοια) rather he used the newly coined word that Philo had begun to use. Philo combined two familiar words [αλλος and αγορεώ] to letterally mean *"speaking other things."* It is best to leave the letteral meaning "speaking other things" and put a footnote in the translation indicating: i.e. speaking analogously. To Paul the analogous nature of Hagar and Mount Sinai allowed "correspondence" — which is part of the vocabulary of typology. Paul did not mean "Hagar is [becomes] Mount Sinai." Paul means "Hagar is [i.e. corresponds to] Sinai." Paul employs the hermeneutic of typology. Paul does not employ allegorization. Today's readers miss the deliberate use of the neologism[125] and its letteral meaning to address Paul's use of typology. Instead we transliterate the word "allegorization" and plug our 1500 years of misuse of interpretive allegorization.

ὑπονοια (huponoia) is the Old Testament and classical word for interpretive allegorization. Letterally it means "that which lies under the sense." Paul clearly condemns interpretative allegorizations using this classical term.[126]

> If any one teaches otherwise and does not agree with the
> sound words of our Lord Jesus Christ and the teaching
> which accords with godliness, he is puffed up with

---

[125] According to Büchsel, "αλληγορέω" *Theological Dictionary of the New Testament*, ed. Kittel, trans. G. W. Bromiley (Grand Rapids: Eerdmans, 1964), Volume 1, p. 260: Plutarch c. 50–120 A.D.) wrote that by the start of the second century (100 A.D.) the former term (ὑπονοια) had totally been replaced by Philo's new term (αλληγορέω).

[126] See Hilary A. Nixon, *Suggested Principles for New Testament Allegory*, (a M.S.T. thesis presented to Biblical School of Theology, Hatfield, Pa., 1972), p. 17–45; 116–130. The name of the school has changed: In 1978 Biblical Theological Seminary; October 2018 it changed again to Missio Seminary.

conceit. He knows nothing; he has a morbid craving for controversy and for disputes about words, which produce envy, dissension, slander and *base suspicions* (υπονοιαι πονηραι letterally "evil allegorizations"). 1 Timothy 6:3–4B NASB [My italics.]

B.2. Typological Interpretation

Typology, like all symbolism, employs the analogy of proportionality. We first consider mathematical proportions; then we move to theological proportions. In the mathematical proportion [(3 is to 6) as (4 is to 8)], the analogates are 3 and 4. Though both are numbers, they would not be correlated by themselves. However, since each analogate has a (hidden) common multiplier of 2, there is correlation between the sets of data. Note the common multiplier is not obvious. The *intrinsic* common character of each set of data is the multiplier 2: (3 corresponds to 6) because of the multiplier, similarly (4 corresponds to 8). Thus, the analogy of proportionality maintains a harmony through the common intrinsic characteristic while recognizing the differences in the analogates. This is paradoxical; similarity is maintained while holding to differences.

Figure 3
Criteria to Evaluate a Type

1. Correspondence refers to the intrinsic qualities of each analogate.
2. Correlation refers to the relationship between two analogates.
3. Coherence is the quality of being logically integrated, or complete. When analogates are very similar to each other, then more coherence exists.

In theological types (or analogies) the same paradoxical tension is at work. In Galatians 4:22– 26, Hagar, Sinai and the present Jerusalem all have a common intrinsic characteristic — bondage to the law.

Thus, Paul wrote, "Hagar corresponds to Jerusalem." In contrast, the allegorical method of exegesis, substitutes one object for another and in that substitution the history or the reality of the initial object gets abandoned.

Types are examples from the past which when correlated to current people or events, have similarities. Application of God's anger at evil become moral principles applicable for us today. Consider God's interaction with the wandering Israelites.

> Now these things happened as examples (types) for us, that we should not crave evil things, as they also craved. And do not be idolaters, as some of them were; as it is written, "The people sat down to eat and drink, and stood up to play." Nor let us act immorally as some of them did, and twenty–three thousand fell in one day. Nor let us try the Lord as some of them did and were destroyed by the destroyer. Now these things happened to them as an example (type) and they were written for our instruction, upon whom the ends of the ages have come. 1 Corinthians 10:6–11B.

Whereas there is only one author–intended meaning to a text, there may be myriads of applications. Typology is the method of making correspondences between the text written then and applications of that text for us now. Romans 15:4 "For whatever was written in earlier times was written for our instruction, that through perseverance and the encouragement of the Scriptures we might have hope." Hence typology, as a method of exegesis, is "the search for linkages between events, persons or things within the historical framework of revelation."[127]

In August 2005 (October 2020 and March 2022), the United States Senate (a legislative branch) decided the next Supreme Court Judge. If the appointee is constitutionally oriented, they see congress make the laws and judges use principles of jurisprudence (typology) to appropriately apply those laws. Over the past few decades the majority on the Supreme

---

[127] K. J. Woolcombe, "The Biblical Origins and Patristic Development of Typology," *Essays on Typology* (London: SCM Press, 1957), p. 40.

Court used other determinates to render their decisions. This is the same sort of divergence that theologians face. Those who want to get the idea from the text (exegesis) are opposed to those who read other ideas into the text (eisegesis). Typology allows one to draw principles and applications from a text. Typology uses correspondence to evaluate the validity of the result.

Typology is by no means as clear as I may make it sound, but at least the results can be tested on the basis of correlation, correspondence and coherence. (Allegorizing cannot). Consider a difficult example of typology — Samson's death, when he brought the house down and two thousand Philistines died along with him (Judges 16:28–31). One typologist may suggest from this that self-sacrifice is justifiable and an honorable end when inflicting destruction against an enemy. Other typologists may not look quite so favorably upon that application, fearing it might give license to suicide bombers. They want closer similarities — like a captured prisoner who dies taking his captor's life. Whether the application to another circumstance is acceptable, may be difficult to sort out, but with typology everyone can work with the text and decide on the basis of illustration by analogy how far they want to illustrate. The closer the correlation between two situations, the more applicable the principles become and the better the analogy. Coherence[128] describes the closeness of the two situations. One illustrates with analogy, but one proves with correlation and coherence.

While the results of typology may be questioned, at least the results provide common ground to evaluate the text, the analogies drawn from

---

[128] Coherence is the quality of being logically integrated. It deals with the appropriateness of correlation. For instance, Pentecost is remarkably similar to Joel 2:28– 31. In both the Holy Spirit descends upon many people. The similarities are enough for correspondence and correlation. With the Holy Spirit's inspiration, Peter clarifies this Pentecost is that [type of thing] spoken by Joel. However, Pentecost lacks the cosmic disturbances of Joel 2:31. This means the fulfilment (the prophetic antitype) did not take place at Pentecost. Appropriate correlation and correspondence exist, but total coherence does not exist. Hence Pentecost is an *escalation*, a step toward culmination, a partial fulfillment, a transitional type, a partial application of truths contained in Joel 2. But Pentecost is not the totally coherent anticipated antitype. Therefore we say "Amen" to Peter's and the Holy Spirit's application of Joel 2 at Pentecost, and we anticipate its still future fulfilment.

the text, verification of the intrinsic characteristics (correspondence) is open for all, the relationship (correlation) between the two objects can be assessed and the appropriateness or fit of the two analogates (coherence) is likewise open for all to work with. Of utmost importance is that the Bible sanctions the typological methodology.

B.3. Allegorical Interpretation

Allegorizing is the search for secondary and hidden meaning underlying the primary and obvious meanings of a narrative.[129]

> "The allegorist takes any narrative (even though the original author gives no indication of having his assertions stand for something else) and after ignoring the primary or obvious meaning, he arbitrarily attaches to the narrative the meaning he wants it to convey. In practice he treats the narrative in such a way as almost to deny its historicity, although in theory he may stoutly defend its historicity."[130]

Allegorization philosophically rests "on a quasi-Platonist doctrine of the relation of the literal sense of Scripture — the outward form or 'letter' of the sacred writings — to the eternal spiritual reality concealed, as it were, beneath the literal sense."[131] In Platonist philosophy the more important aspect is the spiritual, not the physical. The physical (the letter) is a means of spring boarding into the more important "spiritual" areas.

Philo desired to merge Greek Philosophy into the Old Testament. To accomplish this, he used the allegorical method. For example, he saw the four cardinal virtues of Platonism (prudence, self-mastery, courage, and justice) as the four Rivers of Eden.[132] While both the Greek virtues and the Eden rivers had the number "four" in common there is no

---

[129] K. J. Woolcombe, p. 40.

[130] Mickelsen, 238.

[131] G. W. H. Lampe, "The Reasonableness of Typology," *Essays on Typology* (1957), p. 30.

[132] from Philo's allegorical commentary on Genesis 2–4B, *Legum Allegoria* I. 63–78.

correspondence between the intrinsic characteristics of the rivers and the virtues. Hence numbers have significance NOT correspondence.[133]

The method of allegorization is substitution. Allegorization by fiat (not from the original author) makes an identity substitution and often destroys the reality (or historicity) of one of the objects. There is no rationalization for the initial substitution, but once the substitution has been mentally made, then the mind seeks to justify or do something with the results of the magical substitution. Philo allegorized that the fourth river, Euphrates, is the fourth cardinal virtue, Justice. Once the substitution is made, as an allegorizer, I could quickly wax eloquent that "Justice has bends like a river, sometimes moves fast or slow, and at times can be refreshing or tepidly abhorrent." Ironically allegorization can often foster ideas in a quick manner, (like brainstorming or like intuition), however the results of flash thinking are NOT guaranteed as truthful or accurate.

Allegorization can be a simple method to obtain new ideas or to personalize Scripture. Consider Psalm 23. "The Lord is my shepherd, I shall not want." Inadvertently we all allegorize, for we substitute ourselves in the place of the author David. Hence with allegorization the passage is easily personalized. Typology would have us realize David is talking. Then have us draw analogies between David and ourselves. Eventually we find that God shepherds both of us. Truthfully, typology is clumsier than allegorization. But typology, (with its tests of correlation, correspondence and cohesion), helps us check the association and determine the significance. To illustrate, consider this next text: "Judas hung himself" (Matthew 27:5). If I allegorically substitute myself for Judas, then I should go hang myself! Typology would catch that you and the son of perdition are in vastly different circumstances.

Allegorization is NOT a biblically sanctioned method; ironically its quick results may sound reasonable (and seem similar to typological rational)! No wonder there has been confusion!

> In the medieval discipline of biblical exegesis, allegory
> became an important method of interpretation, a habit

---

[133] See John J(ames) Davis, *Biblical Numerology*, a Basic Study of the Use of Numbers in the Bible (Grand Rapids: Baker, 1968).

of seeking correspondences between different realms
of meaning (e.g., physical and spiritual) … It can be
argued that modern critical interpretation continues
this allegorizing tradition.[134]

In summary of the methods of interpretation, we find the original
author's intent as the one meaning of a text. We find applications of that
text using typology, and acceptance of an application is decided by the
strength of correlation, correspondence and coherence between the two
entities. Historically the allegorical method of interpretation has been
sanctioned by the school of Alexandria, Augustine, those embracing
sensus plenior, as well as the fourfold sense passed to us through the
middle ages. We found that Paul did NOT sanction the allegorical
method, although the church has mistakenly thought he did. Instead we
found that Paul in Galatians 4:22–26 employed the typological method.
Paul clearly condemned the allegorization method in 1 Timothy 6:3–4B.

If any one teaches otherwise and does not agree with the
sound words of our Lord Jesus Christ and the teaching
which accords with godliness, he is puffed up with
conceit. He knows nothing; he has a morbid craving
for controversy and for disputes about words, which
produce envy, dissension, slander and *base suspicions*
(ὑπονοιαι πονηραι, letterally "evil allegorizations"). 1
Timothy 6:3–4B NASB [My italics]

So biblical exegesis should only use typology— NOT interpretive
allegorization. Let the method of typology triumph over interpretive
allegorization. Then our thoughts agree with the "sound words of our
Lord Jesus Christ and the teaching which accords with godliness" 1
Timothy 6:3. As we learn to rightly handle the Word of God, we first get
at the original author's intent, then we apply it to our lives using proper
applications of typology. For example in Holy Communion, we use
bread and wine, yet as we by faith remember what Christ has done for
us, the Holy Spirit reconnects us to Christ. In this union we receive all

---

[134] Baldick, s.v. allegory, p. 5.

the benefits Christ has won for us. May we experience the Triune God by applying faith to our understanding of the Eucharist.

C. FIGURES OF RHETORIC

Classical education taught figures of speech as part of rhetoric (oration — speeches). Hence numerous Greek and Latin terms arise. Too often when transliterated into English, different spellings appear. High School students today do not know how to write with cursive letters. Likewise, they have no exposure to classical rhetoric. I present a brief outline to reveal terms and concepts.

Why a speech is given entails the kairos (occasion), the audience, and the decorum (aptness of style using virtues and not vices, and what branches of oratory to use). We have not heard of the five categories (canons): invention, arrangement, style, memory, and delivery. We have not learned the three persuasive appeals: Reason (logos, oration), emotional appeal (pathos), and how to establish the speaker's credibility (ethos). Few know the three 'branches' of oratory: judicial (deliberation from the law), deliberative (legislate to make law), and epideictic (ceremonial or demonstrative oratory as at funerals or a public speech). Fewer yet understand the four categories of change: addition, subtraction, transposition, substitution. But the classical student understood these as ways to modify a word, a phrase, a sentence, a paragraph, a speech or even an entire text.

Figures of reason are broken into 14 variations

1. Informal reasoning, truncated syllogism (enthymeme)
2. Chain of claims which build upon one another. Concatenated enthymemes. (sorites).
3. The use of a remark or an image which calls upon the audience to draw an obvious conclusion (syllogismus).
4. One attributes a cause for a statement or claim made (aetiologia).
5. Reasoning (typically with oneself) by asking questions (ratiocinatio).
6. One asks and then immediately answers his own questions (anthypophora)

7. The rejection of several reasons why a thing should or should not be done and affirming a single one, considered most valid (apophasis).
8. Juxtaposing two opposing statements in such a way as to prove the one from the other (contrarium).
9. After enumerating all possibilities by which something could have occurred, the speaker eliminates all but one (expeditio).
10. When, in conclusion, a justifying reason is provided (proecthesis).
11. Providing a reason for each division of a statement, the reasons usually following the statement in parallel fashion (prosapodosis).
12. Admitting a weaker point in order to make a stronger one (paromologia).
13. A figure by which one balances one statement with a contrary, qualifying statement (dirimens copulatio).
14. Dwelling on or returning to his strongest argument (commoratio).

A speech (oration) is classically broken down into six parts.

1. Introduction (exordium). Here one announces the subject and purpose of the discourse. One usually employs the persuasive appeal of ethos in order to establish credibility with the audience.
2. Narrative Account (narratio) — A statement of facts. A narrative account of what has happened and generally explains the nature of the case.
2B. Quintilian adds a summary of the issues or a statement of the charge (propositio)
3. An outline of what will follow (partitio or divisio), in accordance with what's been stated as the status, or point at issue in the case. Quintilian suggests the partitio is blended with the propositio and also assists memory.
4. Proof (confirmatio) — Here is the main body of the speech full of logical arguments as proof with an emphasis on appeal to logos.
5. Refutation (refutatio) — answers the counterarguments of his opponent.

6. Conclusion (peroratio) — This conventionally employs appeals through pathos, and often includes a summary. The figures of summary: accumulatio, anacephalaeosis, complexio, epanodos, epiphonema, symperasma, synathroesmus.

To delve deeper into figures of rhetoric visit these web sites:

The Forest of Rhetoric http://rhetoric.byu.edu

The Phrontister http://phrontistery.info/rhetoric.html

Glossary of Rhetorical Terms https://mcl.as.uky.edu/glossary-rhetorical-terms

D. *NYM WORDS

Figures of speech are *word (or phrase) to phrase associations*. In contrast, words which end with "…nym" describe *word-to-word associations*. "Nym" derives from the Greek "onoma" meaning name or word. All primary *NYM words are included in the list below. (Derivative words are excluded. (For example: anonym is included, while excluded are anonymity, anonymous, anonymously. This list shows the various relationships one word may have to another word. I have compiled this *nym list of 75 Words over several years. As of May 2020, Wikipedia's has a 68-word list (under "– onym"). Note: some figures of speech (like palindrome) may deal with only one word.

Acronym – Protogram, initialism. Take initial capital letters of a series of words. E.g., NATO (North Atlantic Treaty Organization). E.g., NASA (National Aeronautics and Space Administration).

Allonym – another person's name used by an author as a pen name. Hence a book's author who is not the one the book claims he is. Compare with pseudonym (q.v.).

Ananym – A word derived by spelling another word backwards. A special type of anagram. E.g., Oprah (Winfrey): spell "Oprah" backwards to make "Harpo" as in Harpo Productions.

Anacronym – (combination of anachronism and acronym). Popular small capitalization words that have lost their acronym original meaning. E.g., scuba, radar, laser.

Andronym – husband's name taken on by a wife.

Anepronym – eponym. Trademark name that defines that object. E.g., aspirin, Kleenex.

Anthroponym – study on names of human beings. Subdivisions include Clan and Surnames, Matronyms, Patronyms, Mononyms, Eponyms, Teknonyms, Nicknames, Demonyms, Ethnonyms. Related topics: Exonym and Endonym names; also Toponyms (place names).

Anonym – an anonymous person, a pseudonym (q.v.).

Antonym – a pair of words with (near) opposite meanings: wet/dry, smooth/rough, slow/fast, dead/alive, wife/ husband. From Greek anti (against).

Apronym – acronym or backronym in capital letters that alludes to something else. E.g., PLATO (Programmed Logic for Automated Teaching) alludes to Plato, the teacher philosopher. E.g., SAD means "Seasonal Affective Disorder."

Aptonym – A person's name that matches its owner's occupation or character very well. E.g., Arctic explorer: Will Snow. Tennis player: Margaret Court. Nominative determinism hypothesizes a name may significantly enhance character and work. Similarly aptronym, euonym, charactonym.

Astronym – names for heavenly bodies (star, constellation, etc.)

Autoantonym – A word that can take two (or more) opposite meanings. Irony might have an originating role in these opposite meanings. (Often hyphenated as auto-antonym. Also Antagonym, contranym, contronym, antilogy, enantiodrome, Janus word.)
E.g., Fast means "moving quickly" or "fixed firmly in place",
E.g., Overlook means "to watch over carefully" or "to fail to notice"
E.g., Dust means remove (dust the furniture) or cover (dust the crops).
E.g., Cleave means to "stick together" or "split apart".

Autonym – Self–referential word.
1. A word that describes itself. E.g., A noun is a noun.
2. A person's real name; the opposite of pseudonym.
3. A name by which a social group or race refers to itself. (Also called endonym).
4. In botanical nomenclature, a name automatically created.

Backronym – an ordinary word humorously taken as an acronym. E.g., Fiat: Fix It Again Tomorrow

Bacronym – {From back(wards)}. The reverse of producing an acronym; taking a word which already exists and creating a phrase (usually humorous) using the letters of the word as initials:

E.g., Build Absolutely Nothing Anywhere Near Anybody (BANANA),

E.g., Guaranteed Overnight Delivery (GOD).

Basionym – first name given to biological taxon (genus, specie) which remains even though that taxon has a new name.

Caconym – an incorrect (or undesirable) name especially in taxonomy. Might arise from bad word formation (with mixed Greek and Latin words), too long or bad sounds.

Capitonym – A word which changes its meaning and pronunciation when capitalized.

E.g., polish and Polish, August and August, concord and Concord.

Charactonym – fictional name which describes its character. E.g., Shakespeare's Bottom or Pistol.

Chrematonym – a catch-all name for political, economic, commercial or cultural institution or thing.

Chresonym – biological use of a taxonomic name (which historically was called a synonym). Called orthochresonyms (if usage is correct) or heterochresonyms (if usage is incorrect).

Cohyponym – also called Hyponym. Designates the smaller group, the subordinate term. In Dog/ Animal groupings. Dog is the smaller, subordinate group (Cohyponym or Hyponym). Animal is the larger group (superordinate or generic group, which is called Hyperonym).

Contronym – one word with two meanings that contradict each other. E.g. apology: a defense of faith or declaration of contrition.

Cryptonym – CIA cryptonym. Code names for CIA projects, people, or operations.

Demonym – name of residents from that place. E.g., Utahan – a person from Utah.

Dionym – name with two parts, a binomial zoology name: Homo sapiens.

Endonym – autonym. Name of a place which locals use. E.g., Philly for Philadelphia.

Eponym – A person's name from which another name or word is derived. From Greek epo (on).

Romulus named Rome. "Sandwich" comes from the Earl of Sandwich. Disneyland from Walt Disney. Parkinson's Disease from James Parkinson.

Ergonym – (work name). Substitute name for institution or firm. E.g., Ma Bell for Bell of PA.

Ethnonym – ethnic group name. Outsider names are exonyms. Insider names are endonyms.

Euphonym – pleasant sounding.

Exonym – exo (outside). A place name used by foreigners that differs from the name used by natives. E.g., Londres is the French exonym for London. E.g., English speakers use the exonym Germany; Germans use the endonym Deutschland.

Gamonym – names acquired through marriage. E.g., When the "Mrs." takes husband's last name.

Geonym – names of geographic features.

Glossonym – glottonym, linguonym. Name of a language.

Heteronym – Heterograph. One of two (or more) words that have the same spelling, but different meanings, and sometimes different pronunciation too. (Heteronyms that are pronounced differently are also heterophones.) E.g., sewer, row, entrance, wind. A heteronym is a kind of homonym.

Hodonym – odonym. Name of a street or road.

Holonym – describes a whole entity. E.g., house, car. (Its parts are meronyms.)

Homonym – From Greek homo (same). [Context is critical. Often in puns.] A) words identical in sound but have different meanings (homophone, heteronyms: bough, bow) or B) words identical in spelling but are different in origin, meaning or pronunciation {homograph: lead (metal) / lead (to guide), sewer, row, write and right, way and weigh.}.

Hydronym – names of bodies of water like river or lake.

Hyperonym – (Commonly misspelled Hypernym). Designates the **larger noun group**, the superordinate term, the generic term. A word that has a broader meaning than another. (Cohyponym or hyponym describes the subordinate term.) E.g., in chair/furniture: furniture is the generic or superordinate term (hyperonym); chair is the subordinate term (hyponym, Cohyponym) which is a subset of the larger group. E.g., Tree (hyperonym) includes oak, pine, fir (hyponym). Verb groupings use the word troponym.

Hypocoronym – hypocorism. Unofficial (often shortened) nickname. E.g., Jap for Japanese.

Hyponym – Also called Cohyponym. Designates the **smaller noun group**, the subordinate term. In Dog / Animal groupings. Dog is the smaller group (Cohyponym, Hyponym). Animal is the larger group (superordinate or generic group or Hyperonym).

Isonym – (same name) 1. paronym. Word having same root as another. 2. Identical surnames which may or may not be from the same clans. 3. In biology different names signifying the same group.

Matronym – Metronym. Name derived from a female ancestor. E.g., Regarding the genealogy of Jesus, Luke traces the genealogy through Mary (Luke 3:23–38) explicitly stating "Jesus … being as was supposed the son of Joseph" (v.23). While a female base genealogy is very unusual, so is Luke's virgin conception (Luke 1:34–35). Matthew's genealogy is patronymic — it follows legal descendants of David and ends with Joseph the legal father of Jesus (Matthew 1:2–16).

Meronym – From Greek meros (part). 1. A part or member of a group. E.g., Ankle is a meronym (a part) of the leg. E.g., A brim is a meronym (member) of a hat (the holonym). 2. A term midway between two opposites. E.g., the flat between convex and concave. E.g., present between past and future.

Metonym, Metonymy. From Greek meta (change). These words are historically interchanged. But this distinction is evolving. Metonym is a metaphorical synonym which uses the name of one thing to refer to a closely associated other. E.g., Phishing for information. Only since 1950, has metonymy been narrowing its use to contiguity (associated parts) to describe these close relationships. E.g., The White House issued a news release. Members of the president's staff are closely associated with the White House. E.g., Paul uses the "circumcised" to stand for the Jews (Romans 3:27–30). E.g., The Crown refers to the monarchy. E.g., The bottle refers to alcohol.

Metronym – Matronym (q.v.).

Microtoponym – uninhabited place.

Mononym – a single name which identifies a person. E.g., Madonna, Jesus, Josephus.

Necronym – reference to a dead person. Circumlocution happens if culture taboos direct speech.

Numeronym – is a word based on number. E.g., K9 used for similar sounding "canine."

Oikonym (Greek) – Oeconym (Latin). Name for a house or building.

Oronym – From oral (spoken).

> 1) Neologism for word string which is homophonic with another string of words.
>
> E.g., ice cream and I scream. E.g., Mint spy and mince pie.
>
> 2) [Archaic definition] a mountain. (Toponym is the new replacement word.)

Paedonym – Teknonym: Adult Name given by children. E.g., The child could not remember "oma" (grandmother). he stalled saying "Umm Umm." They called her "Ummies."

Paronym, Paranym – A euphemistic word or phrase whose meaning is contrary to the literal sense. E.g., "Our friend Lazarus has fallen asleep." … Now Jesus had spoken of his death, but they thought that he was speaking of literal sleep. John 11:11 and 13. E.g., Gifted an "inedible pie," the pastor immediately threw it out. His thank you note read, "Thank you Mrs. Jones. A pie like that does not last long in our house."

Patronym – A name derived from the name of one's father, or another male ancestor. E.g., Some theologians think Nathanael (John 1:45–51) is a patronym for Bartholomew (Matthew 10:3).

Phantonym – a word meaning something far different than what it appears to mean. E.g., "Noisome" means unwholesomely smelly, not noisy.

Phytonym – a name for an individual plant. E.g., General Sherman is the largest redwood in Sequoia National Park.

Plesionym – near-synonym. A word almost but not quite synonymous with another. E.g., Fog v. Mist.

Polyonym – (many names). A word which means the same as another word. Swedish proverb: a well-loved child has many names. E.g.,

Philly can be a synonym for Philadelphia, that city's baseball team or a fan of that team. E.g., the city of Magdala (Matthew 15:39) is in the region called Dalmanutha (Mark 8:10.) E.g., Esau had three wives. A) Daughter of Elon the Hittite: called Adah (Genesis 36:2) and Bashemath (Genesis 26:34). B) Daughter of Anah the daughter of Zibeon the Hivite: called Oholibamah (Genesis 36:2) and called Judith (Genesis 26:34. Note: Zibeon is also called Beeri {meaning well–finder} the Hittite in Genesis 26:34. Just how Zibeon is both a Hivite (possibly Horite if text is corrupt) and a Hittite remains a problem!) C) Daughter of Ishmael: called Basemath (Genesis 36:2) and Mahalath (Genesis 28:9). E.g., At times **enigma** is at work with a substitute name. E.g., In Genesis 10:10; 11:2 and Zechariah 5:11, "the Land of Shinar" refers to Babel or Babylon. E.g., Babylon is also called Sheshach in Jeremiah 25:26. (Using backward kabbalah ששך spells בבל). E.g., Edom is called Seir (Deuteronomy 1:2,44; 2:8). E.g., Mount of Olives is called "the mount of corruption" because of idolatries (2 Kings 23:13). E.g., Egypt is called Rahab (Psalm 87:4; 89:10; Isaiah 51:9). E.g., Antichrist is called "the King of Babylon" (Isaiah 14:4). E.g., **Jerusalem** is called Ariel (the Lion of God) in Isaiah 29:1. E.g., Jerusalem is Aholibah (my tabernacle is in her) in Ezekiel 23:4.

Pseudonym – pen name, allonynm, or anonym. An assumed name, especially by an author; E.g., Eric Arthur Blair wrote the novel 1984 under the pseudonym George Orwell.

Retronym — From Greek retro (backward); coined by Frank Mankiewicz. An adjective-noun pairing generated by a change in the meaning of the base noun, usually as a result of technological advance. E.g., Watch became pocket watch when wrist watch arrived. E.g., Pen became fountain pen with the arrival of the ball-point pen.

Socionym – a category is social stratification. E.g., age, income, gender, education, race, spirituality.

Synonym – poecilonym, polyonym. Words that have the same (or very similar) meaning. Synonymous. E.g., big and large, error and mistake, run and sprint. From Greek sun (together).

Tautonym 1. A word composed of two identical parts; E.g., pawpaw, yo-yo, tutu, bye-bye.

2. In taxonomy, when genus and species names are identical; E.g., puffinus puffinus (manx shearwater), apus apus (common swift). From Greek taut (same).

Taxonym – names used for classification. Wikipedia says "Taxonyms include binomens, names of clades or taxons, demonmyms, ethnonyms, and eponyms. Examples include canine, hominid and Dryad."

Theonym – name of a god. Insight in language and a society's understanding of their deity make helpful connections in language and territory. E.g., Tetragrammaton (letterally "he who is") means "I am that I am" Exodus 3:14.

Toponym – From Greek topos (place). 1. A place name. E.g., London, Mount Everest. 2. Word derived from a place. E.g., champagne from Champagne in France; cashmere from Kashmir in India.

Troponym – a verb that more precisely describes a broader verb. E.g., To stroll is to walk slowly. E.g., To duel is to fight with pistols.

Tryonym – three-part name. In taxonomy third name is subspecies.

Zoonym – an animal's common name. E.g., African equids have the zoonym of zebra.

E. FIGURES OF SPEECH

To search for a phrase of words that illustrate vividly or catch attention, we look at figures of speech. (These usually turn the understanding slightly away for letteral interpretation, but they embrace the originator's meaning.) The English word 'figure' is derived from Latin, 'Figura.' Figures symbolize a fact or ideal. For instance, mathematical figures are numbers which represent a count. A fashion (or figure) is stated by the garments one wears. Similarly, the words used to symbolize and portray an idea, fashion the realm of "figures of speech." ('Scheme' is the Greek equivalent to the Latin word 'Figura.') Modern literature usually uses the term figure of speech for A) all types of patterned ways of expression[135] and for B)

---

[135] In this work I have NOT focused on sound rhymes, sound rhythms, versification (stanzas), meters, or poetic devices. I have greatly limited the amount of space given to parallelism and other thought patterns like acrostics. Instead I seek to

figurative language. Older literature used 'trope' to embrace all the figurative means of expression. Anything that can be construed in a letteral sense is NOT a trope. The tropological sense is the figurative sense of a word. Not all rhetoricians agree that **tropes** are figures of *thought,* and **schemes** are *figures of speech.* Generally, they do agree that schemes rearrange the normal order of word meanings; whereas tropes change the meanings of words by a 'turn' of sense. Major figures of speech that are usually classified as tropes are: metaphor, simile, metonymy, synecdoche, irony, personification, and hyperbole. Disputed figures that may be called tropes are: litotes and periphrasis. The method of tropes is typology — it seeks common intrinsic characteristics in associated objects. To understand a trope, first understand the letteral meaning of the figure. Then reflect on the similarities between the two.

Learning the various type of figures of speech is difficult. It is worse than learning a language, because the nomenclatures derive from two languages (Greek and Latin) and often employ the English equivalent. E.W. Bullinger identifies 217 major figures of speech with 30 to 40 synonym variations. So, there are about 250 words in Latin and 250 words in Greek. Therefore, the foreign nomenclature totals around 500 words.[136] Add in the English definitions (equivalents) and the vocabulary increases to 750 words. In my alphabetical figures of speech list, there are 578 entries.

Four Classifications

No agreed upon classification exists. Everyone differs in their attempt to organize figures of speech. I provide four overviews to familiarize you with the range of groupings (and gently introduce you

---

expand the understanding of tropes (the figurative sense of words) and scheme (word arrangement patterns).

[136] E. W. Bullinger, *Figures of speech Used In the Bible* Explained and Illustrated (London: Eyrie & Spottiswoode, 1898). Reprint (Mansfield Centre, CT: Martino Publishing, 2011), p. ix.

to the myriad of terms). Fifteen attempts to organize figures of speech are available on the internet.[137]

A. E.W. Bullinger organizes figures of speech into 3 divisions.

1. Figures made by omission of words (ellipsis).
2. Figures made with addition of words or repetition.
3. Figures which change or alter the meaning, use, arrangement, order or application of words.[138]

B. *Encyclopedia Britannica* CD 99 provides a simple overview to figures of speech.

In European languages figures of speech are generally classified in five major categories:

1. figures of resemblance or relationship (e.g., simile, metaphor, kenning, conceit, parallelism, personification, metonymy, synecdoche, and euphemism);
2. figures of emphasis or understatement (e.g., hyperbole, litotes, rhetorical question, antithesis, climax, bathos, paradox, oxymoron, and irony);
3. figures of sound (e.g., alliteration, repetition, anaphora, and onomatopoeia);
4. verbal games and gymnastics (e.g., pun and anagram); and
5. errors (e.g., malapropism, periphrasis, and spoonerism).

Figures involving a change in sense, such as metaphor, simile, and irony, are called tropes.[139]

---

[137] go to http://rhetoric.byu.edu/
  Then in the search box type in "groupings index"
[138] E.W. Bullinger, p. x, xi.
[139] *Encyclopaedia Britannica CD* (19)99.

C. Berkeley Mickelsen categorizes them functionally[140]:

Short figures of speech

Figures emphasizing comparison:	simile, metaphor
Figures emphasizing association:	metonymy, synecdoche
Figures stressing a personal dimension:	personification, apostrophe
Figures demanding additions to complete thought	ellipsis, zeugma, aposiopesis
Figures involving understatement:	euphemism, litotes (or meiosis)

Figures involving intensification/reversal of meaning hyperbole, irony

Figures involving fullness of thought: pleonasm, epanadiplosis, epizeuxis, climax

Interrogation:	rhetorical questions

Opaque Figures of Speech

Secular Riddle

Sacred Riddle

Fable

Enigmatic sayings

Extended Figures of Speech

Parable and Similitudes

Allegory

D. Professor Grant Williams' internet link categorizes on how the figure is made.[141]

Tropes – figures which change the typical meaning of a word or words: metaphor, metonymy, synecdoche, irony, metalepsis, paradox, oxymoron, anthimeria, litotes, hyperbole.

---

[140] Mickelsen, p. 178 – 235.
[141] After link, look for: II. Modern Classifications, 4. G. Williams' Classification Of Expressive Means
    https://studfile.net/preview/7439698/page:13/

Metaplasmic Figures – figures which move the letters or syllables of a word from their typical place: prosthesis, aphaersis, epenthesis, syncope, paragoge, apocope, antisthecon, metathesis.

Figures of Omission – figures which omit something from a sentence. E.g., a word, words, phrases, or clauses: ellipsis, zeugma, scesis onamaton, anapodoton, aposiopesis, occupatio.

Figures of Repetition (words) – figures which repeat one or more words: epizeuxix, polyptoton, antanaclasis, anaphora, epistrophe, symploce, epanalepsis, anadiplosis, gradatio, congeries, antimetabole, pleonasm.

Figures of Repetition (clauses and ideas) – figures which repeat a phrase, a clause or an idea: auxesis, isocolon, tautology, chiasmus, antithesis, periphrasis.

Figures of Unusual Word Order – figures which alter the ordinary order of words or sentences: anastrophe, hyperbaton, hysteron proteron, hypallage, parenthesis.

Figures of Thought – a miscellaneous group of figures which deal with emotional appeals and techniques of argument: adynaton, aporia, correctio, prosopopoeia, apostrophe.

Alphabetical List of Figures of Speech

For the following definitions, I heavily borrow from E. W. Bullinger, Mickelsen, Baldick, the *Webster's Third international Dictionary* and Professor Grant Williams.[142] E. W. Bullinger's book of 1100 pages is the best source of Latin, Greek and English figures of speech. I provide at least one example from the Bible. My desire is to expose the reader

---

[142] I have extensively used the following works in the list English Figures of Speech

E. W. Bullinger, *Figures of speech Used In the Bible* Explained and Illustrated (London: Eyrie Spottiswoode, 1898). Reprint (Mansfield Centre, CT: Martino Publishing, 2011).

Chris Baldick. *The Concise Oxford Dictionary of Literary Terms*. (New York: Oxford University Press, 1991).

Mickelsen, A. Berkeley. *Interpreting the Bible*. (Grand Rapids Michigan: Eerdmans, 1963).

Webster's Third New International Dictionary, (Springfield, Mass.: G. & C. Merriam Co. Publishers, 1959).

Professor Grant Williams, https://www.academia.edu/6535222/Figures

to the myriad forms of figures of speech. The drawback, of minimal examples, is that you do not get a feel for how often that figure is used. E. W. Bullinger is nearly exhaustive in providing examples from the Bible. E. W. Bullinger's English nomenclature is where I present my primary description of that figure of speech. The foreign words are alphabetically listed with a brief definition and example. But (q.v.) or "See …" will direct you to fuller description. All Zwingli's entries are in the list below. (At least twenty–five were unknown to Google as of 2019.) This list is not exhaustive. Homer Simpson keeps spouting off new ones! I omit E. W. Bullinger's figures which lack a biblical example.

To hear these strange words pronounced: on your computer browser's search line, type "how to say [your word]". E.g., for epiphonema, you type in "how to say epiphonema." Note: Latin nouns are always capitalized: Additio (English equivalent adds an "n": addition). Note: if you find an unfamiliar English word ending in 'n' then look for Latin root word with 'n' removed. E.g., For illation, look for Illatio. A parenthetical phrase clarifies the word either by A) almost letteral translation "Accismus — (almost cut through)." Or B) with illustration.

E.g., Allegory — An extended metaphor (As the Lord is my shepherd Psalm 23). (s) as on "word(s)" means word or words.

Get past the technical names. Start creating your own figures of speech. Use the patterns presented here. When you do, your words become as vivid as the setting sun. I list them alphabetically. The English words have the most complete descriptions. The foreign word may briefly be described. The alphabetized list aids in quick look–up and avoids a complicated index.

Abjection – Abiectio. Emotional rhetoric with despondency, or despair.
Ablatio – See aphaersis. The omission of a syllable or letter at the beginning of a word. A kind of metaplasm.
Abomination – Abominatio (Latin: a detesting). Synonyms: rejection, detestation. See Apodioxis.
Abusus – Anglicized transliteration of Latin Abusio (Catachresis, which see). A rhetorical vice to employ a word at odds with its letteral meaning.
Accismus – (almost cut through). Accido. Apparent or assumed refusal.
    E.g., Matthew 15:22–26. The woman of Canaan cried, "Have mercy

on me, O Lord, thou Son of David." Christ apparently rejects her, as she was one outside of Israel (i.e. a pagan or Gentile), "I was sent only to the lost sheep of the house of Israel." She worshipfully bows to him and responds, "Lord, help me!" Again he apparently rejects her, "It is not good to take the children's bread and throw it to the dogs." At his points she acknowledges that she is a sinner, like the [Gentile] dogs, "Yes, Lord; but even the dogs feed on the crumbs which fall from their masters' table." At this point Christ heals her demon possessed daughter.

Accommodation – Accommodatio. Citing quotations to draw out moral principles [types] to give us knowledge [Gnome] of how to live. E.g., "Now these things happened as examples [types] for us, so that we would not crave evil things as they also craved" 1 Corinthians 10:6. E.g., "Now these things happened to them as an example [type], and they were written for our instruction, upon whom the ends of the ages have come" 1 Corinthians 10:11.

Accumulation – Accumulatio. Bringing together various points made throughout a speech and presenting them again in a forceful, climactic way. A blend of summary and climax. "He [the defendant] is the betrayer of his own self-respect, and the wayfarer of the self-respect of others; covetous, intemperate, irascible, arrogant; disloyal to his parents, ungrateful to his friends, troublesome to his kin; insulting to his betters, disdainful of his equals and mates, cruel to his inferiors; in short, he is intolerable to everyone" Cicero, *Rhetorica Ad Herennium*, 4.40.52

Accusatio Adversa – Adverse accusation, an accusation turned against another. See Anticategoria.

Acope – omit letters from the end of a word. I am Sir Oracle, / And when I **ope** [open] my lips let no dog bark! William Shakespeare, *The Merchant of Venice*, 1.1.93 about 1597.

Acrostic – Acrostichion. First letters of lines form the alphabet (Abecedarian). First letters of words form a word. E.g., RADAR is acronym for **RA**dio **D**etection **A**nd **R**anging. E.g., Acrostic Psalm 9,10, 25, 33, 34, 37, 38, 103, 114, 119, 145; Proverbs 31:10–31; Lamentations 1–4B. See Alliteration.

Acutifatuum – see oxymoron.

Adage – Adagion, Proverb (q.v.), One of several terms describing short, pithy sayings, or traditional expressions of conventional wisdom. E.g., Nothing ventured, nothing gained, Ben Franklin. E.g., "Like mother, like daughter" Ezekiel 16:44.

Addition – Additio. One of four basic strategies in the manipulation of discourse for rhetorical purposes. Addition is related to (and often simply synonymous with) amplification. Figures of addition are metaplasm (q.v.), synonym (q.v.), polysyndeton (q.v.), epitheton (q.v.).

Addubitatio – (begin to doubt or hesitate). See Aporia.

Ad Hominem – an argument attacking a person's character instead of his idea.

Adianoeta(s) – phrase with an obvious meaning and a secondary meaning. E.g., "I will waste no time reading your book." Obvious: right away I will read it. Subtle: I will not read it.

Adjunctum – 2 clauses are joined or yoked together to one verb. The verb may not be appropriate for both clauses. See Synezeugmenon. E.g., "the people **saw** the thunder and lightning" Exodus 20:18.

Adjuration – Deasis (entreating, calling to witness), Obsecratio (beseeching, imploring), Obtestatio (adjure or call God to witness). Key phrases are: "Be it far from me", "The Lord do so unto me, if …". E.g., "I call heaven and earth to witness against you today" Deuteronomy 4:26.

Adumbration – (To sketch [or shadow] out in words.) Representation. See Word–picture.

Adynaton – (plural Adynata). Extreme hyperbole insinuating complete impossibility: E.g., When pigs fly. {A professor told John Steinbeck that he would be an author when pigs fly.} E.g., A snowball's chance in hell. E.g., Not before hell freezes over. E.g., Words cannot convey how much your letters have delighted me. Philipp Melanchthon, *Elementorum Rhetorices Libri*, 44f.

Aenigma – Variant spelling of Enigma (q.v.).

Aequipollentia – a method of saying something by using the **antonym** and "**not**". E.g., Instead of "He **won** the race", the method of aequipollentia changes it to, "He did **not lose** the race."

Aetiologia – Etiologia, Causae Redditio. A figure of reasoning by which one attributes a cause for a statement or claim made, often as a simple relative clause of explanation. E.g., "I mistrust not the judges, for they are just." Synonyms: Apodeixis; Redditio Causae, Ratiocinatio, ratiocination, etiology, rendering a reason, the tell cause, cause shown. "**For** (points out the reason) … **because** (points out the cause." E.g., "For I am not ashamed of the gospel, because it is the power of God that brings salvation to everyone who believes" Romans 1:16 NIV. E.g., Romans 4:14–16 "For … therefore" also point out a clause of explanation.

Affirmation – Affirmatio, (to make steady, strengthen). Words spoken which express positive thought. E.g., "What then? Only that in every way, whether in pretense or in truth, Christ is proclaimed; and in this I rejoice. Yes, and I will rejoice" Philippians 1:18. E.g., "Today, I am brimming with energy and overflowing with joy" Dr. Carmen Harra.

A Fortiori – (Latin: from [the] stronger [reason]). This often uses words like "how much more" or "much more" in order to step to the conclusion. E.g., "If you, then, though you are evil, know how to give good gifts to your children, how much more will your Father in heaven give good gifts to those who ask him!" Matthew 7:11 NIV

Aganactesis – Indignation. E.g., "Then the LORD God said to the woman, "What is this that you have done?" The woman said, "The serpent deceived me, and I ate" Genesis 3:13. E.g., [The Lord said], "What have you done? The voice of your brother's blood is crying to Me from the ground" Genesis 4:10. E.g., Paul spoke to the sorcerer Elymas, "You who are full of all deceit and fraud, you son of the devil, you enemy of all righteousness, will you not cease to make crooked the straight ways of the Lord?" Acts 13:10.

Agnomination – Agnominatio, Adnominatio, adnomination, Paronomasia, Rhyming words. Repetition of word sounds (but not necessarily word sense.). Alliteration repeats initial sounds. Polyptoton repeats sounds. Rhyme repeats end word sounds. See Paronomasia.

Allegory – An extended metaphor (As the Lord is my shepherd Psalm 23) or an extended Hypocatastasis where the association is implied. E.g., In Psalm 89:8–15 the vine by implication refers to Israel. E.g., John 10:11 "I am the good shepherd." Allegory teaches truth by substitution; one noun (element) is supposed to replace another: In so doing the actual history of the first element vanishes. E.g., "The seed is the Word of God" Luke 8:11. When the author intends and interprets his allegories, it is a fine means of illustration. Allegories are fictional (not occurring in real time, have no named characters, and they did not happen at one particular place). Their purpose is to illustrate moral or spiritual truth or an eternal principle. What is not acceptable is for an interpreter to make an allegory when an author did not. (See allegorical hermeneutic.)

Allegorical Hermeneutic – Allegorization. Imparting meanings into a text the author did not intend. Eisegesis. Usually uses substitution of one element for another; (which destroys the reality of the original element). E.g., In Amillennial theology, instead of "Israel", they plug in (or substitute) "the church"; as a result they see none of God's future plans for Israel or the promised land. E.g., When the "body of Christ" gets substituted for bread, the reality of the bread is destroyed. (In contrast see Typological hermeneutic.)

Though historically done; this non–author intended allegorization should NOT be used. It triggers different thought patterns than the author intended. Ironically the allegorical method is quick and easy to use, because it uses a kind of mental short cut (warping). It can come up with interesting insights, but like insight, there may be no validity to it! Verification of the validity and correspondence of the insight must rely upon typology. Paul condemns allegorizing but it is translated as "evil suspicions" in 1 Timothy 6:4.

Allelouchia – (holding together). See Chiasmos.
Alliteration – Homoeopropheron. Repetition of same letter consonant sound that begin successive words or lines. Very difficult to preserve in translation. E.g., The 'B' sound in: "To the bottom of the bog, the boy brought the frog." E.g., Hebrews 1:1 "God, after He spoke long ago to the fathers in the prophets in **many portions and in many ways.**" E.g., Judges 5 is full of alliteration. See acrostic

Alloeosis – allotheta. Also spelled alloiosis. (To make different, to change, otherwise).

A) From grammatical standpoint: alloeosis is a substitution of one case, gender, mood, number, tense, or person for another. Example: <u>Each</u> of the students should bring <u>their</u> notebook. (Where "their" is substituted for his.) Synonymous with enallage, but according to Peacham also includes antiptosis. (Henry Peacham, *The Garden of Eloquence*, 1577.)

B) Substituted theological prospective: the transposed attribute, mutual exchange, changing attributes of one property or nature of a thing or person to another. Because Zwingli emphasized the divine and human natures of Christ, he often used alloeosis to jump from one nature to the other. See footnote 86 for lengthy examples.

C) In a set of lines, initial understanding may be substituted/altered because of later lines. Reason within the context forces the changed understanding. E.g., John 6:56 "Whoever eats my flesh and drinks my blood remains in me, and I in them." The understanding gets totally altered by John 6:63 "The Spirit gives life; the flesh counts for nothing. The words I have spoken to you they are full of the Spirit and life." The explaining set of lines show Christ did not intend his listeners to imbibe in either cannibalism or blood drinking. His explanation is reasonable for "the flesh [body] profits nothing." Christ's words were the means to find life– giving truths; the Holy Spirit gives life.

Ambiguous – Uncertain. Open to more than one interpretation. Synonym amphibolia (q.v.). E.g., Abandon dogmatism; gently suggest your opinion when dealing with ambiguous hendiadys (such as brimstone and fire.) Should there only be one thought "fiery brimstone" or two thoughts: "brimstone" and "fire"?)

Amoebaeon – Repeated phrase at line's end. E.g., "His loving kindness is everlasting" Psalm 118:1–4.

Amphibolia – two true ideas are understood. Sometimes from grammatical structure or improper punctuation. (Not quite ambiguous which means uncertain — where one idea is true and the other may not be true.) E.g., "Go in peace" 2 Kings 5:18. Elisha's answer to Naaman who wished to know if he would be pardoned when he had to bow in the Temple of Rimmon. If Elisha said "Yes

— you may bow", he would have sanctioned idolatry. If he said, "No — do not bow down", Naaman would have violated Elisha's directive. E.g., In John 19:22 Pilate said, "I have written what I have written." Here is double meaning. First is the fact of what he wrote. Second is his ending of discussion on the matter. The Roman soldiers added to it in Matthew 27:37. Finally Luke 23:38 shows a third line. I think Pilate wrote in Hebrew because of the great objection to it by the Jews (Do not write "The king of the Jews" John 19:21). With Latin and Greek as later additions.

Amphidiorthosis – (Double straightening). Corrects a charged statement in two ways. It corrects the speaker's meaning and corrects the hearer's emotion. E.g., "What! Do you not have houses in which to eat and drink? Or do you despise the church of God and shame those who have nothing? What shall I say to you? Shall I praise you? In this I will not praise you" 1 Corinthians 11:22. E.g., "Moreover, the LORD will raise up for Himself a king over Israel who will cut off the house of Jeroboam. This is the day — yes, even today!" 1 Kings 14:14.That prophetic day, is today!

Ampliation(s) – Amplificatio. Enlargement, amplification. Retention of an old name even though a **change** has occurred. E.g., "This is now bone of my bones, And flesh of my flesh; She shall be called Woman, Because she was taken out of Man" Genesis 2:23. The **change** is that it is no longer Adam's bone and flesh. E.g., Aaron's rod that changed into a serpent is still called a rod (Exodus 7:12). E.g., "The wolf will dwell with the lamb" Isaiah 11:6. Although the wolf's nature will change in the millennium, it is still called a wolf. E.g., In John 9:17 the now–healed blind man, is still identified as the "blind man."

Amplification – Amplificatio, Auxesis (q.v.), addition, Pleonasm, redundancy. Using more words than necessary. E.g., "He will not live! He has committed all these abominations, he will surely be put to death; his blood will be on his own head" Ezekiel 18:13. E.g., "God is Light, and in Him there is no darkness at all" 1 John 1:5.

Anabasis – increase or ascent in phrases. Incrementum, Auxesis. (Catabasis is gradual descending). E.g., "How blessed is the man who does not walk in the counsel of the wicked, Nor stand in the path of sinners, Nor sit in the seat of scoffers!" Psalm 1:1. E.g., "You are already filled, you have already become rich, you have become kings without us" 1 Corinthians 4:8.

Anachoresis – return from a regression. Epanaclesis (call back upon, recall). E.g., Eph. 3:14 recalls v.1.

Anachronism– taking something (a person, custom or event) outside its proper historical period. For instance, a town clock is staged in Shakespeare's *Julius Caesar.*

Anachrony – discrepancy between a narrative's presentation of events and the actual sequence of events. The flashback (analepsis) retrospectively jumps back in time; the flashforward (prolepsis) jumps to some future events.

Anaclasis – to break up a poem's rhythm, substitute a long syllable for a short one (or vice versa). E.g., In John Donne, "Batter" is anaclasis:

/ ० ० / ० / ० / ० /

Bat- ter | my   heart| three-   per- | soned   God, | for   you |

Shakespeare's Hamlet. Rhythm (ta Dah) is broken
      by "that is" and "Whether" (Dah ta).
To **be**, or **not** to **be**: **that** is the **ques**tion:
Whether 'tis **nob**ler **in** the **mind** to **suf**fer
The **slings** and **arrows of** out**rage**ous **for**tune'

Anacoenosis – Asking the opinion or judgment of audience. Seeking a common cause by asking: "What do you think about it?" or "What would you say?" Symboulesis, communication. E.g., "And now, O inhabitants of Jerusalem, and men of Judah, judge, I pray you, betwixt me and my vineyard. What could I have done more to my vineyard, that I have not done in it?" Isaiah 5:3–4

Anacoluthon – the expected sequence or grammar gets interrupted because what follows is non sequitur. Often the dash (—) marks the disconnecting point. E.g., Be patient in affliction — let me rest.

Anadiplosis – Reduplication, Reversion (turning back), Epanastrophi, Palillogia. Repetition of a word at end of line and at the beginning of new line. E.g., "He humbled Himself by becoming obedient to the point of **death**, even **death** on a cross." Philippians 2:8. E.g., "the righteous are rewarded with **good** things. A **good** person leaves an inheritance for their children's children," Proverbs 13:21b–22a NIV. E.g., For I have loved long, I crave reward/ Reward me not unkindly: think on kindness,/ Kindness be cometh those of high regard/ Regard with clemency a poor man's blindness. *Fidessa*, sonnet 16 by Griffin 1596.

Anaeresis – aneretic. Distraction used parenthetically. (Parenthetic Tapeinosis.) The clause in a parenthesis is negative and while it appears to take something away, it in fact adds and emphasizes it.

Anagogical – Anagoge. In Middle Ages the 4th sense of interpretation which deals with the mystical and eschatological (final end) of things. (See Appendix B.) As a figure of speech Anagoge is when the sequential clauses build from inferior to superior or from terrestrial to celestial or from mundane to spiritual. (This is a specialized form of Anabasis.) E.g., "What was from the beginning, what we have heard, what we have seen with our eyes, what we have looked at and touched with our hands, concerning the Word of Life" 1 John 1:1.

Anagram – a word or phrase made by using the letters of another word or phrase in a different order: E.g., 'Neat' is an anagram of 'a net'

Analogy – illustration of an idea using a similar but more familiar idea. When teaching about shepherds (Psalm 23) I asked inner city youth, if anyone knew what a shepherd was. Amazingly everyone raised their hands. Choosing the youngest, a six-year-old, I discovered there was a shepherd at the corner gas station whose name was Rex. Ah, they knew German Shepherds. I could now teach, "Just as a German Shepherd guards the gas station, even so a shepherd is a person who guards his sheep." The similarity (parallel or corresponding intrinsic characteristic) is that both guard, even though there are differences such as one is a dog, the other is a person.

Anamnesis – A) In Platonism, it is recollection of ideas a soul remembers from previous existence. B) in a Christian Eucharistic service, it is the remembrance of the Passion, Resurrection and Ascension of Christ. C) As a figure of speech, it **recalls** something to mind. E.g., "I could wish that I myself were accursed, separated from Christ for the sake of my brethren, my kinsmen according to the flesh" Romans 9:3. Paul used to think, to bring to mind.

Anantapodoton – A type of anacoluthon where grammatical expectations are interrupted, leaving the subordinate clause incomplete.

Anaphonema – raising of the voice in Exclamation.

Anaphonesis – (a lifting up of the voice) Exclamation. See Ecphonesis.

Anaphora – Epanaphora, Relatio, relation. Repetition of same word or phrase usually at the start of a line (but repetition may start a clause or sentence). There are many synonyms: Epanaphora, Epembasis, Epibole (several words), Adjectio, Relatio, Repetitio, Repeticio, Repetition, the figure of report. E.g., "Bless the Lord oh my soul, and all that is within me. Bless his Holy name" Psalm 103:1. E.g., **Mad** world! **Mad** kings! **Mad** composition! William Shakespeare, *The Life and Death of King John*, 2.1.561

Anapodoton – omission of a clause. When a speaker interrupts himself without resolving what he began. E.g., "If you think I'm going to sit here and take your insults … ". (The implied clause is "then you would be mistaken"). E.g., "When you decide to promote me to manager then you see more clearly what will benefit this corporation. (Implied clause: then I will be at your service." E.g., "Haply you shall not see me more; or if / A mangled shadow. William Shakespeare, *Antony and Cleopatra*, 4.2.26. [Omitted clause: [if] you do see me again, you will see.]

Anaschesis – taking on one's own self.

Anastrophe – Parallage, Syncategorema, Trajectio, trajection, Inversio, inversion. The **reversal** of the normal order of words for rhetorical effect. "Throw Momma from the train a kiss" is fine Pennsylvania Dutch speak, but gets attention as anastrophe in any other culture. Usually confined to the transposition of one or two words only. (Hyperbation is when several words are out of place.) Normal English structure is a "subject" then a "verb". The *Star Wars* character Yoda spoke object, subject, then verb: "Your path you must decide." "Difficult to see. Always in motion is the future." "Always with you what cannot be done." "Hear you nothing that I say?" "You must unlearn what you have learned." "Try not. Do. Or do not. There is no try." E.g., "You shall not see your countryman's ox or his sheep straying away, and pay no attention to them; you shall certainly bring them back to your countryman" Deuteronomy

22:1. In this verse the verb "shall see" is interrupted by "not" which is out of place. Normal order would read, "if you see your neighbor's critter going astray, you do **not pay no** (or simply you pay) attention to them.

Anesis – Abating, loosening, relaxing. A concluding phrase diminishes what formerly was said. E.g., "Now Naaman, captain of the army of the king of Aram, was a great man with his master, and highly respected, because by him the LORD had given victory to Aram. The man was also a valiant warrior, **but he was a leper**" 2 Kings 5:1.

Annominatio – Agnominatio, Paronomasia or rhyming–words. Two (or more) words have different origin and meaning, but they either sound similar or look alike.

Antanaclasis – See Word–clashing. Repetition of same word in same sentence with two **different** meanings. E.g., Regarding the signers of the Declaration of Independence, Ben Franklin wrote "We must all **hang** together, or most assuredly we shall all **hang** separately." {See Paronomasia which has 2 similar sounding (but different) words. Antanaclasis is akin to Ploce (word folding) but in Ploce the same word is used but with heightened meaning. E.g., "His wife is a wife indeed." "Caesar was Caesar."} "Follow Me, and allow the **dead** to bury their own **dead**" Matthew 8:22 means," Let the spiritually dead bury those that have died." "They are not all **Israel** who are descended from **Israel**" Romans 9:6 means "not all [spiritual] Israel are descendants of [physical] Israel. See Homonym.

Antapodosis – side by side comparison of two things.

Anteisagoge – answer a question, with another question. A simple statement of counter refutation. Anticatallaxis, Anthupophora, Compensation, Contraria Illatio. See Anticategoria which is counter accusation. E.g., "When He entered the temple, the chief priests and the elders of the people came to Him while He was teaching, and said, "By what authority are You doing these things, and who gave You this authority?" Jesus said to them, "I will also ask you one thing, which if you tell Me, I will also tell you by what authority I do these things. "The baptism of John was from what source, from heaven or from men?" Matthew 21:23–25. "You will say to me then, "Why does He still find fault? For who resists His will?" On the contrary, who are you, O man, who answers back to God? The thing molded will not say to the molder, "Why did you make me like this," will it?" Romans 9:19–20.

Antenantiosis – Tapeinosis, demeaning. By speaking less of something, in order to increase it. If clause is in a parenthesis, it is called Anaeresis. In meiosis diminishing one object increases another object. Here this same object is reduced, but heightened. E.g., "A citizen of no mean city" Acts 21:39 meaning an important city. E.g., "Being not weak in faith" Romans 4:19 implies Abraham is strong in faith. E.g., "I praise you not" 1 Corinthians 11:22, means I condemn you in this.

Anteoccupatio – Elimination of anticipated questions or arguments. See Prolepsis.

Antezeugmenon – (yoked before). One verb is joined to two objects. Verb is at the beginning of the sentence. Proepizeuxis, Injunctum. See Zeugma. E.g., "Jabal; he was the father of those who **dwell in tents and [raise] livestock**" Genesis 4:20. "Then the LORD spoke to you from the midst of the fire; you heard the sound of words, but you **saw no form — only a voice**" Deuteronomy 4:12. "Forbidding to marry, and [commanding] to abstain from meats" 1 Timothy 4:3 (KJV) By supplying ellipsis [commanding] the figure looks like an ellipsis, but it really is a zeugma.

Anthimeria – substitution of one part of speech for another. E.g., an adverb for a noun or vice versa. Lord Angelo dukes it well, Shakespeare, *Measure for Measure* 3.2.100.

Anthropopatheia – Condescension, Syncatabasis. Ascribing human feelings, actions or attributes to God. E.g., "Has the LORD's arm been shortened?" Numbers 11:23.

Anthupophora – (reply to an objection). Answering a question with another question. See Anteisagoge.

Anthypallage – The sentence tense shifts to emphasize a point. E.g., "I'm there."

Anthypophora – A figure of reasoning in which one asks and then immediately answers his own questions (or raises and then settles imaginary objections). Reasoning aloud. Anthypophora sometimes takes the form of asking the audience or his adversary what can be said on a matter, and thus can involve both anacoenosis and apostrophe. This is a form of open prolepsis. See Prolepsis. E.g., But someone will say, "How are the dead raised? And with what kind of body do they come?" You fool! That which you sow does not come to life unless it dies" 1 Corinthians 15:35–36B.

Anticatallaxis – Counter with a question. See Anteisagoge. E.g., You will say to me then, "Why does He still find fault? For who resists His will? On the contrary, who are you, O man, who answers back to God?" Romans 9:19–20.

Anticipation – Anticipatio. Expectation. E.g., Anticipating rioters, the mayor set a curfew and requested help from the national guard.

Anticategoria – counter–charge, recrimination. Tu Quoque (an opposite accusation), Accusatio Adversa (an opposite accusation or an accusation turned against another) Translatio in Adversarium (transferring against another.) E.g., "Yet you say, 'The way of the Lord is not right.' Hear now, O house of Israel! Is My way not right? Is it not your ways that are not right?" Ezekiel 18:25. Anteisagoge is a simple question (instead of an accusation).

Anticipation – Anticipatio. A) speaking of something future as though already done or existing (prolepsis q.v.). B) refuting anticipated objections. Synonyms: Procatalepsis, Apantesis, Occupatio, Anteoccupatio, praemonitio.

Anticlimax – a break in intensity by some trivial diversion.

Antimereia – exchange of one part of speech for another. E.g., infinity for a noun: "a man wrestled with him [Jacob] until the **breaking** of the day" Genesis 32:24. Participle for a noun: "But you smear with lies; You are all worthless physicians [healing–ones]" Job 13:4. Participle for adjective: "I call upon the LORD, who is worthy to be praised" Psalm 18:3 [the laudable one]. Preposition for noun: "And who is my neighbor?" Luke 10:29 [near one.] Adverb for adjective: "Do not boast about tomorrow" Proverbs 27:1 [adverb for time to come, later.] Adjective for adverb: "They have beaten us in public [publicly]" Acts 16:37. Adjective for noun: "let the dry [land] appear" Genesis 1:9. Noun for verb: "In His teaching He was saying" Mark 12:38 [During His teaching]. Noun for Adverb: "I will give thanks to You, for I am **fearfully and wonderfully made**" Psalm 139:14. Noun for Adjective: "The steadfast of mind You will keep in perfect peace [peace, peace], Because he trusts in You" Isaiah 26:3.

Antimetabole – a clause which has **words** exactly reversed in grammatical order: AB; BA. (A chiasmus reverses the **thought** or grammatical structure). See Counterchange. E.g., "Woe to those who call evil good, and good evil" Isaiah 5:20. "For My thoughts are not your thoughts, Nor are your ways My ways," declares the LORD, Isaiah 55:8.

Antimetathesis – Polyprosopon (many people), Dialogue. Switching from one person to another. E.g., Romans 3:1–9 is a dialogue between a Jew and Apostle Paul. **Romans is Dialogue**

Figure 4
Romans is Dialogue

Jew:1 Then what advantage has the Jew? Or what is the benefit of circumcision?

Paul:2 Great in every respect. First of all, that they were entrusted with the oracles of God.

Jew:3 What then? If some did not believe, their unbelief will not nullify the faithfulness of God, will it?

Paul:4 May it never be! Rather, let God be found true, though every man be found a liar, as it is written, "that you may be justified in your words, and prevail when you are judged."

Jew:5 But if our unrighteousness demonstrates the righteousness of God, what shall we say? The God who inflicts wrath is not unrighteous, is He? (I am speaking in human terms.)

Paul:6 May it never be! For otherwise, how will God judge the world?

Jew:7 But if through my lie the truth of God abounded to His glory, why am I also still being judged as a sinner?

Paul:8 And why not say (as we are slanderously reported and as some claim that we say), "Let us do evil that good may come"? Their condemnation is just.

Jew:9 What then? Are we better than they?

Paul:9 Not at all; for we have already charged that both Jews and Greeks are all under sin.

Antiphrasis – Permutation. A new and opposite name for an old thing. Ironic use of a single word or phrase. In contrast, irony (q.v.) uses connected sentences. E.g., Give the nickname of "Tiny" to 9.5-foot Goliath. E.g., Death's euphemism: "Lazarus has fallen asleep" John 11:11.

Antipipton – A type of enallage in which one grammatical case is substituted for another.

Note: In English, this is apparent only with pronouns, unlike in inflected languages (Greek, Latin, German, etc.) For Example: "Me Jane, Tarzan". Properly it is "I am Jane, [ellipsis "you are"] Tarzan."

Antiprosopopoeia – (Anti–personification) Persons represented as things. (This is the opposite of prosopopopoeia, which speaks of things as people) E.g., 2 Samuel 16:9 "Why should this **dead dog curse** my lord the king?"

Antirrhesis – vehemently refute an opinion or authority. E.g., Job's wife: "Curse God and die." Job: "You speak like a foolish woman. Should we accept from God only good and not adversity?" Job 2:9–10.

Antisagoge – a counterproposal contradicting an adversary's proposal.

Antistasis – see antanaclasis.

Antistrophe – See epistrophe. See retort.

Antisthecon – It is a misspelling or mispronunciation. E.g., Or, ere they meet, in me, O nature, **cesse**! (properly cease). Shakespeare, *All's Well that Ends Well*, 5.3.75

Antistoixon – a unique word from Zwingli's list. His definition: A sound which is connected with another sound and as such can change.

Antithesis – Contention. Repetition of idea by the exact opposite (or contrast). In rhetoric they are words that contrast or serve to elucidate the opposite idea — usually by balancing the connected clauses with parallel grammatical construction. Akin to antitheton. E.g., One who says to the wicked, "You are righteous,"
Peoples will curse him, nations will scold him; Proverbs 24:24.
E.g., A bliss in proof; and prov'd, a very woe;
Before, a joy propos'd; behind a dream.---Shakespeare, *Sonnets*, 129
E.g., It has been my experience that folks who have no vices have very few virtues, Abe Lincoln.
E.g., For many are called, but few are chosen. Matthew 22:14.

E.g., "If you are living according to the flesh, you must die; but if by the Spirit you are putting to death the deeds of the body, you will live." Romans 8:13'

Antitheton – A proof or composition constructed of contraries. Antitheton is closely related to and sometimes confused with the figure of speech that juxtaposes opposing terms, antithesis. However, it is more properly considered a figure of thought. E.g., Flattery hath pleasant beginnings, but the same hath very bitter endings. R. Sherry

Antitiptosis – a noun is used instead of an adjective. E.g., [kingdom priests] is translated as "kingdom of priests" Exodus 19:6. E.g.,[fullness time] becomes "fullness of the time" Galatians 4:4.

Antonomasia – (literally a different or contrasting name). Instead of proper name or title, use an alternative name (call a wise person, "a Solomon"), title (for teacher use "Rabbonni" [my Master] in John 20:16), or honor (use "your Majesty" for a king). E.g., "Name her Lo-ruhamah [without compassion]" Hosea 1:6.

Apagoresis – The "better not" figure. Often exaggerated to dissuade. E.g., Crude sign in a pharaoh's tomb: If you steal what is here, Your own death will be near.

Apantesis – (meeting). Meeting an objection by anticipation. See Prolepsis.

Aparithmesis – see enumeration.

Apeuche – (to pray something away). See Deprecation.

Aphaersis – omission of letters from the beginning of a word. Often an apostrophe (') replaces the intentional front– cut letters. A kind of metaplasm. E.g., *'scape for escape. 'neath for beneath.* E.g., Coniah replaces Jeconiah in Jeremiah 22:24, "As I live," declares the LORD, "even though **Coniah** the son of Jehoiakim king of Judah …".

Aphodos – (going away from). See Digression.

Aphorism – 1) Sententia (q.v.). A pithy proverb expressed memorially. E.g., "Cleanliness is next to godliness" John Wesley, 1778. E.g., "If it ain't broke, don't fix it." William Satire, 1977. E.g., "Hypocrisy is a homage paid by vice to virtue," La Rochefoucauld. 2) Quotation (q.v.) of known authors or generally accepted truths. E.g., "As some of your own poets have said, 'We are his offspring.'" Acts 17:28. E.g.,

"Bad company corrupts good morals." 1 Corinthians 5:33. E.g., "One of themselves, a prophet of their own, said, 'Cretans are always liars, evil beasts, lazy gluttons.' This testimony is true." Titus 1:12–13. E.g., "Do not handle, do not taste, do not touch!" Colossians 2:21.

Aphorismus – Judgment cast through a question focusing on proper understanding of a word.

E.g., You really think that's what love is?

E.g., You call that a good story?

E.g., For you have but mistook me all this while.

> I live with bread like you, feel want,
>
> Taste grief, need friends: subjected thus,
>
> How can you say to me I am a king? Shakespeare, *Richard II* 3.2.174-177

Apocope – Omitting a letter or syllable at the end of a word. A kind of metaplasm. E.g., yon for yonder. E.g., Jude for Judas. E.g., "Season your admiration for a while With an **attent** ear. [for "attentive"]" Shakespeare, *Hamlet* 1.2.192

Apodeixis – (full demonstration). See Aetiologia.

Apodictic – Apodeixis. "capable of demonstration". Incontrovertible certain self-evident truth. The everybody-knows-it-or-does-it figure. E.g., On earth, you can demonstrate gravity; so gravity is apodictic. E.g., "One thing I do know. I was blind but now I see!" John 9:25.

Apodioxis – Detestation.

Apologue – See fable.

Apomnemonysis – quote an approved authority.

Apophasis – **Implied** insinuation, The deny-it-then-say-it figure. Ironically deny a subject, in order to bring it up. In contrast affirmation (Cataphasis) is **stated** insinuation. "I will not mention the matter, but …" "I will not mention another argument, which, however, if I should, you could not refute." E.g., You spent a lot of money today, not to mention that you borrowed $40.00 from me yesterday." E.g., "I, Paul, am writing this with my own hand, I will repay it (not to mention to you that you owe to me even your own self as well)." Philemon 1:19.

Apopphthegm or apothegm – a pithy aphorism or maxim. E.g., "Patriotism is the last refuge of a scoundrel."

Aporia – See doubt. True or feigned doubt or deliberation about an issue. Asking oneself (or rhetorically asking his hearers) what is the best or appropriate way to approach something. E.g., "What shall I do with you, O Ephraim? What shall I do with you, O Judah? For your loyalty is like a morning cloud And like the dew which goes away early" Hosea 6:4.

Aposiopesis – a sudden silence. It is an unfinished sentence where strong emotion makes the speaker consciously unwilling or unable to continue. Sometimes in print the silent pause shows as a "—". "Get out or else …" E.g., In the parable of the fig tree and the owner wanted to cut the unproductive tree down, the gardener pleads for one more year of cultivation, "if, indeed, it bears fruit for the future, [allow the tree to grow]. Otherwise [if it is not fruitful], cut it down" Luke 13:9). E.g., Moses praying for Israel during the golden calf incident, "But now, if You will, forgive their sin — not, please blot me out from Your book which You have written!" Exodus 32:32. Synonyms are reticentia, parasiopesis. A more intense form is hyposiopesis.

Apostasis – Resumptio. Resumption by repetition of a word after parenthesis. See epanalepsis.

Apostrophe – Sudden diversion in speech from one audience to another. Most often, apostrophe addresses an abstraction, an inanimate object, or someone absent, but the one addressed could be present. This figure often involves emotion, so it can overlap with Exclamation (Exclamatio). This is especially so when a speaker personifies in exclamatory tone. E.g., "O Death, where is your victory? O Death, where is your sting?" 1 Corinthians 15:55. E.g., Within a month … / She married--O most wicked speed: to post/ With such dexterity to incestuous sheets. Shakespeare, *Hamlet*, 1.2.153. E.g., God addressed: "[Tobiah] said, 'Even what they are building — if a fox should jump on it, he would break their stone wall down! **Hear, O our God**, how we are despised! Return their reproach on their own heads and give them up for plunder in a land of captivity. Do not forgive their iniquity and let not their sin be blotted out before You, for they have demoralized the builders." Nehemiah

4:3–5. E.g., "For all of them were trying to frighten us, thinking, "They will become discouraged with the work and it will not be done." **But now, O God, strengthen my hands.**" Nehemiah 6:9. E.g., In Psalm 82:1 God stands to judge, (v. 2–7) the wicked judges are addressed, and by v. 8 the apostrophe addresses God — "Arise, O God, judge the earth! For it is You who possesses all the nations." E.g., Psalm 2:1–9 speaks of king Messiah's millennial rule while v. 10–12 address other kings of the earth. "Now therefore, O kings, show discernment; take warning, O judges of the earth. Worship the LORD with reverence and rejoice with trembling. Do homage to the Son, that He not become angry, and you perish in the way, For His wrath may soon be kindled. How blessed are all who take refuge in Him!" Oneself addressed: E.g., Psalm 103:1,22 "Bless the LORD, O my soul." E.g., Thyself (2nd person) addressed: "Keep your tongue from evil And your lips from speaking deceit" Psalm 34:13. E.g., The city of Tyre addressed: Isaiah 23:16 "Take your harp, walk about the city, O forgotten harlot; Pluck the strings skillfully, sing many songs, That you may be remembered." E.g., Animals addressed: "Do not fear, beasts of the field" Joel 2:22. E.g., Inanimate objects addressed: heavens and earth Deuteronomy 32:1; Mountains of Gilboa 2 Samuel 1:21; court altar 1 Kings 13:2; Sea, Jordan river, mountains Psalm 114:5.

Apposition – Appositio, Appositum. Epithet (q.v.).
   A) Addition of an adjacent, coordinate, explanatory or descriptive element. These normally are noun phrases. (When additional letters are added to a word it is called paragoge.). E.g., Albert Einstein, perhaps the greatest of scientists, seemed not to have mastered the physics of hair combing.
   B) Apposition or naming something by one of its attributes. E.g., 'bowshot' Genesis 31:6.
Ara – See Deprecation.
Archaism – the use of words that are obsolete to the current listeners. E.g., I do you to wit (I want you to know). E.g., I plight you my troth (I pledge to you my truth). E.g., Today a bullock is a castrated male bovine, an ox. Long, long ago ox referred to any male bovine.
Argumentum a fortiori – Argument from strength. If something hard is done, then something easy is more likely to be done.

Ascending Enumeration – a specialized form of diaeresis (where parts are enumerated). Here the enumeration increases (by one) and can mean: A. Emphasis, B. Figurative for Multiple or Myriad, or C. Letteral Significance for the Higher Number.[143] I took every biblical example. Enumeration means to give a detailed list. If the "count of the list" matches the higher number, then sample is place in (C.)Letteral Significance if Higher Number. "Once … twice" uniquely fills (A.)

---

[143] Figurative and Letteral (but not emphatic) uses of "ascending enumeration" are utilized in the Apocryphal book of Sirach (also called Wisdom of Sirach or Ecclesiasticus.)

B. Figurative (when the exact count is not discussed)
E.g., Sirach 23:16 Two sorts of men multiply sin, and the third will bring wrath: a hot mind is as a burning fire, it will never be quenched till it be consumed: a fornicator in the body of his flesh will never cease till he hath kindled a fire. KJV [two specified, third is not.]

C. Number is letterally accurately specified
E.g., Sirach 26:28 There be two things that grieve my heart; and the third maketh me angry: (1) a man of war that suffereth poverty; and (2) men of understanding that are not set by; and (3) one that returneth from righteousness to sin; the Lord prepareth such an one for the sword. KJV
E.g., Sirach 50:25–26 There be two manner of nations which my heart abhorreth, and the third is no nation: (1) They that sit upon the mountain of Samaria, and (2) they that dwell among the Philistines, and (3) that foolish people that dwell in Sichem. KJV
E.g., Sirach 26:5–6 There be three things that mine heart feareth; and for the fourth I was sore afraid: (1) the slander of a city, (2) the gathering together of an unruly multitude, and (3) a false accusation: all these are worse than death. (4) But a grief of heart and sorrow is a woman that is jealous over another woman, and a scourge of the tongue which communicateth with all. KJV
E.g., Sirach 25:7–12 There be nine things which I have judged in mine heart to be happy, and the tenth I will utter with my tongue: (1) A man that hath joy of his children; and (2) he that liveth to see the fall of his enemy: (3) Well is him that dwelleth with a wife of understanding, and (4) that hath not slipped with his tongue, and that hath not served a man more unworthy than himself: (5) Well is him that hath found prudence, and (6) he that speaketh in the ears of them that will hear: (7) O how great is he that findeth wisdom! (8) yet is there none above him that feareth the Lord.(9) But the love of the Lord passeth all things for illumination: he that holdeth it, whereto shall he be likened? (10) The fear of the Lord is the beginning of his love: and faith is the beginning of cleaving unto him. KJV

Emphasis. Otherwise the sample falls into (B) Figurative for Multiple or Myriad.

A. Emphasis. (This group is uniquely filled with "once ... twice" expressions.)

E.g., Psalm 62:11 Once God has spoken; Twice I have heard this: That power belongs to God.

E.g., Job 33:14 Indeed God speaks once, Or twice, yet no one notices it.

E.g., Job 40:5 Once I [Job] have spoken, and I will not answer; Even twice, and I will add nothing more."

B. Figurative for Multiple or Myriad. (Here the enumerated list does not match the higher number.)

E.g., Seven times Amos repeats the phrase "for three transgressions of ... and for four I [the LORD] will not revoke its *punishment*". Only one specific sin is given. Therefore these refer to multiple sins not just 3 or 4. Amos 1:3,6,9,11,13; 2:1,4,6.

E.g., Job 5:19 From six troubles He will deliver you, Even in seven evil will not touch you. Again specific evils are not enumerated, so the numbers mean in multiple ways God delivers from evil.

E.g., Job 33:29 God does all these things to a person— twice, even three times. Both NIV and NASB render "twice, even three times" as oftentimes. The sense is again and again — not just two or three times.

E.g., Ecclesiastes 11:2 Divide your portion to seven, or even to eight, for you do not know what misfortune may occur on the earth. There are not 7 or 8 ways specified, so the intent is to diversify in multiple ways.

C. Letteral Significance for the Higher Number.

E.g., Proverbs 6:16–19. "There are six things which the LORD hates, Yes, seven which are an abomination to Him: 1. Haughty eyes, 2. a lying tongue, 3. hands that shed innocent blood, 4, a heart that devises wicked plans, 5. Feet that run rapidly to evil, 6. A false witness who utters lies, 7. And one who spreads strife among brothers.

E.g., Proverbs 30:15b–16, There are three things that will not be satisfied, Four that will not say, "Enough": 1. Sheol, 2. the barren womb, 3.Earth that is never satisfied with water, and 4. fire that never says, "Enough."

E.g., Proverbs 30:18–19, There are three things which are too wonderful for me, Four which I do not understand: 1. The way of an eagle in the sky, 2. The way of a serpent on a rock, 3.The way of a ship in the middle of the sea, And 4. the way of a man with a maid.

E.g., Proverbs 30:2–23 Under three things the earth quakes, And under four, it cannot bear up: 1.Under a slave when he becomes king, 2. a fool when he is satisfied with food, 3. Under an unloved woman when she gets a husband, and 4. a maidservant when she supplants her mistress.

E.g., Proverbs 30:29–31 There are three things which are stately in their march, Even four which are stately when they walk: 1. The lion which is mighty among beasts And does not retreat before any, 2. The strutting rooster, 3. the male goat also, And 4. a king when his army is with him.

E.g., Micah 5:5 This One will be our peace. When the Assyrian invades our land, When he tramples on our citadels, Then we will raise against him Seven shepherds and eight leaders of men.

E.g., Hosea 6:2 He will revive us after two days; He will raise us up on the third day, That we may live before Him. (I think these numbers are exact, but exactly how they will be prophetically fulfilled is enigmatic to me.)

Asiaticismus – Asiatica abundantia. Oriental expressions derived from Semitic or father east cultures.

Association – Inclusion. When a communicator identifies himself with the audience. E.g., "That they would seek God, if perhaps they might grope for Him and find Him, though He is not far **from each one of us**" Acts 17:27. E.g., "Among them we too" Ephesians 2:3. E.g., "For we also once were foolish ourselves," Titus 3:3.

Assonance – repetition of identical or similar vowel sounds in stressed syllables. Vowel or vocalic rhyme. 'O' sounds in "To the bottom of the bog, the boy brought the frog."

Assumption – Appositio, Proslepsis, Circumductio. When a point supposedly is going to be ignored (Paraleipsis), but it gets fully expanded, it becomes an Assumption. E.g., "And what more shall I say? I **do not have time to tell** about Gideon, Barak, Samson and Jephthah, about David and Samuel and the prophets" Hebrews 11:32. But he goes on to do just that in verses 33–40!

Asterismos – Indicating. Call attention (by making a star or mark). Words used to indicate this are "Lo", "Behold", "verily", and "Yea." E.g., "**Behold** the Lamb of God, the One taking away the sin of the world" John 1:29. E.g., "**Truly, truly**, I say to you, unless one is born again he cannot see the kingdom of God" John 3:3.

Asyndeton – See No–Ands. Omission of connecting words (usually conjunctions) between clauses.

> E.g., "I came, I saw, I conquered." Julius Caesar. E.g., the list of the works of the flesh in Galatians 5:19–21. E.g., List of fruits of the spirit Galatians 5:22.

Athroesmos – See "Concluding Summary"

Attenuation – Extenuatio. Weakening in force or intensity: E.g., Calling a "mortal wound" a "scratch".

Autophasia – (Letterally self-aphasia) which implies one's inability to understand. E.g., Small print bumper sticker: "If you can read this, you're way too close."

Auxesis – (means growth or increasing).

A) Arranging words or clauses in a sequence of increasing force. In this sense, auxesis is comparable to climax and has sometimes been called *incrementum*. E.g., **I may, I must, I can, I will, I do**/ Leave following that which it is gain to miss. Philip Sydney, *Astrophil and Stella*, sonnet 7, circa 1580s.

B) A figure of speech in which something is referred to in terms disproportionately large (a kind of exaggeration or hyperbole). To speak of a scratch by saying, "Look at this wound."

C) Amplification in general, or copy: Erasmus gave 100 variations on, "Your letter pleased me greatly." How many can you think of!

D) See Anabasis (gradual ascent).

Aversion – Adversio. See apostrophe.

Barbarianism, Barbarismus – The use of nonstandard or foreign speech; the use of a word awkwardly forced into a poem's meter; or unconventional pronunciation. E.g., It is barbaric to pronounce Illinois as "Ill– in–noise." E.g., Lan–CASTER' Ohio is accentuated and divided differently than LANC– aster, Pennsylvania. So it is a barbarism to say Lan-CASTER Pennsylvania.

Bathos – an unintentionally failing, feeble or ridiculous anticlimax. In writing it is the unexpected appearance of the commonplace in otherwise elevated style or content. To read a joke (about a blonde who thought a quarterback was a type of refund) in a work primarily about the Eucharist is the height of bathos.

Battologia – Vain repetition. E.g., "when you are praying, do not use **meaningless repetition** as the Gentiles do, for they suppose that they will be heard for their **many words**." Matthew 6:7. E.g., "When they recognized that he was a Jew, a single outcry arose from them all as they shouted for about two hours, 'Great is Artemis of the Ephesians!'" Acts 19:34. E.g., "Then they took the ox which was given them and they prepared it and called on the name of Baal **from morning until noon saying**, 'O Baal, answer us.' But there was no voice and no one answered. And they leaped about the altar which they made." 1 Kings 18:26.

Begging the Question – any argument where the conclusion is inherent in one of its premises. It is akin to circular reasoning: A is true because B is true. B is true so A is true.

Benediction – Benedictio, Blessing. It is both the action of "speaking well of …" and the blessing (or beatitude) itself. A primary duty of a priest is to speak blessings in God's name. "Speak to Aaron and to his sons, saying, 'Thus you shall bless the sons of Israel. You shall say to them.'" Numbers 6:23. E.g., There are three blessings in the creation account: Genesis 1:22,28; 2:3.

Biaeon – a violent retort. See retort.

Blazon – poetic physical description of a lover. E.g., Song of Solomon 4:5 "Your two breasts are like two fawns, Twins of a gazelle Which feed among the lilies."

Bomphiologia (bom-phi-o-LO-gia) – Bombastic bragging speech. The chest-beating figure.

E.g., I am, quite simply, the greatest and most accomplished narrator you will find in the Northern Hemisphere (I have no interest in the South). E.g., Sennacherib's spokesman, Rabshakeh, "Has the god of any nation ever delivered his land from the hand of the king of Assyria? ... Who among all the gods of these lands has delivered his land from my hand? How then can the LORD deliver Jerusalem from my hand?" 2 Kings 18:33,35.

Brachylogy – Breviloquence. Concise but condensed expression. "Morning" instead of "good morning." As a specialized ellipsis, the full meaning of the omitted word(s) can be written with brackets [good] morning or curly brackets {good} morning.

Cacemphaton (cak-EM-pha-ton) – crude, foul or deceptive language. E.g., "warm" in Dutch means not cold, but it could mean very hot.

Cacophonia, Cacophonous – harsh sounding. Cacemphaton deliberately crude (foul) or ill–sounding.

Cacozelia – 1. A stylistic affectation of diction, such as throwing in foreign words to appear learned. 2. Bad taste in words or selection of metaphor, either to make the facts appear worse or to disgust the auditors. E.g., "This is an adultery against the state, to have sex under the trophies of Miltiades." — Seneca.

Candor – Eleutheria, Parrhesia, Licentia. Feeling free to speak boldly, frankly and openly. E.g., "Go and tell that fox" Luke 13:32. "You are of your father the devil," John 8:44.

Casuum Varietas – see "Many Inflections"

Catabasis – see "Gradual Descent."

Catachresis – incongruity. Misapplication of a word or the extension of a word's meaning in a *surprising way*. It usually is a strictly illogical metaphor (— but may be a *surprising* [but proper] translation of a foreign word). Synonyms include: Abusus, abuse, Abusio, abusion. Three forms.

A) Two words link with remote connection. E.g., "Blood of the grape" Deuteronomy 32:14. Men have blood inside them; grapes do not! Yet we understand!

B) Two words connect, but they have different meanings. E.g., "She was foolish enough to order her new Braille book sight unseen. E.g., "Blind mouths." E.g., "Beautiful to the ear." E.g., "Melodious to the eye." E.g., "Sweet to the touch." E.g., Hamlet, "to take arms against a sea of troubles." E.g., "You have made us **stink** in the **sight** of Pharaoh" Exodus 5:21. E.g., Job 4:12 describes an angelic communication as, "Now a word was brought to me stealthily. And my ear received a whisper of it."

C) One word from a foreign language shows up differently. Since words have spheres of understanding, it can be correctly translated in different ways. E.g., The Greek word translated "confess" can also mean "give thanks." Hence Hebrews 13:15 in NIV: "the fruit of lips that openly **profess** his name" and in NASB: "the fruit of lips that **give thanks** to His name."

Catagoge – (origin). Zwingli's term: general expression which means a particular point. (I have not been able to confirm Zwingli's intent, but I associate this with a type of synecdoche where a particular is intended but is referred to by the greater category. E.g., "The law is at the door" means "A policemen is at the door.")

Cataplexis – Threatening or prophesying payback for ill doing. The catastrophic punishment for evil deeds as given in Jeremiah 23:1–2, a jeremiad. E.g., Shakespeare, *The Tempest*, 1.2.321-329 Caliban's curse is rewarded with a threatening prophecy from Prospero:

Caliban: As wicked-dew as e'er my mother brush'd
　　　　With raven's feather from unwholesome fen
　　　　Drop on you both! A south-west blow on ye,
　　　　And blister you all o'er!

Prospero: For this, be sure, to-night thou shalt have cramps,
　　　　Side-stitches, that shall pen thy breath up; urchins
　　　　Shall, for that vast of night that they may work,
　　　　All exercise on thee; thou shalt be pinched
　　　　As thick as honeycomb, each pinch more stinging
　　　　Than bees that made 'em.

Cataploce – Sudden Exclamation. E.g., "Then it came about after all your wickedness ('Woe, woe to you!' declares the Lord GOD)" Ezekiel 16:23.

Catasceue – constructive argument; confirmation of an assumption. This is part of the exordium, the beginning of a speech. For Zwingli this is the prelude to the transition of another part of the speech.

Catastrophe – sensational act, coup de theatre; turning point of an action.

Catch–22 – a long oxymoron akin to synoeciosis. E.g., Space travel is becoming affordable if you die first — ($1000 if dead, $50,000 if alive). Name comes from Joseph Heller's book about the catch in military regulations: to get an insanity discharge, you must request it. But anyone who asks for it, has to be sane!

Categoria – accusatio, criminis reprehensio. Opening an adversary's secret wickedness (often when facing him). E.g., Will you deny your late-night trysts with that man's wife? Shall we discuss your incessant drinking? Your shady business deals? (Silva Rhetoricae). E.g., Jesus reveals the betrayer, Judas (Matthew 26:23). E.g., Paul accuses the sorcerer Elymas (Acts 13:10).

Causae Redditio – See Aetiologia.

Ceratin – Horn (keratin) of dilemma. E.g., Dick Cheney shot and killed a hunter, missing the bird.

Characterismos – See Description of Character.

Charientismus – responding to a harsh verbal attack with soothing mild response. E.g., A soft answer turns away wrath (Proverbs 15:1).

Chiasmus – (from the Greek X "Chi"). Parallelism where the first term is reversed in the second. AB:BA. ABC:CBA. Also called Chiasmos, Chiaston, Decussata Oratio, and Allelouchia. E.g., JFK: "Ask not what your country can do for you, ask what you can do for your country." E.g., "Let us never negotiate out of fear, but let us never fear to negotiate."

E.g., Chiasmus

Figure 5
Format of Zechariah Chapters 1–6

Format of Zechariah Chapters 1–6	Zechariah
A. False peace under Gentile kingdom	1:1–17
B. God breaks empires of Daniel 2 to restore Judah, Israel and Jerusalem	1:18–21
C. Deliverance of true Jerusalem out of Babylon	2:1–13
D. Priesthood and Royalty remodeled before God	3:1–10
D. Priesthood and Royalty remodeled before men	4:1–14
C. The evil of the false Jerusalem sent into Babylon	5:1–11
B. God breaks empires of Daniel 7 to restore Judah, Israel and Jerusalem	6:1–8
A. True peace under Messiah's kingdom	6:9–15

Chleuasmos – Epicertomesis, Mycterismos (turning up the nose). Laugh producing mock, jeer, or scoff. Speaker often turns up the nose. E.g., "He who sits in the heavens laughs, The Lord scoffs at them" Psalm 2:4. E.g., Long scoff in Proverbs 1:22–33. E.g., "you will take up this taunt against the king of Babylon, and say, "How the oppressor has ceased, and how fury has ceased!" Isaiah 14:4. E.g., "How you have fallen from heaven, O star of the morning, son of the dawn! You have been cut down to the earth, You who have weakened the nations!" Isaiah 14:12. E.g., "On that day they will take up against you a taunt And utter a bitter lamentation and say, 'We are completely destroyed! He exchanges the portion of my people; How He removes it from me! To the apostate He apportions our fields.'" Micah 2:4.

Chreia – Quotation. Progymnasmata Exercise. Employing an anecdote which relates a saying or deed **of someone well known.** "Chreia" is from the Greek chreiodes, "useful." In Latin it is Chria. It is a terse enlightening recollection of someone's words or action. To compose:.

1. Praise the speaker, doer or praise the chreia itself
2. Give a paraphrase of the theme
3. Say why this was said or done
4. Introduce a contrast
5. Introduce a comparison
6. Give an example of the meaning
7. Support the saying/action with testimony of others
8. Conclude with a brief epilog or conclusion

Christirismos –Zwingli defines this as using a word or phrase that artfully, exactingly makes the point.

Chronographia – See Description of time. Temporis Descriptio. Pay attention to words of sequence and time: "then," "after that time," "after this," "after these things," etc.

Circular Repetition – Phrase repetition at regular intervals. If at end of passages (as refrain or burden), it is Amoebaeon (q.v.). If repetition is at beginning or middle, it is a Cycloides. E.g., "How the mighty have fallen!" 2 Samuel 1:19,25,27. E.g., "All of them are slain, fallen by the sword" occurs 12 times in Ezekiel 32:20–32! E.g., "His loving devotion endures forever" ends each verse in Psalm 136:1–26. E.g., Revelation 18:21–23, three times "will not be … any longer"

Circumlocution – Circumlocutio, Periphrasis, Circuito. Using many words to "talk around" a subject. Instead of naming it, the speaker describes it. E.g., Washington spin makes everything seem bright. E.g., Instead of "body" — "If the earthly tent which is our house" 2 Corinthians 5:1. E.g., Instead of "I am alive" — "I am in this earthly dwelling" 2 Peter 1:13.

Climax – a sequence of terms linked in chain–like repetition. Climax is the repetition of the last word of one clause or sentence at the beginning of the next, through several clauses or sentences (akin to **repeated** anadiplosis or Epanadiplosis.). It is also called Gradus, gradation, Scala (a ladder), Epiploce (a folding upon). If gradation is upward it is called Anabasis. If gradation is declining or downward, it is called Catabasis. E.g., Romans 5:3–4 "We exult in our tribulations, knowing that tribulation brings about perseverance; and perseverance, proven character; and proven character, hope." E.g., 2 Peter 1:5–7 is another climax. E.g., It is helpful to align the

repeated words to see the structure of the climax in a new way. "But each one is tempted when he is carried away and enticed by his own
lust. Then when
lust has conceived, it gives birth to
sin; and when
sin is accomplished, it brings forth death." James 1:14–15

Closure – the reduction of a work's meaning to a single and complete sense that excludes the claims of other interpretations. "Fear God and keep his commandments." Ecclesiastes 12:13.

Coacervation – Coacervatio. Enumeration (q.v.). Heaping, piling up together; adding together, aggregate (of arguments). Zwingli's Latin word for synathroesmos (q.v.) (also spelled synathroemus).

Coenotes – Commercium. Repetition of two different phrases: one at the beginning and the other at the end of successive paragraphs. Note: Composed of anaphora and epistrophe, coenotes is simply a more specific kind of symploce (the repetition of phrases, not merely words). E.g.,

O give thanks unto the Lord; for He is good: **for his mercy endureth for ever**.

O give thanks unto the God of Gods: **for his mercy endureth for ever**

O give thanks to the Lord of Lords: **for his mercy endureth for ever**. Psalm 136:1–3 KJV.Cohortation – exhortation to encourage or incite the cohort (group). See exultation.

Combination – Syntheton. "And" joins two words expressing two ideas. A synergy (or heightened understanding) may arise, which imparts more than just the two combined thoughts. (In contrast, hendiadys (q.v.) has both words expressing 1 idea.) (In contrast, Syllepsis (q.v.) has 1 repeated word with two different meanings.) Common examples: "tide and time", "rank and fortune", "dust and ashes" Genesis 18:27, "small and great" Psalm 115:13, Moses was "mighty in words and in deeds" Acts 7:22.

Comma – Articulus. Like other modern terms for punctuation, "comma" first referred to a portion of a sentence set off by a "comma mark." Articulus is roughly equivalent to the English "Phrase" — except that the emphasis is on joining several phrases (or words)

successively without any conjunctions (in which case articulus is simply synonymous with the Greek term asyndeton). For example: "Through your ill-will, your injuries, your might, your treachery, you have destroyed the enemy" Cicero, *The Rhetorica Ad Herennium*. (Can you feel the way that the sentence seems to accelerate due to the brief, consecutive phrases — because of the lack of any conjunctions in the series?)

Commercium – see coenotes.

Comminatio – See Deprecation.

Commiseration – Commiseratio. Exciting pity. A feeling of sympathy and sorrow for the misfortunes of others. E.g., "the blind are too often objects of pity".

Commonstratio – see enargia. Zwingli associates commonstratio, demonstratio and epidixis.

Common Cause – English term for anacoenosis.

Comparatio – A general term for a comparison, either as a figure of speech or as an argument. More specific terms are generally employed, such as metaphor, simile, allegory, etc.

Conceit – an unusually farfetched or elaborate metaphor or simile presenting a surprisingly apt parallel between two apparently dissimilar things or feelings. Conceits often employ the devices of hyperbole, paradox and oxymoron. E.g., In some perfumes is there more delight. E.g., "The broken heart is a damaged china pot." E.g., Read Robert Herrick's poem, "The Vine."

Concession – Concessio, Synchoresis (come together, agree on a point), Epichoresis (agreement on a point). Making a concession of one point to gain another. (In contrast, Epitrope is admission or surrender). Admittance, confession. Conceding an argument, either jestingly and contemptuously, or to prove a more important point. A synonym for paromologia. (Admitting a weaker point in order to make a stronger one.) E.g., "Yes, I may have been a petty thief, but I am no felon." E.g., "Righteous are You, O LORD, that I would plead my case with You; Indeed I would discuss matters of justice with You: Why has the way of the wicked prospered? Why are all those who deal in treachery at ease?" Jeremiah 12:1. E.g., "Your eyes are too pure to approve evil, And You cannot look on wickedness with favor. Why do You look with favor On those who deal treacherously? Why are You silent when the wicked swallow up Those more righteous than they?" Habakkuk 1:13. (NASB).

Concluding Summary – Athroesmos, Symperasma. A brief summary, concludes the matter. E.g., Matthew 1:17 summarizes v. 1–16. E.g., Hebrews 11:39 summarizes the chapter on the people of faith, "And all these, having gained approval through their faith, did not receive what was promised."

Condescension – Condescensio. Anthropopatheia, Syncatabasis. Ascribing human feelings, actions or attributes to God. E.g., "Has the LORD's arm been shortened?" Numbers 11:23.

Confirmatio – 4th part of classical oration. This follows propitio (the outline or division) and preceeds refutatio. Here the main body of the speech is presented where one offers logical arguments as proof. The appeal to logos (reason) is emphasized here.

Confutation – Confutatio. A conclusive refutation, which answers counter– arguments of opponent.

Cohabitation – (2 words dwelling together). Synoeceiosis. Repetition of same word in same sentence with an extended meaning. E.g., Least in Matthew 5:19 "Whoever then annuls one of the **least** of these commandments, and teaches others to do the same, shall be called **least** in the kingdom of heaven." There is not a least commandment; therefore that sinner will not be in the kingdom of heaven! E.g., Greatest in Matthew 18:1,4: "Who then is **greatest** in the kingdom of heaven?" … "Whoever then humbles himself as this child, he is the **greatest** in the kingdom of heaven." Here the disciples ask who has the greatest pre-eminence. Illustrating what He Himself did, Jesus illustrates with a child! E.g., Good in Matthew 19:16–17: "Teacher, what **good** thing shall I do that I may obtain eternal life?" And He said to him, "Why are you asking Me about what is **good**? There is only One who is **good**." First good, is human goodness, the second refers to God as the only good one. E.g., Work in John 6:28–29: "What shall we do, so that we may **work the works** of God?" Jesus answered and said to them, "This is the **work** of God, that you believe in Him whom He has sent." "Perseverance in belief that Jesus is the Christ" is the work that saves. Good works do no earn us heaven.

Congeries – a heaping together and piling up of many words that have a similar meaning. But now I am **cabin'd, cribb'd, confin'd, bound in**/ To saucy doubts and fears. Shakespeare, *Macbeth*, 3.4.24. Often congeries is simply the Latin term for synathroesmos ("collection"). However, the Latin term seems to emphasize the emotional amplification of such an accumulation, making congeries akin to climax and grouped among both the Figures of Pathos and the Figures of Amplification (Thus Melanchthon distinguishes incrementum [climax] as a kind of congeries). If the piling up occurs by rapidly touching on one thing and then another, congeries may be considered a type of Epitrochasmus. Some authorities equate congeries with synonymia (such as Melanchthon). See Enumeration.

Conjunction – Coniugative. Synonym for synzeugma as given in *Ad Herennium*. See Zeugma.

Contempt – Exouthenismos, Contemptus. Scorn, disparagement, contemptible, despicable, despised. Seeks audience to look unfavorably on topic. This is the opposite of sympathetic presentation. E.g., Ironic scorn: "What a help you are to the weak! How you have saved the arm without strength!" Job 26:2. E.g., "You who dwell in Lebanon, Nested in the cedars, How you will groan when pangs come upon you, Pain like a woman in childbirth!" Jeremiah 22:23. E.g., "Michal the daughter of Saul came out to meet David and said, "How the king of Israel distinguished himself today! He uncovered himself today in the eyes of his servants' maids as one of the foolish ones shamelessly uncovers himself!" 2 Samuel 6:20.

Contenio – two phrases are set together for contrast. Proverbs abounds in theses contrasts. Synonyms: Contencio, antithesis, antitheton. Opposita, Contraposita. E.g., "The prodigal robs his heir, the miser robs himself." "God demands man's homage; man offers him his patronage." (Quotes from Dr. Robert Anderson, *The Silence of God*, 1897.). E.g., Of Jerusalem, "Righteousness once lodged in her, But now murderers [lodge in her]" Isaiah 1:21. E.g., "We hope for light, but behold, darkness, / For brightness, but we walk in gloom" Isaiah 59:9. E.g., "Through the one man's disobedience the many were made sinners, even so through the obedience of the One the many will be made righteous" Romans 5:19.

Context – text surrounds a phrase that gives further insight into the meaning. Irony must be understood in light of its context.

Contraction – systole. To make short a naturally long vowel. A kind of metaplasm.

In contrast, Diastole lengthens the vowel.

Contraries – Enantiosis. Using opposing or contrary descriptions together, typically in a somewhat paradoxical manner. E.g., "Money is an excellent servant but a cruel master." "I could neither continue listening nor turn away." E.g., "How blessed is the man who does not walk in the counsel of the wicked, Nor stand in the path of sinners, Nor sit in the seat of scoffers!" Psalm 1:1 E.g., "I am God, and there is no other" Isaiah 45:22.

Conundrum – a) a riddle whose answer is or involves a pun. b)a question or problem having only a conjectural answer, c) an intricate and difficult problem. In Matthew 21:23–27 the temple elders wished to trap Jesus with a question regarding "by what authority". In response Jesus gave them a conundrum, "The baptism of John, whence was it? from heaven, or of men? And they reasoned with themselves, saying, If we shall say, From heaven; he will say unto us, Why did ye not then believe him? But if we shall say, Of men; we fear the people; for all hold John as a prophet. And they answered Jesus, and said, "We cannot tell."

Conversion – Conversio. See epistrope. Ending a series of lines, phrases, clauses, or sentences with the same word or words.

Correction – Epanorthosis, Correctio, Diorthosis (set it straight), Epidiorthosis, Metanoea. Recalling in order to correction it. a Retraction. A change of mind, an afterthought. Substitution of a more emphatic word for one just before it. Often amends definition by what it is not. Often employed as an interruption (parenthesis) or as a climax. Three types of correction exist: A) total retraction, B) partial or relative correction and C) conditional changing of the mind.

A) **Absolute** retraction: E.g., I desire not your love, but your submissive obedience. E.g., Regarding the courage of the men in Pickett's Gettysburg charge, "Most brave, nay most heroic act." E.g., "I do believe; help my unbelief" Mark 9:24. E.g., "'Father, save Me from this hour '? But for this purpose I came to this hour" John 12:27.

B) **Partial** correction: E.g., "There are six things which the LORD hates, Yes, seven which are an abomination to Him" Proverbs 6:16. E.g., "King Agrippa, do you believe the Prophets? I know that you do" Acts 26:27. E.g., "In the future there is laid up for me the crown of righteousness, which the Lord, the righteous Judge, will award to me on that day; and not only to me, **but also to all who have loved His appearing**." 2 Timothy 4:8.

C) **Conditional** retraction: E.g., "Did you suffer so many things in vain-- if indeed it was in vain?" Galatians 3:4.

Correspondence – structural repetition of subject matter. Various forms:

1. alternate
2. introverted (or Chiasmus or Epanodos) or
3. complex or combined variously.

E.g., Psalm 19 A 1–4 heavens   Example of Alternate

               B 4–6 The sun in them

          A 7–10 Scriptures

               B 11–14 Your servant in them.

E.g., Leviticus 14:51–52   Example of introverted

A he shall take the cedar wood and the hyssop and the scarlet string

    B with the live bird,

        C and dip them in the blood of the slain bird as well as in the running water,

            D and sprinkle the house seven times.

            D He shall thus cleanse the house

        C with the blood of the bird and with the running water,

    B along with the live bird

A and with the cedar wood and with the hyssop and with the scarlet string.

E.g., Galatians 2:16 Example of introverted

A knowing that a man is not justified

    B by the works of the Law

        C but through faith in Christ Jesus,

        C even we have believed in Christ Jesus,

        so that we may be justified by faith in Christ

    B and not by the works of the Law; since by the works of the Law

A no flesh will be justified.

Counterchange – Antimetabole, Diallelon, Metathesis, Commutatio. A **clause** which has words exactly **reversed** in grammatical order: AB; BA. (A chiasmus reverses the thought or grammatical structure). E.g., "Thy **sea** within a **puddle's** womb is hearsed,/ and not the **puddle** in thy **sea** dispersed." Shakespeare, *The Rape of Lucrece*, 657-658. E.g., "Woe to those who call evil good, and good evil" Isaiah 5:20. E.g., "For My thoughts are not your thoughts, Nor are your ways My ways," declares the LORD Isaiah 55:8.

Cycloides – See circular repetition.

Definition – Horismos, Definitio. Briefly and precisely define the subject. E.g., "Blessed are the **gentle** [meek KJV], for they shall inherit the earth." Matthew 5:5. Strong's defines meekness as mild or gentle. I prefer to think of it as **humble**. But there is more to it, HELPS Ministries, Inc., Word–studies: "It is not weakness but rather refers to exercising God's strength under His [God's] control — i.e. demonstrating power without undue harshness. [The English term "meek" often lacks this blend — i.e. of gentleness (reserve) and strength.]" "Now the man Moses was very humble, more than any man who was on the face of the earth)" Numbers 12:3.

Deiectio – Zwingli's Latin term for exouthenismos — an expression of contempt. Deiectio (dejection in English) refers to a melancholy emotion of feeling deeply sad, low spirited and depressed.

Deliberativus – see Genus Deliberativus.

Demonstration – Demonstratio, enargia. A figure aiming at vivid, lively description.

Deprecation – deprecatio (praying against). Express deprecation feelings. Three types occur.

1. Praying against evil. E.g., "I [Jesus] do not ask You [heavenly Father] to take them out of the world, but to keep them from the evil one" John 17:15. Following the golden calf incident, "Moses returned to the LORD, and said, 'Alas, this people has committed a great sin, and they have made a god of gold for themselves. But now, if You will, forgive their sin and if not, please blot me out from Your book which You have written!' The LORD said to Moses, 'Whoever has sinned against Me, I will blot him out of My book.'" Exodus 32:31–33.

2. Imprecatory (q.v.) prayer. Beseeching God to reward evil doers with His curse. E.g., "When he is judged, let him come forth guilty, And let his prayer become sin. Let his days be few; Let another take his office. Let his children be fatherless And his wife a widow" Psalm 109:7–9.

3. Ejaculatory prayer – short prayer of aspiration such as "Praise the Lord!", "Hallelujah!", and "Amen!" E.g., The Jesus Prayer: "Lord Jesus Christ, Son of God, have mercy on me, a sinner." E.g., "Deliver us from evil" Matthew 6:13.

Derivation – Derivatio. Paregmenon. Repetition of words similar in origin and sound, but not similar in sense. This figure is common in all languages but rarely can be translated into another language. E.g., "You are Peter [πετρος], and upon this rock [πετρα] I will build My church" Matthew 16:18. "Peter" letterally means a rock which is small enough to be thrown by hand. The rock, which the church is built upon, is a huge cliff, like the Rock of Gibraltar. In context that rock is not Peter, but the confession that "Jesus is the Christ, the Son of the living God" (v. 16.). E.g., "For as through the one man's [Adam's] disobedience [παρακοης] the many were made sinners, even so through the obedience [ὑπακοης] of the One [Christ] the many will be made righteous" Romans 5:19.

Description – Descriptio. Broad category to description a: thing, person, place, time, or action.

See: Description of Actions, Description of Character, Description of Circumstances, Description of Feelings, Description of Manners, Description of Order, Description of Persons, Description of Place, Description of Sayings, Description of Time, Word–picture, and Word–portrait.

Description of Actions – Pragmatographia. Detailed description of an event. E.g., Great Tribulation (Matthew 24:21,15–31. Daniel 9:27, 12:1, 11; Revelation 7:13–14.) Christ's return to earth (Matthew 24:29–31B; Zechariah 14; Revelation 19:11–21).

Description of Character – Characterismos. Description of a person's character or morals. E.g., "The Word became flesh, and dwelt among us, and we saw His glory, glory as of the only begotten from the Father, full of grace and truth" John 1:14. E.g., Cornelius was "a devout man and one who feared God with all his household, and gave many alms to the Jewish people and prayed to God continually" Acts 10:2.

Description of Circumstances – Peristasis, Circumstantiae Descriptio. Description of setting or circumstances. (If description is given to move passions, it is called Diaskeue.) E.g., "Jacob's well was there. So Jesus, being wearied from His journey, was sitting thus by the well" John 4:6.

Description of Feelings – Pathopoeia. Expression or description of feelings or affections. E.g., "When He approached Jerusalem, He saw the city and wept over it" Luke 19:41.

Description of Manners – Ethopoeia, Notation, Morum Expressio. Description of customs or characteristics of person or place (natural propensities, manners and affections, etc.). A kind of enargia. E.g., "The daughters of Zion are proud And walk with heads held high and seductive eyes, And go along with mincing steps And tinkle the bangles on their feet" Isaiah 3:16.

Description of Order – Protimesis. Sequence uses first, then, again, second, etc. E.g., Regarding witnesses to the resurrection 1 Corinthians 15:5–8B uses "He appeared to Cephas, **then** to the twelve. **After that** He appeared to more than five hundred brethren at one time, most of whom remain until now, but some have fallen asleep; **then** He appeared to James, **then** to all the apostles; and **last of all**, as to one untimely born, He appeared to me [Paul] also."

Description of Persons – Prosopographia, Personae Descriptio. Vivid description of a person. E.g., "Now John himself had a garment of camel's hair and a leather belt around his waist; and his food was locusts and wild honey" Matthew 3:4.

Description of Place – Topographia, Loci Descriptio. Description of a place. E.g., New Jerusalem Revelation 21:9–22:3B.

Description of Sayings – Mimesis, Imitatio. Emphasis by way of imitation on another's way of saying [accent] or use of particular words to describe something. E.g., Thus says the Lord GOD, "Because the enemy has spoken against you, 'Aha!' and, 'The everlasting heights have become our possession,' Ezekiel 36:2. E.g., But someone will say, "How are the dead raised? And with what kind of body do they come?" 1 Corinthians 15:35.

Description of Time – Chronographia, Temporis Descriptio. Chronology. Pay attention to words of sequence and time: "then," "after that time," "after this," "after these things," etc. E.g., John is told to "write the things which you have seen, and [even] the things which are, and the things which **will take place after these things**" Revelation 1:19. Present Things are in the seven churches (Revelation 2–3). Future things that will take place are in Revelation 4–22:7. We know this because of the wording of Revelation 4:1: "Come up here, and I will show you what must happen **after these things**."

Figure 6
Revelation's Chronology

Revelation 1:19		Rev. Chapter
write the things which you have seen,	<= Past	1
and the things which are,	<= Present	2–3 (90 AD)
and the things which will take place		4–22:7
after these things	<= Future	

Detestation – Detestatio. Apodioxis. The figure of Detestation or banishment. Reject argument as irrelevant, needless, false, wicked, absurd. Synonyms abomination, rejection, detestation. E.g., Jeremiah 9:2 "Oh that I had in the desert A wayfarers' lodging place; That I might leave my people And go from them! For all of them are adulterers, An assembly of treacherous men."

Diaeresis or Dieresis – in rhetoric, a figure by which the parts or attributes of anything are enumerated. E.g., Proverbs 30:18–19: "There are three things too wonderful for me, four that I cannot understand: the way of an eagle in the sky, the way of a snake on a rock, the way of a ship at sea, and the way of a man with a maiden." See ascending enumeration.

Dialogue – Dialogismos, Subjectio (substituting), Responsio (responding). Conversation between two or more people. Logismus is when one speaker presents both sides. Sermocinatio is when another's words are used. Dianoea is animated dialogue. E.g., Those who see you will gaze at you, **They** will ponder over you, **saying**, "Is this the man who made the earth tremble, Who shook kingdoms, Who made the world like a wilderness And overthrew its cities, Who did not allow his prisoners to go home?" Isaiah 14:16–17. E.g., "On that day they will take up against you a taunt And utter a bitter lamentation and **say**, 'We are completely destroyed! He exchanges the portion of my people; How He removes it from me! To the apostate He apportions our fields.'" Micah 2:4. Romans is dialogue, see Antimetathesis.

Diaporesis – being without passage or resource. See Aporia.

Diasyrmos – See Raillery.

Diastole – To lengthen a vowel or syllable beyond its typical length. A kind of metaplasm. The third syllable of "serviceable" is normally short, but as this word occurs in the following line of iambic pentameter, that syllable is lengthened because it takes the stress of the meter's rhythm (stressed syllables are in italics): I *know* thee *well*; a ser*vice*able villain. Shakespeare, *King Lear* 4.6.251

Diatribe – Archaic use: critical dissertation: Romans is a diatribe that the "just shall live by faith" (Romans 1:17) addressing Jewish and Gentile perspectives. Modern use: bitter criticism.

Diazeugma – one noun is linked to several verb phrases, usually arranged in a parallel series. E.g., "A wise man will hear and increase in learning, And a man of understanding will acquire wise counsel" Proverbs 1:5.

Diexodos – See Expansion.

Digression – an excursus or temporary departure from one subject to another related topic before returning to the main subject. Synonyms: Parecbasis, Parabasis, Ecbole, Aphodos. E.g., Genesis 2:7 God forms man. A digression about the Garden of Eden occurs in 2:8–14. After this, the subject returns to man:" Then the LORD God took the man and put him into the garden of Eden to cultivate it and keep it. The LORD God commanded the man, saying, "From any tree of the garden you may eat freely; but from the tree of the knowledge of good and evil you shall not eat, for in the day that you eat from it you will surely die." Genesis 2:15–17B. E.g., The generations of Isaac (Genesis 25:19–35:29B). A digression, on Esau's generations, follows in Genesis 36–37B. Then Joseph (Isaac's offspring) continues Genesis 37–50. Excursus is a digression in written material.

Dilemma – Offering to an opponent a choice between two (equally unfavorable) alternatives. Either your client is guilty of perjury, or of murder.

Distribution – Merismos, Epimerismos, Diallage, Distributio, Discriminatio. Enumeration of parts of a whole that is mentioned. The effect is to enhance and amplify — (not divide). E.g., **Behold, the LORD lays the earth waste**, devastates it, distorts its surface and scatters its inhabitants. And the people will be like the priest, the servant like his master, the maid like her mistress, the buyer like the seller, the lender like the borrower, the creditor like the debtor. The earth will be completely laid waste and completely despoiled, for the LORD has spoken this word" Isaiah 24:1–3.

Doubt – Aporia. True or feigned doubt or deliberation about an issue. Asking oneself (or rhetorically asking one's own hearers) what is the best or appropriate way to approach something.

Dubitatio (doubt, wavering, uncertainty), Addubitatio (begin to doubt or hesitate). E.g., "What shall I do with you, O Ephraim? What shall I do with you, O Judah? For your loyalty is like a morning cloud And like the dew which goes away early" Hosea 6:4. "The manager said to himself, 'What shall I do, since my master is taking the management away from me? I am not strong enough to dig; I am ashamed to beg" Luke 16:3. E.g., "Whether he took them from his fellows more impudently, gave them to an harlot more lasciviously, removed them from the Roman people more wickedly or altered them more presumptuously, I cannot well declare.—Henry Peacham, *The Garden of Eloquence*, 109

Druckfehler – misprint, typo, or erratum.

Dubitatio – (doubt, wavering, uncertainty). See Aporia.

Duplication – Epizeuxis, Gemination, Iteration, Conduplicatio, Subjunctio. **Repetition** of the same word in the same sense. Geminatio (doubling), Iteratio, Conduplicatio is when the word is repeated right after itself. When the two words are separated, it is called Epizeuxis (yoked upon) or Subjunctio. E.g., "Behold, **I, even I** am bringing the flood of water upon the earth" Genesis 6:17. "The water prevailed more and more upon the earth" [more more] Genesis 7:19. "But the angel of the LORD called to him from heaven and said, "**Abraham,**

Abraham!" Genesis 22:11. "Until **Your people pass over**, O LORD, **Until the people pass over** whom You have purchased" Exodus 15:16. "Then the LORD passed by in front of him and proclaimed, **"The LORD, the LORD** God, compassionate and gracious, slow to anger, and abounding in loving kindness and truth" Exodus 34:6. "My God, my God, why have You forsaken me?" Psalm 22:1 (Matthew 27:46). "for He is coming, for He is coming to judge the earth" Psalm 96:13. "They kept on calling out, saying, "Crucify, crucify Him!" Luke 23:21. "Truly, truly, I say to you" John 1:51.

Echoism – See Onomatopoeia. Words that echo or accurately reflect the sound: Buzz, hiss, peep.

Ecbole – See Digression.

Ecphonesis – Anaphonesis (lifting up the voice), Exclamatio. Expression of feeling by way of exclamation. See exclamation. E.g., "My heart is steadfast, O God, my heart is steadfast; I will sing, yes, I will sing praises!" Psalm 57:7. Then I said, "Woe is me, for I am ruined! Because I am a man of unclean lips, And I live among a people of unclean lips; For my eyes have seen the King, the LORD of hosts" Isaiah 6:5. "Which one of the prophets did your fathers not persecute? They killed those who had previously announced the coming of the Righteous One, whose betrayers and murderers you have now become" Acts 7:52. "Wretched man that I am! Who will set me free from the body of this death?" Romans7:24.

Effictio – See Word–portrait.

Eironeia – See irony.

Either/Or – Neither/Nor, Paradiastole, Disjunctio. Repeated disjunction (lack of correspondence). E.g., "Who will separate us from the love of Christ? Will tribulation, or trouble, or persecution, or famine, or nakedness, or danger, or sword? Romans 8:35.

　　E.g., "For I am convinced that neither death, nor life, nor angels, nor principalities, nor things present, nor things to come, nor powers, nor height, nor depth, nor any other created thing, will be able to separate us from the love of God, which is in Christ Jesus our Lord." Romans 8:38–39.

　　E.g., "Those who are sickly you have not strengthened, the diseased you have not healed, the broken you have not bound up, the scattered you have not brought back, nor have you sought for the lost; but with force and with severity you have dominated them." Ezekiel 34:4.

Ellipsis – Brachylogy. Words omitted from a sentence that usually can be auto supplied (non-repetitive) or known from the context (repetitive). Three dots ' … ' grammatically show the omission. "I will … to Ireland" means "I will [go] to Ireland." "Your blood upon your head" (Acts 18:6) filled out becomes "Your blood [will be] upon your head." Sometimes the addition is put in italics. "Jesus took some bread, and after a blessing, He broke *it* and gave *it* to the disciples" Matthew 26:26.

There are many, many types of complex ellipsis. I will briefly illustrate Concisa Locutio (concise or abbreviated speech) where the omitted word is contained in another word. This is also called composition, Syntheton, Synthesis, Constructio Praegnans, where the verb derives added force. E.g., Slaughter (to kill an animal) can be either for meat or for sacrifice. Deuteronomy 12:15, 22 allow for slaughter anywhere to produce food. Leviticus 17:3 seems to contradict this until the context reveals that slaughter [for sacrifice] must only be done at the court altar. "Any man from the house of Israel who slaughters [for sacrifice] an ox or a lamb or a goat in the camp, or who slaughters it [for sacrifice] outside the camp, **and has not brought it to the doorway of the tent of meeting** to present it as an offering to the LORD before the tabernacle of the LORD, blood guiltiness is to be reckoned to that man. He has shed blood and that man shall be cut off from among his people."

Emblem – a picture with symbolic meaning, visual allegory. E.g., In heraldry or butter imprints.

Emphasis – force or intensity of expression that gives impressiveness and calls for importance to those words. Speakers may vary the tone, pitch or speed of speech. Writers *italicize* important words. Quietly reading "Repent" does injustice to the emphasis by which John the Baptist uttered that word (Matthew 3:2).

Enallage – Enallaxis. See Exchange. A grammatical substitution which makes a sentence semantically equivalent but grammatically different. E.g., Use king's English where 'we' is used instead of 'I'. Enallage never substitutes one noun for another but allegory does!

Enantiosis – Using opposing or contrary descriptions together, typically in a somewhat paradoxical manner. E.g., "Money is an excellent servant but a cruel master." E.g., "I could neither continue listening nor turn away." E.g., "Blessed is the man that walketh not in the counsel of the ungodly, nor standeth in the way of sinners, nor sitteth in the seat of the scornful." Psalm 1:1 (KJV). E.g., "I am God, and there is no other" Isaiah 45:22.

Enargia – Generic name for a group of figures aiming at vivid, lively *description* usually visual: diatyposis, hypotyposis, demonstratio, descriptio, commonstratio, epidixis. (Not energia.)

Energia – A general term referring to "energy". Energia is not necessarily visual, and not necessarily descriptive. (Not enargia.)

Enigmatic Saying – Obscure or dark saying. A mysterious riddle where the words that are known, but their meaning or interpretation is not readily understood. Parables usually have explanations, enigmatic sayings may not. English translations: dark saying Psalm 49:4, 78:2; dark sentence Daniel 8:23; dark speech Numbers 12:8; hard question 1 Kings 10:1. 2 Chronicles 9:1; proverb Habakkuk 2:6; riddle Judges 14:12,13,14,15,16,17,18,19, Ezekiel 17:2. E.g., Samson's riddle: "Out of the eater came something to eat, and out of the strong came something sweet" Judges 14:14. Answer: "What is sweeter than honey? And what is stronger than a lion?" Judges 14:18. E.g., Belshazzar's feast was interrupted by writing on the wall: MENE, MENE, TEKEL, UPHARSIN. [In English these words mean: Numbered, Numbered, Weighed, Divided.] Daniel supplied the interpretation: "This *is* the interpretation of the thing: MENE; God hath numbered thy kingdom, and finished it. TEKEL; Thou art weighed in the balances, and art found wanting. PERES; Thy kingdom is divided, and given to the Medes and Persians." Daniel 5:25–28.

Enthymeme – Enthymema. Commentum (a thought) and Conceptio (draw up a statement) are the Latin words for this.

    A) A figure of speech which bases a conclusion on the truth of its contrary. "If to be foolish is evil, then it is virtuous to be wise."

    B) An abbreviated syllogism where a premise is missing. This enthymeme typically occurs as a conclusion coupled with a reason. When several enthymemes are linked together, this becomes sorites.

E.g., "We cannot trust this man, for he has perjured himself in the past. (The major premise is missing: Those who perjure themselves cannot be trusted.)

E.g., We are dependent   (minor premise)

Therefore we should be humble.   (Conclusion)

Dependent people should be humble (unstated major premise)

E.g., Romans 7:1–6.   v.

A husband and wife are bound by law to be faithful to each other.   2

If her husband is alive and she joins with another, then she is   3 an adulterous.

If her husband dies, she is free and not an adulterous even if   3 she remarries.

                (unstated: If she dies, she is free)

Law has dominion over a man while he is alive.   1

We were made to die to the Law through the body of Christ.   4

So that we might be joined to Him who was raised from the dead.   4

E.g., Syllogism: 1. It is wicked to punish a righteous [or innocent] man.

                  2. Jesus is a righteous man.

                  3. Therefore, have nothing to do with punishing him.

Note: three testify to the righteous and innocent character of Jesus

A) Pilate's wife: "Have nothing to do with that righteous Man" Matthew 27:19.

B) The prisoner crucified with Jesus, "This man has done nothing wrong." Luke 23:41.

C) The Centurion, "Certainly this man was innocent." Luke 23:47.

Enumeration – Enumeratio, Synathroesmos, Aparithmesis, Congeries, Eirmos. Count off differing individual parts, where there is no mention of the whole group (or sum of the parts). Some identify these as amplification. Similarly "Ascending Enumeration" q.v. may be figurative or letteral.

    E.g., "What are your multiplied sacrifices to Me?" Says the LORD.

"I have had enough of burnt offerings of rams / And the fat of fed cattle;
And I take no pleasure in the blood of bulls, lambs or goats." Isaiah 1:11.

E.g., See: Isaiah 3:16–23; Romans 1:29–31; 1 Timothy 4:1–3B; 2 Tim.
3:1–7; 1 Peter 4:3.

At times the number letterally means that number.

E.g., Proverbs 30:24–28 Four things are small on the earth, But they
are exceedingly wise: 1. Ants are not a strong people, But they
prepare their food in the summer; 2. Shephanim [Hebrew root
word means "hiders" — hyrax syriacus] are not mighty people,
Yet they make their houses in the rocks; 3. Locusts have no king,
Yet all of them go out in ranks; 4. Lizard [E.g., geckos] you may
grasp with the hands, Yet it is in kings' palaces.

The following are **NOT** enumeration because they mention the
whole group:

Merismus — because it has an overall name given to the collection.

Synonymia — it groups all synonyms.

Symperasma — has the grouping in a conclusion.

Epadiplosis – Double encircling. Repeated Epanadiplosis. When words
are repeated at both the beginning and end of a line. E.g., "Sing
praises to God, sing praises; Sing praises to our King, sing praises"
Psalm 47:6. E.g., "For if we live, we live for the Lord, or if we die, we
die for the Lord; therefore whether we live or die, we are the Lord's"
Romans 14:8.

Epanadiplosis or Epizeuxis – Inclusion, Cyclus. Repeated word
made for emphasis with no other intervening words. Sometimes
extremely difficult to translate. E.g., "Holy, Holy, Holy" (Revelation
4:8). E.g., "Babylon the Great has fallen, has fallen" (Revelation
14:8, 18:2). E.g., "Before him there was no king **like him** who
turned to the LORD with all his heart and with all his soul and
with all his might, according to all the law of Moses; nor did any
like him arise after him" 2 Samuel 23:25. E.g., "Hope that is seen
is not hope; for who hopes for what he already sees?" Romans
8:24. E.g., "Rejoice in the Lord always; again I will say, rejoice!"
Philippians 4:4. E.g., "**What use is it**, my brethren, if someone says
he has faith but he has no works? Can that faith save him? 15If

a brother or sister is without clothing and in need of daily food, 16and one of you says to them, "Go in peace, be warmed and be filled," and yet you do not give them what is necessary for their body, **what use is that**? Even so faith, if it has no works, is dead, being by itself." James 2:14–17.

Epanalepsis – Resumptio, resumption. Repetition (or taking up again) of the beginning at the end. The echo may be a single word (Iteratio), whole phrase (Repetitio), or before and after long intervening passages (Inclusio) or parenthesis (Apostasis). E.g., "**Rejoice** in the Lord always: and again I say, **Rejoice**" (Philippians 4:4). E.g., Blood hath bought blood, and blows have answer'd blows:/ Strength match'd with strength, and power confronted power. Shakespeare, *King John*, 2.1.329–30.

Epanodos – In rhetoric, Reditus is a return to a theme after an excursus. As a figure of speech, it is a repetition of words in reverse order. Synonyms: Inversion, Regressio, Chiasmus, Synantesis.

> E.g., Blessed be the God   2 Corinthians 1:3
> and Father of our Lord Jesus Christ,
> the Father of mercies
> and God of all comfort,.

> E.g., Now the flax   Exodus 9:31
> and the barley were ruined,
> for the barley was in the ear
> and the flax was in bud.

Epanorthosis – See Correction.

Epenthesis – add letters, sound, or syllable to the middle of a word. A kind of metaplasm.
Note: Epenthesis is sometimes employed in order to accommodate meter in verse; sometimes, to facilitate easier articulation of a word's sound. It can, of course, be accidental, and a vice of speech. E.g., Lie blist'ring fore the **visitating** sun.

Epexegesis – See Fuller Explaining.

Epibole – Repetition of same **phrase** at **irregular** intervals.

E.g., when Jael killed Sisera, "Between her feet he bowed, he fell, he lay; Between her feet he bowed, he fell; Where he bowed, there he fell dead" Judges 5:27. E.g., "The voice of the LORD" occurs 7 times in Psalm 29:3,4,4,5,7,8,9.

A| Do not store up for yourselves
    B| treasures on earth,
        C| where moth and rust destroy,
            D| and where thieves break in and steal.
A| But store up for yourselves
    B| treasures in heaven,
        C| where neither moth nor rust destroys,
            D| and where thieves do not break in or steal.
Matthew 6:19–20.

Epichirema – A syllogism in which the proof of the major or minor premise, or both, is introduced with the premises themselves, and the conclusion is derived in the ordinary manner. Zwingli sees ancient speeches drawing the full conclusion, and later development tied together all the arguments here.

Epiclesis – inclusion. See Epanalepsis. Letterally it means "calling upon." 1) As a rhetorical figure of speech, Zwingli used it to recall a cause after a long interruption. 2) For Catholics, epiclesis is the specialized prayer by a consecrated priest which calls upon God to change the Eucharistic elements into the body and blood of Christ. 3) For Greek Orthodox, the "communion epiclesis" is the call for the Holy Spirit to join the congregation's hearts to the words and actions of the priest. The "consecratory epiclesis" makes the gifts of bread and wine holy (and is absolutely necessary in Greek Orthodoxy). See epiclesis in the glossary.

Epicrisis – See Judgment. A standalone short sentence, often at the end of a paragraph, which adds judgment or clarification. E.g., "These things took place in **Bethany** beyond the Jordan, where John was baptizing" John 1:28. They had come from Jerusalem (v.19), so they had traveled a good bit.

Epididosis – concession, Concessio. Conceding an argument, either jestingly and contemptuously, or to prove a more important point. A synonym for paromologia.

Epidixis – Enargia: a figure aiming at vivid, lively description. Zwingli's Synonyms: Commonstratio, commonstration, Demonstratio, demonstration.

Epilogue – Providing an inference of what is likely to follow.

Epimone – Commoratio, Synonymia, Communio. lingering (q.v.). Dwell repeatedly on a point using different words. E.g., Zechariah 1:3–6 the people did not listen to God, therefore they brought this trouble on themselves. E.g., In Matthew 7:21–23 being a channel for Pentecostal power is no guarantee of salvation! Jesus does not deny that they prophesied, cast out demons and did miracles in His name! They did not do the will of the Father v.21] and they practiced lawlessness.

Epiphonema – An exclamation (q.v.) at the conclusion. An epigrammatic summary which gathers into a pithy sentence what has preceded. A striking, summarizing reflection. If it is very brief and emphatic, it is called Deinosis. E.g., "Thus let all Your enemies perish, O LORD" Judges 5:31. E.g., "How blessed are all who take refuge in Him!" Psalm 2:12. E.g., "Salvation belongs to the LORD; Your blessing be upon Your people!" Psalm 3:8. E.g., "He who has ears to hear, let him hear" Matthew 11:15. E.g., "A voice out of the cloud said, 'This is My beloved Son, with whom I am well-pleased; **listen to Him**!'" Matthew 17:5. E.g., "For many are called, but few are chosen" Matthew 22:14. E.g., "He who testifies to these things says, 'Yes, I am coming quickly.' **Amen. Come, Lord Jesus**" Revelation 22:20. E.g., "Thus is the haughty miller soundly beat, And thus he's lost his pay for grinding wheat, And paid for the two suppers, let me tell, of Alain and of John, who've tricked him well, His wife is taken, also his daughter sweet; **Thus it befalls a miller who's a cheat**." Chaucer, *The Reeve's Tale*.

Epiphoza – Argument repeating same words at end of successive sentences.

E.g., Are they Hebrews?	So am I. 2 Corinthians 11:22.
Are they Israelites?	So am I.
Are they descendants of Abraham?	So am I.

Epistrophe – Conversion, Antistrophe, Epiphora, Repetition of words at the end of a clause, line, or sentence. E.g., "We are born to **sorrow,** pass our time in **sorrow,** end our days in **sorrow.** I'll have my **bond**!/ Speak not against my **bond**!/ I have sworn an oath that I will have my **bond**." Shakespeare, *The Merchant of Venice*, 3.3.4. E.g., "Who is this **King of glory**? The LORD of hosts, He is the **King of glory**" Psalm 24:10. E.g., "He is their help and their shield" is repeated in Psalm 115:9–12B.

Epitasis – Intentio. The addition of a concluding sentence that merely emphasizes what has already been stated. A kind of amplification. E.g., "Clean your bedroom. All of it." E.g., "But I know that the king of Egypt will not permit you to go, except under compulsion." Exodus 3:19.

Epitherapeia – (to apply additional remedy). Adding a sentence to heal, soften or modify what was previously said so that feelings might not be offended. It may serve as an apology. (See Protherapeia and Prodiorthosis) E.g., "He came to the disciples and found them sleeping, and said to Peter, "So, you men could not keep watch with Me for one hour? Keep watching and praying that you may not enter into temptation; **the spirit is willing, but the flesh is weak**." Matthew 26:40–41. E.g., "I rejoiced in the Lord greatly, that now at last you have revived your concern for me; indeed, you were concerned before, **but you lacked opportunity**" Philippians 4:10.

Epithet – Epitheton, Appositum, apposition. Naming a thing by describing it. Attributing to a person or thing a quality or description — sometimes by the simple addition of a descriptive adjective; sometimes through a descriptive or metaphorical apposition. Note: If the description is given in place of the name, instead of in addition to it, it becomes antonomasia or periphrasis. E.g., unfettered joy. Rosy-fingered dawn. Swift-footed Achilles. Often a measure: "bowshot" Genesis 31:6, "hand–breadth Exodus 25:25, "hair–breadth" Judges 20:16. "stone's–throw" Luke 22:41.

Epitimesis – See Reprimand. Feelings expressed by rebuke, reproof or reproach. E.g., "O foolish men and slow of heart to believe in all that the prophets have spoken!" Luke 24:25.

Epitrechon – Subcontinuatio. Running Along. A short explanatory sentence is put parenthetically inside another. E.g., God said to Abram, "Know for certain that your descendants will be strangers in a land **that is not theirs, where they will be enslaved and oppressed** four hundred years." Genesis 15:13. E.g., "But so that you may know that the Son of Man has authority on earth to forgive sins "-- **then He said to the paralytic**, "Get up, pick up your bed and go home." Matthew 9:6. E.g., "(but the servants who had drawn the water knew)" John 2:9. E.g., "There came a woman of Samaria to draw water. Jesus said to her, "Give Me a drink." **For His disciples had gone away into the city to buy food**." John 4:7–8.

Eitrochasmos – See Summarizing. A quick running through a summary. E.g., "And what more shall I say? For time will fail me if I tell of Gideon, Barak, Samson, Jephthah, of David and Samuel and the prophets" Hebrews 11:32.

Epitrope – Permissio (giving up). Admission of wrong in order to gain what is right. E.g., "He took and gave it to Judas, the son of Simon Iscariot. After the morsel, Satan then entered into him. Therefore Jesus said to him, "**What you do, do quickly**." John 13:27 Jesus permits the evil; he does not sanction it.

Epizeuxis – See Duplication. Repeated word made with intervening words. E.g., "Before him there was no king **like him** who turned to the LORD with all his heart and with all his soul and with all his might, according to all the law of Moses; nor did any **like him** arise after him" 2 Samuel 23:25. E.g., "Hope that is seen is not hope; for who hopes for what he already sees?" E.g., Romans 8:24. "Rejoice in the Lord always; again I will say, rejoice!" Philippians 4:4. E.g., "What use is it" James 2:14,16.

Equipollency – Equipollence, Aequipollentia. A Figure of rhetoric from Greek *isodynama*, meaning "equal in power." Hence equal in power, force, signification, or application. Equipollency, equipollence, aequipollentia, duplication, iteratio, heratio, isotimon are all synonymous.

Erotesis – See Interrogation. Asking questions without waiting for an answer. E.g., "The Jews began to argue with one another, saying, "How can this man give us His flesh to eat?" John 6:52.

Ethologia – letterally means; a reasoning (logia) on the character (ethos). Hence the question is raised as to whether the objective is right or not.

Ethopoeia – See Description of Manners

Euche – Prayer, wish, vow, Votum. If prayer is to curse, it is imprecatory (deprecation q.v.). E.g., "O LORD, do save, we beseech You; O LORD, we beseech You, do send prosperity!" Psalm 118:26.

Euphemism – Euphemy, Euphemismos, involution. A nicely worded phrase for a harsh reality. Periploce is a figure in which its unpleasantness is wrapped around and made to appear agreeable. Chroma means embellishment. E.g., "Lazarus sleeps ... is dead" John 11:11–14. "Blood, which is poured out for you" in Luke 22:20 (NIV) connotes Christ's death.

Euphony – a pleasing smoothness of sound, experienced by the ease to make or listen to the words. In English, long vowels, liquid consonants (l, r) and semi–vowels (w, y) contribute to euphony along with the avoidance of adjacent stresses. The meaning of the words is also important.

Exaggeration – See Hyperbole

Exallage – Zwingli's transliterated Greek word, commonly known as enallage: where a word form is interchanged with another form. Grammatically the phrase is the same, but semantically things differ. "We [I] liked the play" — enallage shifts the number. English Royalty speak in the plural when they are speaking for themselves.

Example – Exemplum. A conclusion by way of example. E.g., "On that day, the one who is on the housetop and whose goods are in the house must not go down to take them out; and likewise the one who is in the field must not turn back. "**Remember Lot's wife**." Luke 17:31–32.

Exchange – Enallage, Enallaxis. Exchange one word for another. A grammatical substitution which makes a sentence semantically equivalent but grammatically different. Switch a part of speech (Antimeria) or gender or number or verb tense or mood (Heterosis); or one case for another (Antiptosis). Hypallage interchanges word connection by grammatical means (not by logical connections. [Enallage never substitutes one noun for another.] E.g., Use king's English where 'we' is used instead of 'I'. See Antimeria, Heterosis, Antiptosis, and Hypallage.

Exclamation – A concluding pithy exclamation is called Epiphonema. (See Epiphonema.) If it is an application of feeling, it is called Ecphonesis or Exclamatio. (See Ecphonesis.) If exclamation is parenthetical it is called Interjectio. (See Interjection).

Exectratio – See Imprecatory.

Exemple – exemplum, paradigma. Amplifying a point by providing a true or feigned example.

Exergasia – See Working Out.

Exhortation – Paraenesis. A) In ancient rhetoric, this is the deciphering of the plot, or "the moral of the story." B)In more modern usage it is usually the **exhortation**. It can be a warning of impending evil. (Ominatio is a prophecy of evil.) Synonyms: admonition, sapienta, foretelling, foreboding. E.g., "But seek first His kingdom and His righteousness, and all these things will be added to you." Matthew 6:33.

Exordium – A beginning; an introduction; especially, the introductory part of a discourse or written composition, which prepares the audience for the main subject (narratio). The first or opening part of an oration. The goal of exordium is to win the sympathy of the listeners.

Exouthenismos – Expression of contempt, scorn, disparagement. Irony may be part of this. Zwingli subsumed 5 Latin terms under this Greek heading: abiectio (throwing away), contemptus (contempt), deiectio (dejection), extenuatio (diminish or make it of less importance), humiliation. Ironic scorn: "What a help you are to the weak! How you have saved the arm without strength!" Job 26:2. E.g., "You who dwell in Lebanon, Nested in the cedars, How you will groan when pangs come upon you, Pain like a woman in childbirth!" Jeremiah 22:23. E.g., "Michal the daughter of Saul came out to meet David and said, "How the king of Israel distinguished himself today! He uncovered himself today in the eyes of his servants' maids as one of the foolish ones shamelessly uncovers himself!" 2 Samuel 6:20. E.g.,

Expansion – Diexodos. A digression to lengthen out by supplying many facts. (This is the opposite of Syntomia which abridges or shortens.) E.g., "suffering wrong as the wages of doing wrong. They count it a pleasure to revel in the daytime. They are stains and blemishes, reveling in their deceptions, as they carouse with you, having eyes full of adultery that never cease from sin, enticing unstable souls, having a heart trained in greed, accursed children; forsaking the right way, they have gone astray, having followed the way of Balaam, the son of Beor, who loved the wages of unrighteousness" 2 Peter 2:13–15B. E.g., "These men are the hidden reefs in your love feasts, shamelessly feasting with you but shepherding only themselves.

They are clouds without water, carried along by the wind; fruitless trees in autumn, twice dead after being uprooted. "They are wild waves of the sea, foaming up their own shame; wandering stars, for whom blackest darkness has been reserved forever" Jude 1:12.

Exultation – Paeanismos, cohortation. Calling others to rejoice over something, like a victory in war. (This is not a factual statement.) E.g., "Rejoice, O nations, with His people; / For He will avenge the blood of His servants, / And will render vengeance on His adversaries, / And will atone for His land and His people." Deuteronomy 32:43. E.g., "Rejoice greatly, O daughter of Zion! Shout in triumph, O daughter of Jerusalem! Behold, your king is coming to you; He is just and endowed with salvation, Humble, and mounted on a donkey, Even on a colt, the foal of a donkey." Zechariah 9:9. E.g., "Rejoice in the Lord always; again I will say, rejoice!" Philippians 4:4.

Fable – Apologue. A brief fictional tale that conveys a moral message. Often beasts or inanimate things are given human voice or manners so that they might show human weakness. They usually end with a general moralization. Parables are believable; in contrast fables deal with unbelievable things. E.g., Judges 9:8–15 is not called a fable, but it depicts one. The moral and prophetic fulfilment follow (v. 16–57). Another fable is 2 Kings 14:9 "Jehoash king of Israel sent to Amaziah king of Judah, saying, "The thorn bush which was in Lebanon sent to the cedar which was in Lebanon, saying, 'Give your daughter to my son in marriage.' But there passed by a wild beast that was in Lebanon, and trampled the thorn bush." See Myth (mythos is the Greek word for Fable.)

Figure of Speech – see trope.

Figura I – see schema.

Figura II – see type.

Fuller Explaining – Epexegesis, Epichrema. A re–interpretation of what has just been said. A kind of redefinition or self-interpretation (often signaled by constructions such as "that is to say … "). The repetition enables further explanation. Exegesis is explanation from the text. Ecphrasis is explaining or recounting. Epichrema furnishes needful information. E.g., I'm afraid we've run up against the bamboo curtain—that is to say, an economic and political barrier in the East as real as the iron curtain has been in the West. Epexegesis has three divisions: 1) developing (or working out) what was previously said (Exergasia), 2) lingering to create a deeper impression (Epimone) and 3) adding to what was said by way of interpretation (Hermeneia). (See Working Out, Lingering, and Interpretation.)

Geminatio – Iteratio, Conduplicatio. Repetition of same word in the same sense twice (with nothing in between). E.g., "But the angel of the LORD called to him from heaven and said, "Abraham, Abraham!" Genesis 22:11. E.g., "Then the LORD passed by in front of him and proclaimed, "The LORD, the LORD God, compassionate and gracious, slow to anger, and abounding in loving kindness and truth" Exodus 34:6. E.g., "My God, my God" Psalm 22:1 (Mark 15:34, Matthew 27:46).

Genus Deliberativum – (Zwingli's term) speech to encourage toward or to advise against something.

Genus Demonstrativum – Zwingli's term for speech of praise. His synonyms are ἐπιδεικτικως and ἐπιδειξις (epidixis can mean either commonstratio or demonstratio).

Gnome – (a knowing). Quotation, Sententia (sentiment). Proverb, a brief sentient saying of common acceptance (without quoting the author's name). Every proverb is a gnome, but every gnome is not a proverb. See Quotation. E.g., Proverbs 1:2 "Words of understanding (NASB)" "Understanding words of insight (NIV)."

Gradation – Gradatio. Repeating anadiplosis. My conscience hath a thousand several **tongues**,/ And every **tongue** brings in a several **tale**,/ And every **tale** condemns me for a villain. Shakespeare, *Richard III*, 5.3.194

Gradual Ascent – See Anabasis.

Gradual Descent – Catabasis (going down), Decrementum. Emphasis on humiliation, degradation, sorrow. (This is the opposite of Anabasis which ascends). E.g., Isaiah 40:31 "Yet those who wait for the LORD Will gain new strength; They will mount up with wings like eagles, They will run and not get tired, They will walk and not become weary." The descent is flying, running, walking.

Hebraism – Hebraismus. Phrases derived from the Hebrew culture. By fasting, "your gloom will be like the midday" (Isaiah 57:10).

Parallelism (q.v.) is common to both Hebrew and Oriental cultures; it helps understanding by saying the concept with other words.

Hendiadys – One idea expressed with two words joined with an "and". Two words (usually nouns or verbs) joined with an "and" but expressing a single idea. The two words must be related, have the same case and enhance but one idea.[When the two words express two ideas, this is Syntheton (combination), not a hendiadys]. **Note: with hendiadys, cautious care is needed.** The original speaker knows if a hendiadys is intended. The listener may not! Try intersecting the phrase as 1 idea (hendiadys) or two ideas (syntheton). Above all avoid dogmatism! [The last example illustrates the need to cautiously suggest.] E.g., Law and order, house and home, come and get it, nice and juicy. E.g., "Then the LORD rained on Sodom and Gomorrah **brimstone and fire** from the LORD out of heaven" Genesis 19:24 [brimstone — burning brimstone.] E.g., 2 Chronicles 2:9 "The house which I am about to build will be **great and wonderful**" [great — wonderfully great]. E.g., Jeremiah 22:3 "Do justice and righteousness" [do justice — and righteous justice]. E.g., Jeremiah 29:22 ";For I know the plans that I have for you,' declares the LORD, 'plans for welfare and not for calamity to give you a **future and a hope**'" [future — a hopeful future.] E.g., Daniel 8:10 "caused some of the host and some of the stars to fall to the earth" [1 starry host or 2 stars and hosts.] E.g., Matthew 3:11 "He will baptize you with the **Holy Spirit and fire**" [Holy Spirit — fiery {purifying} Spirit]. E.g., Matthew 24:30 "when they see the Son of Man coming on the clouds of heaven, with **power and great glory**." [power — great and glorious power.] E.g., Luke 1:17 "in the spirit and power of Elijah" [in the spirit — Elijah's powerful spirit]. E.g., John 1:17 "For the Law was given through Moses; **grace and truth** were realized through Jesus Christ" [grace — true grace]. E.g., John 4:24 "God is spirit, and those who worship Him must worship in **spirit and truth**" [worship in spirit — truly worship with the spirit]. E.g., Colossians 2:8 "See to it that no one takes you captive through **philosophy and empty deception**" [philosophy — empty deceptive philosophy]. E.g., 2 Timothy 1:10 "brought life and immortality" [brought life — immortal life]. E.g., Revelation 5:10 "You have made them to be a **kingdom and priests** to our God; and they will reign upon the earth." Taken as a hendiadys (the plural priests implies greatness) becomes "kingdom — great priestly kingdom." This is the sense of Exodus 19:6 "you shall be to Me a kingdom of priests and a holy nation." E.g., Matthew 13:23 "the man who **hears** the word **and understands** it." E.g., Revelation 20:4 "they **lived and reigned** with Christ a thousand years" (KJV) As a hendiadys it means "they reigningly lived." Taken as 2 individual verbs, it means, they lived [came back to life] and reigned with Christ. **This last example shows the need to cautiously suggest if the phrase intends a hendiadys or syntheton.**

Hendiatris – One idea expressed by three words. (Hendiadys uses two words.) E.g., Jeremiah 4:2, "You will swear, 'As the LORD lives,' In truth, in justice and in righteousness" [swear in truth — justly and righteously.]. E.g., Daniel 3:7 "all the **people, nations, and languages** fall down and worshiped the gold image" (NKJV) [all the people — of all nations and languages]. {We know this is a hendiatris because "nations do not letterally fall down" neither do "languages letterally fall down". E.g., Matthew 6:13 "Yours is the kingdom and the power and the glory" [yours is the kingdom yes — indeed the powerful and glorious kingdom.] E.g., John 14:6 "Jesus said to him, "I am **the way, and the truth, and the life**; no one comes to the Father but through Me" [the way — the true and living way].

Hermeneia – See Interpretation.

Heterogenium – Avoiding an issue by changing the subject to something different. Sometimes considered a vice. E.g., "Has our logging company endangered the spotted owl? I'll tell you what we've endangered: the unemployment rate in Oregon."

Heterosis – (another, different). A figure of speech by which one form of a noun (number, gender {but not case which is Antiptosis}], verb (voice, mood, tense, person), adjective, adverb or pronoun, is used for another. E.g., "What is life to such as _me_?" [technically "_I_" should be used.] These are not grammatical mistakes — they are means to draw attention at the unusual construction. E. W. Bullinger gives 25 pages of examples! Because this figure demands a deep understanding of Hebrew and Greek grammar, I will only give two biblical examples. E.g., "Tremble and do not sin" Psalm 4:4 is meant to mean "Stand in awe [of the Lord] and [you] will not sin." E.g.,

God often speaks through His prophets in the "**prophetic perfect tense**." Here, the past tense ("came") or perfect tense ("have come") instead of the future tense ("will come"). God is so sure of His word that He speaks of the future as if it already has happened! E.g., "For we have become partakers of Christ, if we hold fast the beginning of our assurance firm until the end," Hebrews 3:14. E.g., "But you have come to Mount Zion and to the city of the living God, the heavenly Jerusalem, and to myriads of angels" Hebrews 12:22.

Hiatus – a gap or omission in pronunciation is called elision (th' expense), or in text. Special hyperbaton occurs in manuscripts with pieces missing called lacuna or plural lacunae.

Homoeosis – Beautifying, enforcing and enlarging language through comparison. Bede identifies three figures that perform this: icon, parabola, and paradigma.

Homoeopropheron – See Alliteration. The same letter begins successive words or lines. Very difficult to preserve in translation. E.g., Hebrews 1:1 "God, after He spoke long ago to the fathers in the prophets in **many portions and in many ways.**"

Homoeoptoton – See Like Inflections.

Homogene – (same kind) where the verb and its infinitive or participle are alike. See Polyptoton. E.g., Genesis 2:16 "From any tree of the garden you may **eat freely**" [letterally: eating you shall eat.] E.g., Genesis 2:17 "but from the tree of the knowledge of good and evil you shall not eat, for in the day that you eat from it you **will surely die**"[letterally: dying you will dye.] E.g., Genesis 3:4 "The serpent said to the woman, "You surely will not die!" [letterally: dying you will not die.] E.g., "I will **greatly multiply** Your pain in childbirth" [letterally multiplying multiple.] E.g., Exodus 19:12 "whoever touches the mountain shall surely be put to death" letterally: stoning, he shall be stoned.]

Homoioteleuton – Similarity of endings of adjacent or parallel words. The "og" sound in the next sentence. "To the bottom of the bog, the boy brought the frog." There are several variant spellings of this word: homoeoteleuton, omoioteliton, omoioteleton, similiter desinen. English equivalent is "like endings" E.g., "He is esteemed eloquent which can invent wittily, remember perfectly, dispose orderly, figure diversly [sic], pronounce aptly, confirme strongly, and conclude directly" Henry Peacham. E.g., Mark 12:30 "this is the first commandment" (KJV) [hautee protee entolee].

Homoioptoton – The repetition of similar case endings in adjacent words or in words in parallel position. Since this figure only works with inflected (non-English) languages, it has often been conflated with homoioteleuton and (at least in English) has sometimes become equivalent to simple rhyme: "To no avail, I ate a snail"

Homonym – a word identical in sound (homophone: bough, bow) or in spelling {homograph: lead (metal) / lead (to guide)}. Context is critical. Often in puns.

Humiliation – Humiliatio. Expression of strong feelings of embarrassment. Scornful, pejorative presentation of a cause. Seeks to evoke blame.

Hypallage – An interchange of words which attracts attention. A) (Transferred Epitaph) and adjective appropriate for one noun is attached to another. "Sick room" refers to the "sick [people] in the room." B) A reversal of words which seems to change the sense. Open the **day**, and see if it be the **window**, Henry Peacham, *The Garden of Eloquence,* 1577. Yet I'll not shed her blood,/ Nor scar that whiter skin of hers than snow … Shakespeare, *Othello,* 5.2.3. E.g., [a hunting man of strength] becomes "a mighty hunter" Genesis 10:9. E.g., [righteousness of the law] becomes "law of righteousness" Romans 9:31.

Hyperbaton – Transposition. Normal sentence word order is greatly altered. Yoda speak: "Do you in, I could." When parchments have missing pieces, the word order is also altered, this hyperbaton is called lacuna (or in the plural lacunae). E.g., "The sky will be rolled up like a scroll" (Isaiah 34:4 NASB) puts the translation in normal word order. But Young's Literal Translation preserves the hyperbaton: "rolled together as a book have been the heavens."

Hyperbole – Epauxesis, Hyperoche, Hyperthesis, Superlatio. A conscious unbelievable exaggeration for sake of emphasis but NOT intended to be taken letterally. E.g., "If thy right eye makes you to stumble, tear it out" Matthew 5:29. Tearing out one or two eyes, does not help get to the heart [v.28] of the matter, so the reader understands this as overstatement or hyperbole. E.g., The last verse of John has an impressive hyperbole: "There are also many other things which Jesus did, which if they were written in detail, I suppose that even the world itself would not contain the books which were written" John 21:25. E.g., "Among all these soldiers there were 700 select left-handers, each of whom could **sling a stone at a hair without missing**." Judges 20:16. E.g., Hypothetical hyperbole: "For I could wish that I myself were cursed and cut off from Christ" Rom. 9:3.

Hypocatastasis – A special type of analogy where the association of two nouns is implied. E.g., In Psalm 89:8–15 the vine by implication refers to Israel. See Implication.

Hypokeimenon – See subiectum.

Hyposiopesis – a more intense form of aposiopesis.

Hypostygma – Zwingli's synonym for "comma."

Hypotactic, hypotaxis – when words link together. E.g., I am tired *because* it is hot. In contrast paratactic juxtaposes clauses. E.g., I am tired; it is hot.

Hypotimesis – Meiligmata. Under–estimating. A parenthetical remark given as an apology in order to excuse some bold language. Commonly used phrases include: "If I may so say," "so to speak," or "as it were." E.g., "But if our unrighteousness demonstrates the righteousness of God, what shall we say? The God who inflicts wrath is not unrighteous, is He? (**I am speaking in human terms**.)" Romans 3:5. E.g., "Are they servants of Christ?-- **I speak as if insane**-- I more so; in far more labors, in far more imprisonments, beaten times without number, often in danger of death" 2 Corinthians 11:23

Hypotyposis – See Word–picture.

Hypozeugma – (end yoking). A) Placing last, in a construction containing several words or phrases of equal value, the word or words on which all of them depend. E.g., Mark Anthony, "Friends, Romans, countrymen, lend me your ears." Shakespeare, *Julius Caesar*. B) Zeugma toward end of sentence. (A zeugma has two objects and one verb — where grammatically only one object is suitably used with that verb.) E.g., "They did what your **power and will had decided** beforehand should happen" Acts 4:28. See Zeugma.

Hysteresis – Subsequent narration of prior events. When huge time elapses between event and its written account, it is called "historical hysteresis." I believe the Holy Spirit can accurately add to former scripture accounts; those who do not believe in the Spirit of truth, see human error. E.g., 1 Chronicles 16:8–36B is (a compilation of Psalm 105:1–15; 96:2–13; 106:47–48.) The writer (Ezra ? about 450 BC ?) writes that these scriptures were used by David when the ark was brought up to Jerusalem. I have no reason to doubt the accuracy and historicity of this account.

Hysterologia – The first, of two **events,** is put last. (This is the opposite of hysteron proteron). A form of hyperbaton or parenthesis in which one interposes a phrase between a preposition and its object. E.g., (Bold letters are interruption phrase) I jumped into **with as much enthusiasm as a teenager has hormones** my speech on abstinence. E.g., Genesis 10 dispersal of nations (Noah's clan genealogies). Genesis 11:1–9 Reason for nation dispersal, tower of Babel. Also, a synonym for hysteron proteron

Hysteron Proteron – (last first) reversal of normal rational, temporal or natural order of **words.** What should be second, is put first. E.g., "the people saw the thunder and lightning" Exodus 20:18. We see lightning first, then hear thunder second. Synonyms are prothysteron, hysterologia (q.v.).

Icon – A) figure which paints the likeness of a person by imagery. B) A figure of comparison in which a person is held up against the explicit image of another. A major subset of homoeosis (q.v.).

Idiom – a phrase which means more than the letteral meaning of its words. Idioms are few in words. They say one thing, but mean something else. Like symbols and figures, idioms require the mind to unscramble the cultural meaning. Translation of idioms into another language cannot be letterally done because it takes may more words to convey its meaning. E.g., "Monday week" means "the Monday a week after next Monday." The language of the New Testament is Koine Greek. But Aramaic was what Jews spoke. (Both Aramaic and Hebrew are dialects of the Semitic language group.) Hebraisms are Greek words expressing the Hebrew minds and idioms. E. W. Bullinger writes, "unless the translation be idiomatic, there must be grave mistakes made; and that, if a translation be absolutely literal [letteral], it will be a fruitful source of errors."[144]A) In Hebrew an active verb can mean **attempt**. E.g., Hence 1 John 1:10, "If we say that we have not sinned, we [**attempt to**] make Him a liar and His word is not in us." E.g., "As many as are [**would be or try to be**] perfect" Philippians 3:15.

B) In Hebrew an active verb can express permission (and not the actual doing). E.g., Exodus 4:21 "I [God] will harden his [Pharaoh's] heart" idiomatically means "I will permit Pharaoh's heart to be hardened." E.g., Matthew 6:13, "do not lead us into temptation" idiomatically means "permit us not to be led into temptation."

C) Two imperatives may unite so that the first is a condition and the second becomes a future. E.g., "Search, and see" becomes "search and you will see." John 7:52. E.g., 1 Corinthians 15:34 "Awake to righteousness, and sin not" (KJV) becomes "Awake to righteousness, and you will not be sinning." Likewise the NASB "Become sober-minded as you ought, and stop sinning" becomes "Become sober-minded as you ought, and you will stop sinning."

Idiotimus – for Zwingli, the common, everyday idiom.

Illation – Illatio. See inference.

Image – motifs, recurring themes. Messiah is both the suffering servant and coming king.

Imitation – Imitatio. Imitation was a primary pedagogical method in ancient Roman and in Renaissance humanist curricula. Students were given models to copy on any of a number of linguistic levels. Mimesis is the Greek word for this. See Description of sayings.

Imminution – Imminutio. A lessening; diminution; decrease. See litotes and meiosis.

Implication – Hypocatastasis. I implied analogy between two nouns.

Metaphor	You are a beast.
Simile	You are like a beast.
Implication	Beast! [you implied]

E.g., "For dogs have surrounded me; A band of evildoers has encompassed me;" Psalm 22:16. Parallelism links dogs with evildoers.

---

[144] E.W. Bullinger, p. 820.

E.g., "Every plant which My heavenly Father did not plant shall be uprooted" Matthew 15:13. Each plant by implication is a person. (Jesus most frequently used interrogation and implication!) E.g., "Watch out and beware of the leaven of the Pharisees and Sadducees" Matthew 16:6. Leaven by unstated implication (hypocatastasis) is "doctrine." E.g., Psalm 89:8–15 the vine by implication refers to Israel). E.g., "Destroy this temple, and in three days I will raise it up" John 2:19. Temple is by implied implication his physical body, which is clarified in v. 21: "But He was speaking of the temple of His body."

Imprecatory – Deprecation (q.v.), Imprecative, Imprecatio, malediction, execration, commination, Ara, execration, Misos, Apeuche. To pray for divine vengeance on sinners because of their sins. God promises to bless obedience and curse disobedience to His laws (Deuteronomy 27–28). Imprecatory prayer asks God to deal now for other's wickedness. E.g., "Let his days be few; Let another take his office. Let his children be fatherless and his wife a widow" Psalm 109:8,9 see 6–19. "Woe, shepherds of Israel who have been feeding themselves! Should not the shepherds feed the flock?" Ezekiel 34:2. "Where you die, I will die, and there I will be buried. Thus may the LORD do to me, and worse, if anything but death parts you and me" Ruth 1:17. Imprecatory psalms are 69, 109, 5, 6, 11, 35, 37, 40, 52, 56, 57, 58, 59, 79, 83, 94, 137, 139, 143.

Inclusion – A)Repetition of the same word or thought (as in redditio and prosapodosis) but usually after a long interruption. See Epanalepsis. B) See association — where a communicator identifies himself with the audience. E.g., "That they would seek God, if perhaps they might grope for Him and find Him, though He is not far **from each one of us**" Acts 17:27. "Among them we too" Ephesians 2:3. "For we also once were foolish ourselves," Titus 3:3.

Indignation – See Aganactesis.

Inference – Illation. The closing arguments. The reasoning involved in making a logical judgment on the basis of circumstantial evidence and prior conclusions rather than on the basis of direct observation.

Innuendo – oblique allusion, hint, insinuation. It may be veiled and open to different interpretations. E.g., A crowd wanted to stone Jesus for saying "My Father and I are One" (Note, the crowd correctly interpreted this to mean Jesus is God.) But Jesus by innuendo confused them. He quoted Psalm 82:6, "You are gods". At first glance it appears that the people were called gods too, but deeper reflection into the context of Psalm 82 shows the "gods" to be corrupt judges. Just as the godlike judges had to make decisions regarding right and wrong, so the people needed to decide if Jesus and God were one!

Insertion –

A) Simultaneum. A parenthetic insertion between two simultaneous **events**. E.g., People shouting is inserted within Pilate's words. "Pilate said to them, "Then what shall I do with Him whom you call the King of the Jews?" They shouted back, "Crucify Him!" But Pilate said to them, "Why, what evil has He done?" But they shouted all the more, "Crucify Him!" Mark 15:12–14.

B) Parembole, Epembole, Paremptosis. Addition of a sentence that could stand elsewhere by itself. (You might mistakenly think it is an insertion by a later scribe.)

E.g., An **insertion** is in verses 3–4 of Mark 7:1–5, "1The Pharisees and some of the scribes gathered to Him after they came from Jerusalem, 2and saw that some of His disciples were eating their bread with unholy hands, that is, unwashed. 3(For the Pharisees and all the *other* Jews do not eat unless they carefully wash their hands, *thereby* holding firmly to the tradition of the elders; 4and *when they come* from the marketplace, they do not eat unless they completely cleanse themselves; and there are many other things which they have received *as traditions* to firmly hold, *such as* the washing of cups, pitchers, and copper pots.) 5And the Pharisees and the scribes asked Him, "Why do Your disciples not walk in accordance with the tradition of the elders, but eat their bread with unholy hands?"

E.g., Revelation 16:13–16 has a **parenthetic insertion** in v.15: "13And I saw coming out of the mouth of the dragon and out of the mouth of the beast and out of the mouth of the false prophet, three unclean spirits like frogs; 14for they are spirits of demons, performing signs, which go out to the kings of the whole world, to gather them together for the war of the great day of God, the

Almighty. 15("Behold, I am coming like a thief. Blessed is the one who stays awake and keeps his clothes, so that he will not walk about naked and men will not see his shame.") 16And they gathered them together to the place which in Hebrew is called Har-Magedon."

Interjection – Parenthetical exclamation (q.v.). E.g., "My soul thirsts for God, for the living God; **When shall I come and appear before God?**" Psalm 42:2. E.g., "Then it came about after all your wickedness (**'Woe, woe to you!' declares the Lord GOD**)," Ezekiel 16:23.

Interlocutor – subjects of a speech. E.g., the NT book of Romans addresses Jew and Greek interlocutors. See Antimetathesis.

Interposition – See parenthesis. Interrupting remark.

Interpretation – Hermeneia, Interpretatio. Repetition to interpret more clearly what has already been said. E.g., "Your way was in the sea And Your paths in the mighty waters, **And Your footprints may not be known.**" Psalm 77:19. E.g., "How the faithful city has become a harlot, She who was full of justice! Righteousness once lodged in her, But now murderers. Your silver has become dross, Your drink diluted with water. **Your rulers are rebels And companions of thieves**; Everyone loves a bribe And chases after rewards. They do not defend the orphan, Nor does the widow's plea come before them." Isaiah 1:21–23.

Interrogation – Erotesis, Peusis, Pysma, Percontatio, Interrogatio, Erotema. A) Asking rhetorical questions without waiting for an answer. B) Asking questions and waiting for an answer. Jesus did this often! The Bible uses this figure a lot! E. W. Bullinger[145] provides the following statistics. Questions in OT number 2274 and in the NT 1024. The book of Job has 329 questions; Jeremiah has 195. E.g., Then the Jews began to argue with one another, saying, "How can this man give us His flesh to eat?" John 6:52. E.g., "Where then is boasting? It is excluded. By what kind of law? Of works? No, but by a law of faith" Romans 3:27. E.g., "Where is the wise? Where is the scribe? Where is the debater of this age? Has not God made foolish the wisdom of the world?" 1 Corinthians 1:20.

---

145 16.E.W. Bullinger, p. 944.

Inversion – Anastrophe (q.v.). Reversal of normal word order: E.g.,
Sweetly blew the breeze

Irony – reversal of meaning of a phrase as dictated by its context. Actors impart a changed tone to imply irony, but tone is not a written element. Several speech figures exploit this twist in meaning: antiphrasis, litotes, meiosis, permutatio, sarcasmos, peirastic, paralipsis and paraprosdokian. There are five types of Irony.

1. A) One word cast in opposition (Antiphrasis, q.v.). Here a word is used that is opposite of what is meant. E.g., "Tiny Goliath." E.g., Replace "court of justice" with "court of vengeance." E.g., "glory" is meant negatively as "faded diminished glory": "They will be like the **glory** of the sons of Israel … Now in that day the glory of Jacob will fade, And the fatness of his flesh will become lean" Isaiah 17:3–4. E.g., "What right has My **beloved** [hated one] in My house When she has done many vile deeds?" Jeremiah 11:15. B). A phrase case in opposition (litotes q.v.) E.g., By fasting, "your gloom will be like the midday" (Isaiah 57:10). C). Meiosis (q.v.)— understatement in extreme irony E.g., "We became like grasshoppers in our own sight, and so we were in their sight" Numbers 13:33.

2. Permutation – counter–charge(q.v.) phrases, sentences and longer expressions which say one thing but mean the opposite. E.g., "You are sons of those who murdered the prophets. Fill up then [irony for you have filled up] the measure of guilt of your fathers" Matthew 23:32. Irony **can revise** what is thought to be said. Consider, "But give that which is within as charity [or alms], and then all things are clean for you" Luke 11:41. At first you think, "giving alms from the heart is what matters." But this internal attitude accompanied with the external alms–giving is what the Pharisees taught. In this context, Christ lambasts the Pharisees. "Now you Pharisees clean the outside of the cup and of the platter; but inside of you, you are full of robbery and wickedness. "You foolish ones, did not He who made the outside make the inside also?" Luke 11:39–40. "But woe to you Pharisees! For you pay tithe of mint and rue and every kind of garden herb,

and yet **disregard justice and the love of God**; but these are the things you should have done without neglecting the others. Woe to you Pharisees! For you love the chief seats in the synagogues and the respectful greetings in the market places. Woe to you! For you are like concealed tombs, and the people who walk over them are unaware of it." Luke 11:42–44. So take the verse in question [v. 41] as ironic and it becomes partially true — give alms with a heart of love. Then **add** God's justice, mercy and love (which enables you to be His channel — showing His love). Now you get the full picture of charitable giving!

3. Sarcasm – Sarcasmos (q.v.) (A tear the flesh" as dogs do). Wounding with cutting words as in a taunt or ridicule. **A)** Here the **tone of mockery is obvious**. Jeering is obvious. Synonyms: Chleuasmos (q.v.), Epicertomesis, Mycterismos (q.v.). E.g., "The Lord laughs at the wicked, for he knows their day is coming" Psalm 37:13. E.g., "The kings of the earth take their stand And the rulers take counsel together Against the LORD and against His Anointed, saying, "Let us tear their fetters apart And cast away their cords from us! **He who sits in the heavens laughs, The Lord scoffs at them.**" Psalm 2:2–4. E.g., "Elijah mocked them [prophets of Baal] and said, "Call out with a loud voice, for he [Baal] is a god; either he is occupied or gone aside, or is on a journey, or perhaps he is asleep and needs to be awakened" 1 Kings 18:27. E.g., "And he [Pilate] said to the Jews, "Behold, your King!" John 19:14. "They knelt down before Him and mocked Him, saying, "Hail, King of the Jews!" Matthew 27:29. E.g., Context helps to perceive the ironic flip–side of words. "Teacher, we know that You are truthful and teach the way of God in truth, and defer to no one; for You are not partial to any. "Tell us then, what do You think? Is it lawful to give a poll-tax to Caesar, or not?" But Jesus perceived their malice, and said, "Why are you testing Me, you hypocrites? Matthew 22:16–18. **B)** Deceptive Irony. Here there is **no overt tone of mockery. Evil uses a sincere tone**. Eironeia is dissimulation which conceals one's thoughts, feelings and character. E.g., "The serpent said to the woman, "You surely will not die! "For God knows that

in the day you eat from it your eyes will be opened, and you will be like God, knowing good and evil." Genesis 3:4–5. The serpent's half-truths and sincere tones put evil poison into our lives. Physically Adam and Eve began to die that day. Spiritually they died — making a very grave mistake! E.g., Herod to the wise men "Go and search carefully for the Child; and when you have found Him, report to me, so that I too may come and **worship** Him." Matthew 2:8. Herod wanted to slay him — not worship him! How many innocents have been led into sexual relationships with insincere words of "love"?

4. Trying or testing irony – Peirastic (q.v.). Words not really meaning what is said, but rather given to **test** another's commitment. This **trial** of words probes one's own sincerity. E.g., Lot offered hospitality, but the angels **tested** his resolve with: "No, but we shall spend the night in the square." Yet he urged them strongly, so they turned aside to him and entered his house" Genesis 19:2–3. E.g., God **tested** Moses concerning Israel's worship of the golden calf. "Now then let Me alone, that My anger may burn against them and that I may destroy them; and I will make of you a great nation." Exodus 32:10. But Moses interceded for them (Exodus 32:11–13). "So the LORD changed His mind about the harm which He said He would do to His people" Exodus 32:14. God never intended to destroy all of Israel! He does not change (Malachi 3:6, James 1:17). But by testing Moses (so that Moses interceded for Israel), the circumstances changed. So God showed partial mercy instead of only anger. In the end only three thousand died instead of the whole nation (Exodus 32:28). E.g., Jesus **tested** the Syrophoenician woman Matthew 15:24–28 "I was sent only to the lost sheep of the house of Israel." But she came and began to bow down before Him, saying, "Lord, help me!" And He answered and said, "It is not good to take the children's bread and throw it to the dogs." But she said, "Yes, Lord; but even the dogs feed on the crumbs which fall from their masters' table." Then Jesus said to her, "O woman, your faith is great; it shall be done for you as you wish." and her daughter was healed at once. E.g., "God **tested** Abraham" (Genesis 22:1)

with these words: "Take now your son, your only son, whom you love, Isaac, and go to the land of Moriah, and offer him there as a burnt offering on one of the mountains of which I will tell you." Genesis 22:2. God stopped the sacrifice of Isaac, "Do not stretch out your hand against the lad, and do nothing to him; for now I know that you fear God, since you have not withheld your son, your only son, from Me." Genesis 22:12. This place became the site of Solomon's temple! Here God substituted a ram for Isaac. Here God substituted His Son, the Lamb of God for the sins of the world (John 1:29).

5. Paralipsis (q.v.) – ironic pretense to skip over a topic, which then is spoken of. E.g., "For time will fail me if I tell of Gideon, Barak, Samson, Jephthah, of David and Samuel and the prophets, who by faith conquered kingdoms, performed acts of righteousness, obtained promises, shut the mouths of lions" Hebrews 11:32–33.

Isocolon – repetition of phrases of equal length and corresponding grammatical structure. E.g., I speak Spanish to God, Italian to women, French to men, and German to my horse., Line of Charles V character in Shakespeare. *Edward III*. 1596.

Iugum – Latin for yoke, or the beam of scales held by the blindfolded statue of Justice. Hence linking of two items of the same kind. For Zwingli it is repetition of a word at the beginning/end of a phrase or synonyms used at the end of a phrase. Zwingli likened it to redittio, geminatio (doubling).

Jeremiad – prolonged lamentation or prophetic warning of disaster because of evils. The Prophet Jeremiah gave name to this term with God's pronouncements on many nations. E.g., Jeremiah 23:1–2.

Judgment – Epicrisis. A stand-alone short sentence, often at the end of a paragraph, which adds judgment or clarification. E.g., "These things took place in **Bethany** beyond the Jordan, where John was baptizing" John 1:28. The had come from Jerusalem (v.19), so they had traveled a good bit. E.g., "John had not yet been thrown into prison" John 3:24 is the reason John still baptized. E.g., "Now it was a Sabbath on the day when Jesus made the clay and opened his eyes" John 9:14. This addition gives context to the discourse. E.g., "Now Jesus had spoken of his death, but they thought that He was speaking of literal sleep" John 11:13. This clarifies what Jesus meant by "sleep."

Justification – Proecthesis. A Sentence added to the end of a conclusion that justifies what was said. E.g., "But go and learn what this means: 'I desire compassion, and not sacrifice,' for I did not come to call the righteous, but sinners" Matthew 9:13. "How much more valuable then is a man than a sheep! So then, it is lawful to do good on the Sabbath" Matthew 12:12.

Kenning – Poetic circumlocution, often two words with a hyphen. Fire-water (whiskey). Lord God (for the unspoken name of God — the tetragrammaton, יהוה). Old English used kenning abundantly as in descriptions of 'ocean:' "whale's bath", "foaming fields", "sea–street."

Latinismus – Expression derived from Roman or Latin speaking cultures. E.g., "All roads lead to Rome." Alain de Lille, 1175 AD.

Letteral – Wooden language. Grammatically the sense of a phrase **without** using figures of speech or idioms. Hermeneutically forcing an author's intended figurative speech into non-figurative language. E.g., Regarding Herod and "Go tell that fox" (Luke 13:32): Letterally it means a fox named Herod. Literally (as author intended) King Herod is attributed a fox–like characteristic through metaphor.

Leitmotif – (or Leitmotiv). The main, major or key note, frequently repeated images or themes. "Hell" and the "kingdom is at hand" are the two primary leitmotifs of Jesus. Seems a misnomer in English, for these are really major or "heavy motifs.".

Lexophile – (lover of words). A person who loves word games, like cross words, anagrams, palindromes, and other word puzzles. E.g., "A will could be called a 'death wish', but I prefer to call it 'a dead giveaway.'"

Like Beginnings – See Alliteration.

Like Endings – Homoioteleuton. Similarity of endings of adjacent or parallel words. The "og" sound in the next sentence. "To the bottom of the bog, the boy brought the frog." There are several variant spellings of this word: homoeoteleuton, omoioteliton, omoioteleton, similiter desinen. E.g., "He is esteemed eloquent which can invent wittily, remember perfectly, dispose orderly, figure diversly [sic], pronounce aptly, confirme strongly, and conclude directly" Henry

Peacham. E.g., Mark 12:30 "this is the first commandment" (KJV) [hautee protee entolee]. It does not translate well.

Like Inflections – Homoeoptoton. Similar end sounds like rhyme, but here caused by inflection where the noun has the same case or the verb is an infinity or participle. It does not translate well. E.g., Romans 12:15 "Rejoice with those who rejoice, and weep with those who weep." A free rendering which preserves the rhyme: "Be cheerful with those that are glad, / Be tearful with those that are sad."

Like sounding inflections – Paromoeosis. Similar sounds. See assonance. Also called Paromoeon. Similar to Parechesis (which properly describes a foreign word whose translation does not sound the same). It does not translate well. E.g., Matthew 11:17 "'We played the flute for you, and you did not dance [orche**sasthe**]; we sang a dirge, and you did not mourn [ekop**sasthe**.].'

Lingering – Epimone. Repetition so as to dwell upon a subject and impress it in the listener's mind. Commoratio. E.g., In the passage below, the point dwelt upon is that the people neglected God's word. Zechariah 1:3–6 "Therefore say to them, 'Thus says the LORD of hosts, "Return to Me," declares the LORD of hosts, "that I may return to you," says the LORD of hosts. "Do not be like your fathers, to whom the former prophets proclaimed, saying, 'Thus says the LORD of hosts, "Return now from your evil ways and from your evil deeds."' But they did not listen or give heed to Me," declares the LORD. "Your fathers, where are they? And the prophets, do they live forever? "But did not My words and My statutes, which I commanded My servants the prophets, overtake your fathers? Then they repented and said, 'As the LORD of hosts purposed to do to us in accordance with our ways and our deeds, so He has dealt with us.'"

Lipogram – literary device where a particular letter is dropped. E.g., Shakespeare's *Hamlet* has no 'I' in it. E.g., Ernest Vincent Wright's *Gadsby* has no 'e' in it.

Literal – grammatically the author's sense of a phrase **including** the use of figures of speech and idioms. Hermeneutically taking an author's intended figure of speech as figurative language. See Letteral. {Caution. This definition is contrary to usual usage. What I define as letteral, most define as literal. Modern development of figures of speech, sees them as a twist from normal usage. However figures of speech were part of rhetoric in ancient times. When you take the author's or orator's intended sense, you include figures of speech as literal language (as the school at Antioch which championed typology). If you exclude figures of speech as literal author intended language, you fall into another camp. (The school at Alexandria championed allegory which does not stick to the author's intended meaning.)

Litotes – (Meiosis) — to indirectly affirm by saying the opposite, often with understatement. E.g., By fasting, "your gloom will be like the midday" (Isaiah 57:10). E.g., "I am not averse to a drink of water." E.g., "I hurt not a little." E.g., "But you all will be baptized with the Holy Spirit *not long after these days* [shortly]" Acts 1:5.

Locution – Locutio, oration, pronunciation, expression, phrase, idiom used by a particular region or group. Zwingli's example: Hebraic locution. E.g., Philadelphians use "irregardless", Southerners say "Ye all"; Appalachians say, "crick" instead of "creek."

Macrologia – Long windedness. Using more words than are necessary in an attempt to appear eloquent. Polonius exemplifies macrologia in the following speech.

My liege, and madam, to expostulate
What majesty should be, what duty is,
Why day is day, night night, and time is time,
Were nothing but to waste night, day, and time;
Therefore, [since] brevity is the soul of wit,
And tediousness the limbs and outward flourishes,
I will be brief. Your noble son is mad:
Mad call I it, for to define true madness,
What is't but to be nothing else but mad? Shakespeare, *Hamlet* 2.2.86-94

Malapropism – Acyrologia. Confused, improper, inappropriate, (maybe comically) inaccurate use of a word. E.g., "Cleopatra got bit by a wasp [asp]."

Many Ands – Polysyndeton, Polysyntheton. This is a specialized Anaphora where each line begins with "and". E.g., Genesis 22:9, 11. E.g., 1 Samuel 17:34–36B. E.g., The widow of Nain, Luke 7:11–18.

Many Inflections – Polyptoton, Metagoge, Casuum Varietas. Here the same word is repeated in the same sense, but with some grammatically different inflection. If a verb, the mood, tense or person can vary. If a noun, the case, gender or number may vary. E.g., verb: "who **delivered** us from so great a peril of death, and **will deliver** us" 2 Corinthians 1:10. E.g., "From any tree of the garden you may **eat freely**" [Hebrew: eating you shall eat]" Genesis 2:16. E.g., "you will **surely die**" [Hebrew, dying you shall die] Genesis 2:17. E.g., "To the woman He said, "I will **greatly multiply** your pain in childbirth" [Hebrew multiplying, I will multiply] Genesis 3:16. E.g., "They became **very much afraid**" [Greek they feared a fear] Mark 4:41. E.g., "**Blessed** be the God and Father of our Lord Jesus Christ, who has **blessed** us with every spiritual **blessing** in the heavenly places in Christ" Ephesians 1:3. E.g., "For **through the Law** I died **to the Law**, so that **I might live** to God. I have been crucified with Christ; and it is no longer **I who live**, but Christ **lives** in me; and the life which I now **live** in the flesh **I live** by faith in the Son of God, who loved me and gave Himself up for me" Galatians 2:19–20. E.g., Noun: "Holy of Holies" [most holy] Exodus 26:33. E.g., "Vanity of vanities" [the greatest vanity] Ecclesiastes 1:2. E.g., "Adjective: "He came to His own [neuter so possessions], and those who were His own [masculine so people] did not receive Him" John 1:11.

Maxim – A short memorable statement of a general truth. See sententia. E.g., Ben Franklin wrote: "Three may keep a secret, if two are dead."

Meiosis – understatement or belittling. E.g., A mortal wound is called a scratch. E.g., A writer is called a scribbler. Note the substitute diminishes the importance. Synonyms: tapinosis, tapeinosis, miosis, antenantiosis, humiliatio, abbaser, a demeaning, minution, attenuation/extenuatio. E.g., "We became like grasshoppers in our own sight, and so we were in their sight" Numbers 13:33. E.g., Abraham replied, "Now behold, I have ventured to speak to the Lord, although I am but dust and ashes" Genesis 18:27. E.g., David speaking to King Saul, "Whom are you pursuing? A dead dog, a single flea?" 1 Samuel 24:14. E.g., "This would be unprofitable for you" Hebrews 13:17. Disobedience to your leaders is understated as "unprofitable" — it is disastrous. E.g., "I am a worm and not a man"

Psalm 22:6 belittles his humanity. Yet the metaphor, "I am a worm" carries far more depth than meets the eye. To get the crimson (or scarlet) color to dye clothing, a special worm (coccus ilicis) was crushed to squeeze out the scarlet dye! Messiah's passion included "He was crushed for our iniquities" Isaiah 53:5. So the metaphor, "I am a worm" indicates Messiah was born to die in a bloody way to cover over (atone) the sins of His people — "Though your sins are as scarlet, They will be as white as snow; Though they are red like crimson, They will be like wool" Isaiah 1:18.

Merismos – See Distribution.

Mesarchia – Repetition at the beginning or middle of successive sentences. (Resembles Epizeuxis where repetition is close together. Slightly differs from Anaphora where the sentences are independent.) E.g., "Vanity of vanities," says the Preacher, "Vanity of vanities! All is vanity." Ecclesiastes 1:2. E.g., "If sometimes the cloud remained a few days over the tabernacle, according to the command of the LORD they remained camped. Then according to the command of the LORD they set out" Numbers 9:20. E.g., "Near is the great day of the LORD, Near and coming very quickly; Listen, **the day** of the LORD! In it the warrior cries out bitterly. **A day** of wrath is that day, **A day** of trouble and distress **A day** of destruction and desolation, **A day** of darkness and gloom, **A day** of clouds and thick darkness, **A day** of trumpet and battle cry Against the fortified cities And the high corner towers." Zephaniah 1:14–16. E.g., "He who receives you receives Me, and he who receives Me receives Him who sent Me. He who receives a prophet in the name of a prophet shall receive a prophet's reward; and he who receives a righteous man in the name of a righteous man shall receive a righteous man's reward." Matthew 10:40–44.

Mesodiplosis – Mesophonia. Repetition in the middle of sentences. E. g. "We are afflicted in every way, but not crushed; perplexed, but not despairing; persecuted, but not forsaken; struck down, but not destroyed" 2 Corinthians 4:8–9.

Mesoteleuton – Repetition in middle and end of successive sentences. This repetition emphasizes the fact stated. E.g., "Behold, I will put a spirit in him so that he will hear a rumor and return to **his own**

land. And I will make him fall by the sword in **his own land**."' 2 Kings 16:7. E.g., "You are not to say, 'It is a conspiracy!' In regard to all that this people call a conspiracy" Isaiah 8:12. E.g., "He was met by a man with an unclean spirit, who was coming from **the tombs**. This man had been living in **the tombs**" Mark 5:2–3.

Metabasis – Transition, Interfactio (putting something in between). A transitional statement in which one explains what has been and what will be said. E.g., "You have heard how the proposed plan will fail; now consider how an alternative might succeed." There are eight forms of metabasis, according to Smith based on relationship of what was and what will be said. 1. Equal. E.g., "The matters you have heard were wonderful, and those that you shall hear are no less marvelous." 2. Unequal. E.g., "You have heard very grievous things, but you shall hear more grievous." 3. Like. E.g., "I have spoken of his notable enterprises in France, and now I will rehearse his worthy acts done in England." 4. Contrary. E.g., "As I have spoken of his sad adversity and misery, so will I now speak of his happy prosperity." 5. Differing. E.g., "I have spoken of manners; now it remains that I speak concerning doctrine." 6. Anticipating Objection. E.g., "You may think me too long in the threats of the law; I will now pass to the sweet promises of the gospel." 7. Reprehension. E.g., "Why do I dwell on these things? I shall hasten my speech unto that which is the principle point of the matter in question." 8. Consequents. E.g., "You have heard how he promised, and now I will tell you how he performed." For Zwingli metabasis is the transition from one aspect of a speech to another. E.g., 1 Corinthians 11:17 "But in giving this instruction" is a transition from hair length to the Lord's Supper. E.g., 1 Corinthians 12:31 "But earnestly desire the greater gifts. And I show you a still more excellent way." This is Paul's transition to a discussion of Love (1 Corinthians 13). E.g., Hebrews 6:1–3B discusses "elementary teachings" then transitions to formerly empowered people who have fallen away (v. 4–8). "For in the case of those who have once" (Hebrews 6:4) is the transitional phrase.

Metabole – also spelled Metabola. A change or mutation. Abrupt change in the dramatic action.

Metagoge – see "Many Inflections."

Metalepsis – a double metonymy in which an effect is represented by a remote unstated cause. E.g., Consider "Pallid death." Death causes the body to become pale. So putting the effect of death to death itself is this remote connection. E.g., "She has a lead foot" [She drives fast, as if her foot was made of lead.] Synonyms are transumption, postsumptio. E.g., "Only do nothing to these men, inasmuch as they have come under the shelter of my **roof**." Genesis 19:8. Lot's hospitality is meant when he speaks of his home's roof which protects those inside. E.g., "To Him who loves us and released us from our sins **by His blood**" Revelation 1:5. His blood purchased our atonement which freed us from our sin.

Metallage – A change over. Substitution of a thought away from the original thought. E.g., "I don't want to hear another 'I'll do it later.' Do it now." E.g., "Their liquor gone; They play the harlot continually; Their rulers dearly love shame" Hosea 4:19.

Metamorphosis – Zwingli's definition: transformation, switch from normal to figurative language.

Metanoia – See Correction.

Metaphor – is stated representation. Designated metaphors are those the author intends to make. Context, usually but not always with certainty, distinguishes designated from undesignated metaphors. Allegories are extended metaphors. In simile the **resemblance** is stated: "he is like a pig." In metaphor the **representation** is boldly stated: "he is a pig." There are several special metaphors: Anthropomorphism (ascribing human body parts to God, E.g., "The arm of the Lord.") Anthropopathism — ascribing human feelings to God: grief, anger, or wrath. (Caution: metaphorical language embraces all figurative speech — not just the metaphor.) E.g., Simile: "all flesh is as grass" 1 Peter 1:24. Metaphor: "All flesh is grass" Isaiah 40:6. E.g., Simile: "All of us like sheep have gone astray" Isaiah 53:6. Metaphor: "We are His people and the sheep of His pasture" Psalm 100:3.

Metaplasm – A general term for changes to the spelling of words (figures). This includes alteration of the letters or syllables in single words, including additions, omissions, inversions, and substitutions.

Such changes are considered conscious choices made by the artist or orator for the sake of eloquence or meter, in contrast to the same kinds of changes done accidentally and discussed by grammarians as vices (see barbarism).

Metaplasm by addition: diastole, epenthesis, paragoge, prothesis, diaeresis

Metaplasm by transposition: metathesis

Metaplasm by substitution: antisthecon

Metaplasm by subtraction or omission: aphaeresis, apocope, ellipsis, ecthlipsis, synaloepha, synaeresis, syncope, systole

Metastasis – (Letterally means to "place in another way.") Hence repeated usage of the word/phrase taken in a different (perhaps playful) way. Denying and turning back on your adversary's word/ arguments used against you. E.g., "And it came to pass, when Ahab saw Elijah, that Ahab said unto him, 'Art thou he that **troubleth** Israel? And he answered, I have not **troubled** Israel; but thou [have troubled Israel], and thy father's house, in that ye have forsaken the commandments of the LORD, and thou hast followed Baalim." 1 Kings 18:17–18 KJV.

Metathesis – Transposition of a letter, sound, or words out of its normal order. E.g., **Frevent** [for fervent]", Shakespeare, *The Merry Wives of Windsor*, 2.1.122.

Metonym – A substitute name is used for something else closely related to it. "Met" means "other." E.g., Washington is a metonym for the federal government of the United States. E.g., Press substitutes for reporters. E.g., Crown substitutes for the king or monarch. Caution: use of this word began to be popular after 1950. Prior to that the word was metonymy (s.v.). today many think metonym and metonymy are identical. I suspect they are changing into two distinct concepts. Metonymy uses contiguity (attribute of the object, like "fishing for oysters"); whereas metonym uses metaphor, (like phishing for information.)

Metonymy – a synonym which uses the name of one thing to refer to something closely associated with it. Contiguity describes these close relationships. Nouns are interchanged by switching **cause** or **effect**,

symbol or signified, associated thing or object. E.g., The White House issued a news release. Members of the president's staff are closely associated with the White House. E.g., Paul uses the "circumcised" to stand for the Jews (Romans 3:27–30). At times the sign is used for the signified, an author for his work, the cause for the effect. E.g., "Coastlands, listen to Me in silence" Isaiah 41:1 Coastlands means "People of the coastlands." E.g., "The spirits [spiritual gifts] of prophets are subject to prophets" 1 Corinthians 14:32. E.g., "Do not quench the Spirit" 1 Thessalonians 5:19 means "Do not hinder the use of spiritual gifts." E.g., "That which is born of the flesh is flesh, and that which is born of the Spirit is spirit." John 3:6 — "spirit" is synonymous with the "new born again nature", "flesh" is the "old nature" (see Romans 8:1–15). E.g., "Spirit" substituted for "spirit's operations" in 2 Kings 2:9 a double portion of your spirit be upon me." E.g., "'They have Moses [i.e. his writings] and the Prophets [i.e. his writings]; let them hear them" Luke 16:29. E.g., "You will not abandon my soul to Sheol" Psalm 16:10 [for soul substitute the whole individual. (See Acts 2:27,31). E.g., "For the lips of an adulteress drip honey And smoother than oil is her speech [letterally mouth]" Proverbs 5:3. E.g., "Their **line** has gone out through all the earth, And their **utterances** to the end of the world" Psalm 19:4. The "line" is difficult to understand. The word can refer to a "plummet line". Figuratively it can represent rule [correct measure as in Isaiah 28:11]. Parallelism connects "utterances" to it. Hence "their voice goes out into all the earth" (NIV and "voice" is how Paul quotes the verse in Romans 10:18). Regardless of the exact meaning of this one word. The whole sentence means "everywhere on earth, the knowledge of God's creative glory is seen." E.g., "Having made peace through the blood of His **cross**" Colossians 1:20. "Cross" is interchanged for "death [with its meritorious rewards.]. A synecdoche (s.v.) is a specialized metonymy. Metonym (s.v.) may be similar to metonymy but may have more metaphor.

Mezozeugma – (middle yoking). Conjunctum. One verb or adjective joins two objects in the middle of a sentence. E.g., "At that time people will see the Son of Man coming in clouds with **great power and glory**" Mark 13:26. "And at once **his mouth was opened and his tongue** [loosed], and he began to speak in praise of God" Luke 1:16.

Micrologia – Paying attention to petty differences. Pedantic recital of unnecessary trifles.

Mid–cut – Tmesis, Disssectio, Diacope, Diaeresis, Diastole, Ectasis, Dialysis, Divisio. Interjecting a word or phrase between parts of a compound word or between syllables of a word. E.g., a whole nother story. E.g., "here appear after." [appear interjected in hereafter.] Related to hyperbaton, anastrophe, parenthesis, and diacope. E.g., "knowing that **whatever good thing** each one does, this he will receive back from the Lord, whether slave or free" Ephesians 6:8. A letteral interlinear translation of the bold words is [**if whatever he might have done good**.]. The normal 3 Greek words get jumbled. (Instead of normal word order of 1 2 3, the word order becomes 1 3 2.)

Mimesis – see "Imitation Sayings" and "Description of Sayings."

Minution – Minutio. See meiosis.

Miosis – see meiosis.

Mnemonic – formats helpful in remembering (learning) something. E.g., "Thirty days hath September." E.g., Remember Christ's 12 disciples with "52 Bam St" with 5 J's and 2 P's.

Motif – a recurring general theme. When an element is repeated significantly. See Leitmotif.

Mycterismus – Nasus (q.v.). A mock given with an accompanying gesture, such as a scornful countenance. E.g., In some smiling sort of way, looking aside or by drawing the lip awry or shrinking up the nose, as he had said to one whose words he believed not, "No doubt, sir, of that," George Puttenham, *The Arte of English Poesie*, 1589. Usually **irony** is involved since the words are contrary to one's own gesture or one's own position. Zwingli describes it as a talk with nose and mocking grimace.

Myth – a traditional story "through which a given culture ratifies its social customs or accounts for the origins of human and natural phenomena, usually in supernatural or boldly imaginative terms."[146] This vocabulary is not used by those who believe in the inspiration of the Bible who understand Adam and Eve as an actual historical account

---

[146] Baldick, s.v. myth, p. 143.

given by God's inspiration. There are basically two versions of the myth camp. The 'rationalistic' say "a myth is a false or unreliable story or belief; they use the adjective: **mythical**. The second camp is called 'romantic.' 'Myth' is a superior intuitive mode of cosmic understanding (adjective: **mythic**). In most literary contexts, the second kind of usage prevails, and myths are regarded as fictional stories containing deeper truths, expressing collective attitudes to fundamental matters of life, death, divinity, and existence (sometimes deemed to be 'universal'). Myths are usually distinguished from legends in that they have less of an historical basis, although they seem to have a similar mode of existence in oral transmission, re-telling, literary adaptation, and allusion." "**mythology** is a body of related myths shared by members of a given people or religion, or sometimes a system of myths evolved by an individual writer[147] Mythopoeia or mythopoesis is the making of myths, either collectively in the folklore and religion of a given (usually pre-literate) culture or individually by a writer who elaborates a personal system of spiritual principles.[148] The word myth stems from Aristotle who stressed the plot (mythos) above everything else (see 'plot' below).

The New Testament uses the Greek word "mythos" five times — each time negatively. E.g., "As I urged you upon my departure for Macedonia, remain on at Ephesus so that you may instruct certain men not to teach strange doctrines, nor to pay attention to **myths** and endless genealogies, which give rise to mere speculation rather than furthering the administration of God which is by faith" 1 Timothy 1:3–4B E.g., "You will be a good servant of Christ Jesus, constantly nourished on the words of the faith and of the sound doctrine which you have been following. But have nothing to do with worldly **fables** fit only for old women." 1 Timothy 4:6–7. E.g., "For the time will come when they will not endure sound doctrine; but wanting to have their ears tickled, they will accumulate for themselves teachers in accordance to their own desires, and will turn away their ears from the truth and will turn aside to **myths**." 2 Timothy 4:3–4. E.g., "This testimony is true. For this reason reprove them severely so that they may be sound in the faith, not paying attention to Jewish **myths** and commandments

---

[147] Baldick, s.v. myth, p. 143.
[148] Baldick, s.v. mythopoeia, p. 144.

of men who turn away from the truth." Titus 1:13–14B. E.g., "For we did not follow cleverly devised **tales** when we made known to you the power and coming of our Lord Jesus Christ, but we were eyewitnesses of His majesty." 2 Peter 1:16.

Narration – Narratio. An account describing the statement of facts, incidents or events. This is the second part of classical oration (speech). Follows the introduction (exordio). Here the speaker provides a narrative account of what has happened and generally explains the nature of the case. The next part of classical oration is either propositio or partitio (see both).

Nasus – Mycterismus (q.v.). Letterally nasus means "nose" hence to turn up the nose or mock. A mock given with an accompanying gesture, such as a scornful countenance.

Negation – Spontaneous negative. E.g., "To whom we gave place by subjection, no, not for an hour" Galatians 2:5. E.g., "He instructed them that they should take nothing for their journey, except a mere staff — no bread, no bag, no money in their belt" Mark 6:8.

Neither/Nor – see Either/Or.

No–Ands – Asyndeton. Omission of connecting words (usually conjunctions) between clauses. E.g., "I came, I saw, I conquered." Also called: Asyntheton, Dialysis, Dialyton, Solutum, Dissolutio, Epitrochasmos, Percursio. E.g., the list of the works of the flesh in Galatians 5:19–21. E.g., List of fruits of the spirit Galatians 5:22.

Noema, Noemata (plural) – A quotation applied to a certain person, time or place or with particulars about it. See Quotation.

Numerology – Do numbers in the Bible have meaning beyond their significance as a number? The answer to this question deserves a book. I prefer an extremely limited approach (as advocated by John J Davis, *Biblical Numerology. A Basic Study of the Use of Numbers in the Bible.*) Basically gather every use of a number in the Bible, analyze and classify those uses. (That is the approach I used in ascending enumeration, q.v.). Hence 7 suggests completion and 40 suggests trial. (See also symbolism.)

Every numerologist does what is right in his own yes. Examining one system alone, you may see their rationale, but have no way to evaluate their allegorical redefinition. Try combining several numerologist systems — then you discover how arbitrary and indefinite their archetype meanings become!

Hidden meaning in numbers (numerology) began with Pythagoras (570 – c. 495 BC). It also has roots in Platonism and Neoplatonism (where reality is in the ideal). It is akin to allegorical interpretation in which the "spiritual" significance of a number is more important that the number itself. It is often used in divination, astrology and paranormal arts. God's Word speaks plainly about these abuses: "There shall not be found among you … one who uses divination, a soothsayer, one who interprets omens, or a sorcerer" Deuteronomy 18:10.

What about 666? "Here is wisdom. Let him who has understanding calculate the number of the beast, for the number is that of a man; and his number is six hundred and sixty-six" (Revelation 13:18). The Apostle John wrote 666 in Greek. Each Greek letter signified a specific number value. Take the name, translate name to Greek, substitute the Greek letter value for each letter, then calculate by summing all letter values (which is the meaning of gematria.). This riddle seems strange to us because we use the Arabic number system, John used the Greek Ionic number system. (Do not use Latin or Hebrew number systems to try to solve this riddle.)

Figure 7
How to Calculate the Number of the Beast: 666

(ΧΞϚ). The rigid historic rules to cipher this number were intimately known in John's day, but are totally foreign to us today. I use the literal, historical, grammatical approach. It hinges on the Greek letters/numbers and accords with examples and witness of Irenaeus, <u>Contra Haereses</u> 5:28 & 30. [Caution: "Against Heresies", also translates Irenaeus <u>Adversus Haereses</u>, but is a different work.]

The Text: Revelation 13:16–18 And he [the second beast – the false prophet] causes all, the small and the great, and the rich and the poor, and the free and the slaves, to be given a mark on their right hands, or on their foreheads. 17and he decrees that no one will be able to buy or to sell, except the one who has the mark, either the name of the [first] beast [Antichrist] or the number of his name. 18Here is wisdom. Let him who has understanding <u>calculate</u> the number of the beast, for the number is that of a man; and his number is six hundred and sixty-six. NASB (My <u>underline</u> and [my interpretation in brackets].) Note: Each letter of a person's name has a number value. "Calculate" means to use arithmetic and add up each letter's value to get a sum total (or **gematria**). The sum total of XΞϚ is (600+60+6= 666).

Background John wrote XΞϚ (666) with Koine Greek letters, so a Greek "letter to number system" solves the puzzle. This forces us to select the Greek Ionic numeral system, in common use since 300 BC. See table below. (Note: XΞϚ does not use Hebrew or Latin letters so the riddle is not solved with a Hebrew or Latin number system!!!) Each Greek letter represents a different numeral. (Only capital letters existed in Christ's day; but lowercase letters supplied to simplify!) Three letters of Phoenicia had significance — vau, qoph, sampi. Note: Greek numeral 6 varies over time: Ϝ vau or digamma (ancient) = Ϛ Stigma (Christ's time)= ΣΤ (Modern). Caution: Ϛ Stigma is not ς (final sigma as in Jesus below. Confusingly Modern Greek calls this final "s" (ς) letter form stigma, but they know it is not the [stigma] numeral 6 (Ϛ) . Stigma as a numeral always has a small lift at upper right: Ϛ while final s stigma does not (ς).

The Rules
A. Write down the name   Example=> Jesus
B. Convert to Greek   => Ιησους (stigma)
    (Use Google translator; do not transliterate***)
C. Substitute Ionic Numeral value for each Greek letter.
    (Use table: Greek Ionic Numerical System
                              =>10+8+200+70+400+200
D. Calculate the Greek gematria:
        sum up the numerical values   = 888

Greek Ionic Numeral System
(from Encyclopedia Britannica under "Numerals")

Value	1	2	3	4	5	6	7	8	9
Symbol	Αα	Βϐ	Γγ	Δδ	Εε	Ϝ,ϛ,ΣΤ	Ζζ	Ηη	Θθ
Name	alpha	beta	gamma	delta	epsilon	stigma	zeta	eta	theta

Value	10	20	30	40	50	60	70	80	90
Symbol	Ιι	Κκ	Λλ	Μμ	Νν	Ξξ	Οο	Ππ	Ϙ
Name	iota	kappa	lambda	mu	nu	xi	omicron	pi	qoph

Value	100	200	300	400	500	600	700	800	900
Symbol	Ρρ	Σσς	Ττ	Υυ	Φφ	Χχ	Ψψ	Ωω	ϡ
Name	rho	sigma	tau	upsilon	phi	khi,chi	psi	omega	sampi

Note: Irenaeus supplied these 3 potential solutions, confirming use of the Greek Ionic Numerals.

E   Y   A   N   Θ   A   Σ
50 + 400 + 1 + 50 + 9 + 1 + 200)   => 666

Λ   A   T   E   I   N   O   Σ
30 + 1 + 300 + 5 + 10 + 50 + 70 + 200   => 666

T   E   I   T   A   N
300 + 5 + 10 + 300 + 1 + 50   => 666

Note: Nero Caesar=>Νερο Καισαρ

N   ε   ρ   ο   K   α   ι   σ   α   ρ
50 + 5 + 100 + 70 + 20 + 1 + 10 + 200 + 1 + 100 => 557

(Incorrect use: Hebrew letter gematra becomes 666 or 616. BUT Irenaeus cites witnesses who asked John and John said, "It is 666 (ΧΞϛ)." See Wikipedia: The Number of the Beast." A few texts (A,C, P115) read 616 (ΧΙϛ).

Note: if Google transliterates, translate from Greek to English then check box of "type phonetically." E.g., Barack Obama => βαρακκ Οβαμα =>

β   α   ρ   α   κ   κ   O   β   α   μ   α
2 + 1 + 100 + 1 + 20 + 20 + 2 + 70 + 1 + 40 + 1 => 258

[End of **Numerology**.]

Obiter Occurrens – Latin term for antipipton (q.v.).

Objurgatory – Obiurgatorius. Designed to objurgate or chide; containing or expressing reproof; culpatory. E.g., When the tennis ball was in, but the referee called it out, John McEnroe began to chide, "How could you not see that the ball was clearly in? Shall I take up a collection so we can buy you new glasses?"

Obscurity – Enigmatic, hard to understand. E.g., Jesus said, "I speak to them in parables: because they seeing see not; and hearing they hear not, neither do they understand." Matthew 13:13.

Occupation – when a speaker elaborates on the very thing he just said he would not speak of.

Also the opposite. "I will make no mention of his drunken banquets nightly, and his watching with bawds, dicers, whore masters. I will not name his losses, his luxurity, and staining of his honesty." Henry Peacham, *The Garden of Eloquence*, 131.

Ode – is an elaborate lyric poem praising an event (or an individual) expressing inspired feelings in a sincere and dignified way. There are **3 forms: Pindaric, Horatian, and irregular**. All three forms use rhyme but only the first two use meter. Often these were sung with lyre accompaniment.

A **Pindaric** ode is usually short with 3 parts. The chorus looks left to give the strophe (the opening) and turns right (back the other way) to give the antistrophe — which often mirrors the strophe in repeated phrase, words or metrical form. The closing section (epode) has a different meter and length.

B) **Horatian** odes are often long epic poems with regular stanza patterns of either two or four lines.

Ode Synonyms: anacreontic, clerihew, dithyramb, eclogue, elegy, English sonnet, epic, epigram, epode, epopee, epos, georgic, idyll (also idyl), jingle, lament, limerick, madrigal, pastoral, pastorale, psalm, rondeau, rondel (or rondelle), rondelet, sonnet, triolet, villanelle

Ode near synonyms: lyric, poem, rune, song; rhyme (also rime); ballad, lay, haiku, senryu, tanka, blank verse, free verse, minstrelsy, poesy, poetry, versification, vers libre.

Oeonismos – See wishing.

Onomatopoeia – Echoism. Nomenclature that phonically imitates the sound. Comics are loaded with these. Oddly they do not transliterate into other languages: pig's grunt (English "oink") in German is "grunz." E.g., Buzz, hiss, peep, whip-poor-will, whack, gurgle, whoosh. E.g., Jokes often use echoism. What type of sock does a pirate wear? Aaarg - yle [argyle] socks!

Ostentus – Latin for paradigma. An argument from example whose purpose is to exhort or dissuade.

Oxymoron, Acutifatuum – (sharp foolishness). combination of incongruous or contradictory words. A paradox condensed to a phrase. A wise saying that at first sounds foolish. E.g., cruel kindness, hellish heaven, act naturally, alone together, clearly confused, deafening silence, definitely maybe. E.g., "No one goes to that restaurant anymore. It's always too crowded." - Yogi Berra E.g., "You have … stripped the naked of their clothing" Job 22:6 (KJV). E.g., "But if your eye is bad, your whole body will be full of darkness. If then the light that is in you is darkness, how great is the dark-ness!" Matthew 6:23. E.g., "God has chosen the foolish things of the world to shame the wise, and God has chosen the weak things of the world to shame the things which are strong" 1 Corinthians 1:27. E.g., "To me, the very least of all saints, this grace was given" Ephesians 3:8.

Paeanismos – See Exultation.

Palindrome – a word, phrase or sentence with the same letters whether read forwards or backwards. E.g., kayak, madam, 02/02/2020. "nurses run." James Joyce in *Ulysses* coined "tattarrattat."

Palinodia – See retracting.

Parable – is a repeated or continued simile. It is an illustration in which one set of circumstances is **likened** to another set. (Technically it is not an extended metaphor, which uses representation.) Parables use likeness. A parable has one particular purpose or specific occurrence. Verb action is past tense, as with the parable of a lost son (Luke 15:11–32). (In contrast, a *similitude* has a timeless general truth, or customary habit, and the verbs are in present tense.) When an author tells the reader to substitute one for another, the allegorical hermeneutic is at work and it is legitimate to get at what the author is intending. Note parables do not have a historic time and place, for when you substitute the interpretive key into the illustration, the reality of the original is lost. Parables are illustrations made up to make a point; they usually are brief in the illustration of that moral point. Note: seek the likeness; do not press in all points or extend it in all directions. For example "the day of the Lord will come just like a thief in the night" 1 Thessalonians 5:2. The likeness is the "unexpected" timing, not the character of dishonesty in a thief. Synonym: parabole, similitude, comparison, resemblance mystical. Parables are a major subset of homoeosis (q.v.).

Paradiastole – See Either/Or.

Paradigma – An argument from example whose purpose is to exhort or dissuade. Synonyms: example, resemblance by example, exemplum and ostentus. A major subset of homoeosis (q.v.).

Paradox – a statement that is seemingly contradictory or opposed to common sense and yet is perhaps true. E.g., Light behaves both like a wave and like a particle. E.g., "Whosoever wishes to save his life will lose it, but whoever loses his life for My sake, he is the one who will save it" Luke 9:24.

Paragoge – add letters at the end of a word. A type of metaplasm. E.g., Call spirits from the **vasty** deep – Shakespeare, *Henry IV* part I, 3.1.52. Akin to apposition.

Paregmenon – See derivation. Word repetition with different inflection or with the same root word in different words. Greek word is παραγμενον, but in ancient Greek it was παρηγμενον. E.g., "my loving and beloved wife."

Paralepsis – See Prolepsis. Anticipation. The presentation of a future event as if it has already happened. Many prophetic (yet to be fulfilled) prophecies are given in the past tense, as if they had already happened.

Paralipsis – Stating and drawing attention to something in the very act of pretending to pass it over. A kind of irony. E.g., "It would be unseemly for me to dwell on Senator Kennedy's drinking problem, and too many have already sensationalized his womanizing." Synonyms: paraleipsis, paralepsis, antiphrasis, parasiopesis, occultatio, occupatio, praeteritio, preteritio, praetermissio, the passager, preterition. E.g., "And what more shall I say? For time will fail me if I tell of Gideon, Barak, Samson, Jephthah, of David and Samuel and the prophets" Hebrews 11:32.

Paraenesis – A) In ancient rhetoric, this is the deciphering of the plot, or "the moral of the story". B)In more modern usage it is usually the **exhortation**. It can be a warning of impending evil. (Ominatio is a prophecy of evil.) Synonyms: admonition, sapienta, foretelling, foreboding. E.g., "But seek first His kingdom and His righteousness, and all these things will be added to you." Matthew 6:33.

Parallelism – an oriental language device in which *thoughts* are repeated in various formats or patterns. A partial list of parallelism types is given: synonymous, antithetical, synthetic, emblematic, stair like, introverted, incomplete, chiastic, Epanodos. (Parallelism gives insight on unique words because the next line gives the same thought in different words.) E.g., "Bless the Lord, O my soul; and all that is within me, bless His holy name.Bless the Lord, O my soul; and forget none of His benefits;

> Who pardons all your iniquities; who heals all your diseases;
> Who redeems your life from the pit;
> who crowns you with loving kindness and compassion
> who satisfies your years with good things,
> so that your youth is renewed like the eagle." Psalm 103:1–5.

Paraphrase – Paraphrasis — reworded for clarification. E.g., "I do you to wit" paraphrased into modern English means "I want you to know."

Parapleromaticos – Supplementary. Zwingli's definition: Adding unnecessary, redundant words. Zwingli translated the expression with "impletive ac obiter" or "obiter implendi."

Paraprosdokian – Para (alongside or despite) prosdokian (the expectation). It consists of a sentence with two parts: the first is a statement upon which the second gives an intriguing variation. The first part becomes a figure of speech, because the second causes you to reinterpret the first part. Comedians and satirists use them because they typically have humorous, anticlimax or dramatic effect. According to William Gordon Casselman paraprosdokian is a twentieth century neologism. Some paraprosdokians not only change the meaning of an early phrase, but they also play on the double meaning of a particular word, creating a form of syllepsis.` E.g.,

- War does not determine who is right - only who is left.
- Going to church doesn't make you a Christian any more than standing in a garage makes you a car.
- The last thing I want to do is hurt you. But it is still on the list.
- If I agreed with you, we'd both be wrong.
- We never really grow up; we only learn how to act in public.
- Knowledge is knowing a tomato is a fruit; Wisdom is not putting it in a fruit salad.
- The early bird might get the worm, but the second mouse gets the cheese.
- How is it one careless match can start a forest fire, but it takes a whole box to start a campfire?
- Dolphins are so smart that within a few weeks of captivity, they can train people to stand at the edge of a pool and throw fish.
- I didn't say it was your fault, I said I was blaming you.
- A clear conscience is usually the sign of a bad memory.
- You don't need a parachute to skydive, but you do need one to skydive again.
- The voices in my head may be fake, but they have good ideas!
- Hospitality is making your guests feel like they're at home, even if you wish they were.
- I scream the same way whether I'm about to be eaten by a shark or seaweed touches my foot.
- Some cause happiness wherever they go, others whenever they go.
- There's a fine line between cuddling and holding someone down so they can't get away.
- Sometimes my mind wanders and other times it goes away completely.
- Never complain about growing old, far too many people have been denied that privilege.
- I live in my own little world, but that's okay, they like me there
- "He was at his best when the going was good." Alistair Cooke on the Duke of Windsor

- "I've had a perfectly wonderful evening, but this wasn't it." Groucho Marx
- "If I could say a few words, I'd be a better public speaker." Homer Simpson
- "I sleep eight hours a day and at least ten at night." Bill Hicks

Parasiopisis – see aposiopesis.

Parataxis – Place unrelated clauses one after another without any connective. E.g., Electric cars do not pay gasoline tax; the banana has brown spots.

Parecbasis – A digression. More specifically, a digression that often comes following the narration and has some bearing on the case, although it appears to be a departure from the logical order. Excursus is a more familiar term. Several variations exist: parecnasis, pareonasis, digressio, egressus, egressio, the straggler or figure of digression.

Paregmenon – Derivation (q.v.). A general term for the repetition of a word or its cognates in a short sentence. Often, but not always, polyptoton. E.g., "I will destroy the wisdom of the wise; the intelligence of the intelligent I will frustrate." 1 Corinthians 1:19.

Parembole – See insertion.

Parenthesis – a word, phrase, or sentence inserted as an aside in a sentence. There are two types: A) Parenthesis, which adds to the understanding, or B) Interposition which if omitted does not enlarge the understanding. Both forms could stand completely by itself. In written text, its demarcation may be with parentheses ( ), em dash —, or commas. E.g., But now my Deere (for so love makes me to call you still)/ That love I say, that luckless love, that works me all this ill. *George Puttenham, The Arte of English Poesie*, 141. E.g., "But from those who were of high reputation (what they were makes no difference to me; God shows no partiality) well, those who were of reputation contributed nothing to me." Galatians 2:6. E.g., "But we do see Him who was made for a little while lower than the angels, namely, Jesus, **because of the suffering of death crowned with glory and honor,** so that by the grace of God He might taste death for everyone" Hebrews 2:9. E.g., "So we have the prophetic word made more sure, to which you do well to pay attention **as to a lamp**

shining in a dark place, until the day dawns and the morning star arises in your hearts" 2 Peter 1:19.

Paroemia – One of several terms describing short, pithy sayings. E.g., "Like a dog that returns to its vomit Is a fool who repeats his folly." Proverbs 26:11. Related figures: adage, apothegm, gnome, maxim, proverb, sententia. Also related to maxim, proverb and Chreia. Variant spellings: paremia, parimia, adagium.

Paronomaion – Zwingli's term for alliteration (q.v.). Similar to homoeoprophoron.

Paronomasia – Rhyming words. Repetition of word sounds (but not necessarily word sense.). Alliteration repeats initial sounds. Polyptoton repeats sounds. Rhyme repeats end word sounds. A) words similar in sound (homonyms) are set in opposition so as to give antithetical force. More commonly B) the same word is used in different senses (homographs and homonyms). Puns are one kind of paronomasia, for the same sound is interpreted differently. E.g., Three puns are intended when the comedian joked, "I have to punish you." Did he letterally mean to "punish you"? Or was he trying to make a "Pun issue"? Perhaps it was to declare "Pun – ish OOOOO." Synonyms: Adnomination (repetition of root words) or Agnomination, Allusion, the nicknamer. All languages have this and it is very difficult to translate. E.g., "She shall be called Woman, Because she was taken out of Man" Genesis 2:23 from "man" God created "Wo– man". E.g., "Well, I'd rather have a bottle in front of me than a frontal lobotomy" (Tom Waits on Fernwood2Night, 1977). E.g., "Your children need your presence more than your presents" (Jesse Jackson).

Pathetic Fallacy – ascription of human traits or feelings to inanimate nature. E.g., "cruel sea;" Category IV hurricanes are "pitiless storms;" Hellfire has "devouring and unquenched flames."

Pathopoeia – Pathos. Description of feelings or affections. E.g., "When He approached Jerusalem, He saw the city and wept over it" Luke 19:41.

Partitio – In this third section of the oration, the speaker outlines what will follow, in accordance with what's been stated as the status, or point at issue in the case. It follows the narratio (and perhaps the propositio). It comes before the confirmatio.

Pericope – Pericopa. A selection or extract from a book (especially from the Bible), appointed to be read in the churches or used as a text for a sermon.

Period – The periodic sentence, characterized by the suspension of the completion of sense until its end. This has been more possible and favored in Greek and Latin, languages already favoring the end position for the verb, but has been approximated in uninflected languages such as English. Note the long delay prior to the occurrence of the sentence's main verb ("sing"):

> Of man's first disobedience and the fruit
> Of that forbidden tree, whose mortal taste
> Brought death into the world, and all our woe,
> With loss of Eden, till one greater Man
> Restore us, and regain the blissful seat,
> **Sing** Heav'nly Muse … John Milton, *Paradise Lost*

Synonyms: hirmos, hirmus, ambitus, circumductum, continuatio, conclusio, long loose.

Periphrasis – Circumlocution, Circuitio. Instead of directly and briefly naming it, one speaks round about it. Usually the replacement of a single word by several which together have the same meaning; a substitution of more words for less. E.g., Instead of "Zechariah, a prophet– "Zechariah, who had understanding through the vision of God" 2 Chronicles 26:5.

Peristasis – See Description of Circumstances.

Peroratio – 6th or final part of a classical oration. Follows refutatio. Here are appeals through pathos and often a summing up. E.g., "Do not worry about tomorrow, for tomorrow will worry about itself" Matthew 6:34.

Personification – Personificatio, Prosopopoeia, Personae Fictio, Conformation. Abstract characteristics are given human shape. The absent are addressed as present. The dead are spoken of as alive. E.g., "All my **bones will say**, 'LORD, who is like You'" Psalm 35:10. E.g., "He [leviathan) **laughs** at the rattling of the javelin. E.g., "The voice of your brother's blood is crying to Me from the ground" Genesis 4:10. E.g., "Sin is crouching at the door" Genesis 4:7. E.g., "Our sins testify against us" Isaiah 59:12 (likewise in Jeremiah 14:7).

Phasma – Zwingli's Greek word for spectrum (an apparition, specter, or ghost).

Pleonasm – Needless repetition of a word/phrase; a tautology on the level of a phrase. E.g., "God swore with an oath [took an oath with an oath]" 2 Samuel 7:12–16B. E.g., "You will say to the household master of the house" Luke 22:11. E.g., Sober he seemed, and very sagely sad,/ And to the ground his eyes were lowly bent,/ Simple in shew, and voyde of **malice bad** ... Edmund Spenser, *The Faerie Queene,* Book 1, 1.29

Ploce – (word folding) The same word is repeated but with heightened meaning. E.g., "His wife is a wife indeed." E.g., "Caesar was Caesar." Other synonyms are Homogene, Anaclasis, Antitasis, Dialogia, Refractio, Reciprocatio (interchange of words). (These are not homonyms which has two words (identically spelled but different meanings.) E.g., "Do they **provoke** me to anger? saith the LORD: do they not **provoke** themselves to the confusion of their own faces?" Jeremiah 7:19 (KJV). 1st provoke is people provoking God's anger. 2nd provoke is God's wrath on the people. E.g., "But I see a different **law** in the members of my body, waging war against the **law** of my mind and making me a prisoner of the **law** of sin which is in my members." Romans 7:23. 1st & 3rd law: old nature. 2nd law: new nature.

Plot – a writer's arrangement of presenting events which may differ from the chronological order (or story). For emphasis flash-backs and flash-aheads may occur. Plots in ancient times were termed *mythos* beginning with Aristotle who put utmost importance to it as the overarching principle of development and coherence. Characters and all other elements in a drama are secondary to the plot for Aristotle.

Poetic – Zwingli's term means erudite rhetoric, or speaking like a poet in contexts that are not poetry.

Polyptoton – repetition of the same word or root in different grammatical functions or forms. See "Many Inflections". E.g., Disturb his hours of **rest** with **restless** trances,/ Afflict him in his **bed** with **bedrid** groans;/ Let there **bechance** him **pitiful mischances**,/ To make him **moan** but **pity** not his **moans**. *Shakespeare, The Rape of Lucrece,* 974-977.

Polysyndeton – See Many Ands.

Portmanteau – a new word morphed from two words. E.g., Redox reactions can "reduce" or "oxygenate"

Postsumptio – see metalepsis.

Praefixio – see proposition.

Praemonitio – defending beforehand, obviating objections. See Prolepsis.

Pragmatographia – See Description of Actions

Prayer – Euche, Votum. Prayer, wish, vow. If prayer is to curse, it is imprecatory (deprecation q.v.). E.g., "do save, we beseech You; O LORD, we beseech You, do send prosperity!" Psalm 118:26.

Probation – For Zwingli the positive evidence for the assertions, the positive part of a speech.

Procatalepsis – (a seizing beforehand), a pre-occupation. See Prolepsis.

Prodiorthosis – Words (to heal, soften, mitigate, or modify) come as a warning of later shock.

Proecthesis – See Justification.

Prolepsis – (from the Greek to 'leap ahead' or 'anticipate.'). Prolepsis anticipates objections and answers them. The application of an epithet or description, before it becomes applicable. Two categories of Prolepsis exist: A) Future Time Anticipated and B) Future Anticipated Arguments.

A) Future Time Anticipated. Anticipation of a future **time** which currently cannot be held onto but must be **deferred**. Speaking of something future as though already done or existing. Many of the Bible's future predictions are written in the perfect tense, as if it has already happened. This is called the "prophetic perfect." E. W. Bullinger identifies this as a figure of speech, which he calls Heterosis (q.v.). The concept of prolepsis is hard to grasp, so let me illustrate. E.g., 1 Corinthians 15:54–57B. "Death is swallowed up in victory. "O death, where is your victory? O death, where is your sting?" The sting of death is sin, and the power of sin is the law; but thanks be to God, who gives us the victory through our Lord Jesus Christ." In Christ Jesus the power of sin and death are **already** broken — Christianity stands or falls on the resurrection of Jesus from the dead. But why then is death not totally done away with? This proleptic anticipation sees the end of death, even though **we do not yet have its total defeat.** It is as if we stand between World War II's D–day (Defeat Day) and V–day (Victory Day). The enemy was defeated, but not totally defeated until the final victory. For the Christian, at the cross death was defeated, but not yet is it totally done away with. Even when Messiah rules as king (in the future millennium), death will be greatly diminished, but still linger. "No longer will there be in it an infant who lives but a few days, Or an old man who does not live out his days; For the youth will die at the age of one hundred And the one who does not reach the age of one hundred Will be thought accursed." Isaiah 65:20. Ampliatio means **adjourning** (a putting off of dealing with the anticipation). E.g., "Moses said, "You are right; I shall never see your face again!" Exodus 10:29 this anticipates but is proleptic, since Moses leaves Pharaoh again in Exodus 11:8. E.g., "This is My body which is given for you; do this in remembrance of Me" Luke 22:19. This is proleptic for it anticipates the future crucifixion as if it was happening at that moment. Hence we connect the "broken bread" with Christ's death where his body was broken from his spirit.

B) Future Anticipated Arguments. Anticipation which **deals** with the anticipated argument. Synonyms: Occupatio, Prolepsie, anticipation, propounder (to propose an idea), Procatalepsis, Procatalepsis, Apantesis, Occupation, anteoccupation, Praemonitio. Further classification depends on how the anticipated arguments are dealt with.

1) Techa or Closed Prolepsis:

    a) anticipated objection is **either** stated (or implied), but not answered (Hypophora), **or**

    b) answered, but not stated. E.g., "But it is not as though the word of God has failed. For they are not all Israel who are descended from Israel" Romans 9:6. The unstated question is "If Israel is rejected, then does not God's word fail?" E.g., "God has not rejected His people, has He? May it never be!" Romans 11:1. Unanswered answer to stated objection, "God has not rejected His people, has He?"

3) Aperta or Open Prolepsis anticipated objection is **both** stated and answered. Anthypophora (a substitution by stealth — take opponent's objection and use it for our own). Schesis (checking), Anaschesis (taking on one's own self). Prosodoton (a giving back to or besides), Hypobole (throwing under). E.g., [objection] "Zion said, "The LORD has forsaken me, / And the Lord has forgotten me." [Answer] "Can a woman forget her nursing child / And have no compassion on the son of her womb? / Even these may forget, but I will not forget you" Isaiah 49:14–15. E.g., "Do not suppose that you can say to yourselves, 'We have Abraham for our father'; for I say to you that from these stones God is able to raise up children to Abraham" Matthew 3:9. E.g., "What shall we say then? Is the Law sin? May it never be! On the contrary, I would not have come to know sin except through the Law" Romans 7:7. E.g., "But someone will say, "How are the dead raised? And with what kind of body do they come?" You fool! That which you sow does not come to life unless it dies"1 Corinthians 15:35–36B.

Prooemium – Latin for preface, prelude, introduction of a speech.

Proparoxytonos – (acidify). Zwingli's definition for sharp (or pointed) wording.

Propositio – Coming between the narratio and the partitio of a classical oration, the propositio provides a brief summary of what one is about to speak on, or concisely puts forth the charges or accusation. This is also known as the divisio.

Proposition – the first assertion of a syllogism. Prothesis. Propositum.

Prosapodosis – Redittio, Sejugatio, Disjunctio, Diezeugmenon. After announcing two or three subjects, there is a return to each subject. The reasons usually follow the presented order. E.g., Notice the three subjects are returned to in the order presented. "And He, when He comes, will convict the world concerning **sin** and **righteousness** and **judgment**; concerning **sin**, because they do not believe in Me; and concerning **righteousness**, because I go to the Father and you no longer see Me; and concerning **judgment**, because the ruler of this world has been judged." John 16:8–11.

Prosopographia. See Description of Persons.

Prosopopoeia – Personification (q.v.). Representing an imaginary or absent person as speaking or acting; attributing life, speech or inanimate qualities to dumb or inanimate objects. E.g., With how sad steps, O Moon, thou climb'st the skies,/ How silently, and with how wan a face! Philip Sidney, Astrophil and Stella, *sonnet 31*, c1580s.

Prosthesis – addition of letters to the beginning of a word. E.g., "I all alone **beweep** my outcast state" Shakespeare, *Sonnets*, 29.

Protherapeia – Proepiplexis. Words (to heal, soften, mitigate, or modify) come at the beginning in order to secure an indulgence or conciliation. E.g., "Rabbi, we know that You have come from God as a teacher; for no one can do these signs that You do unless God is with him." John 3:2. E.g., "In regard to all the things of which I am accused by the Jews, I consider myself fortunate, King Agrippa, that I am about to make my defense before you today; especially because you are an expert in all customs and questions among the Jews; therefore I beg you to listen to me patiently" Acts 26:2–3. E.g., Paul stood in the midst of the Areopagus and said, "Men of Athens, I observe that you are very religious in all respects" Acts 17:22.

Prothesis – see proposition.

Prothysteron – see hysteron proteron.

Protimesis – See Description of order.

Proverb – Paroemia. A general truth in short form. A common saying, usually of unknown authorship. If author is known, technically it is an aphorism. A) Quotations indicate a known proverb. E.g., "the saying is true, 'One sows and another reaps.'" John 4:37. B) Probable common expressions. E.g., "I will surely prosper you and make your descendants **as the sand of the sea, which is too great to be numbered.**" Genesis 32:12. C) Scriptural proverb that has become common place. E.g., "Do not muzzle an ox while it is treading out the grain." Deuteronomy 25:4, 1 Corinthians 9:9, 1 Timothy 5:18.

Pun – Paronomasia. An expression that adds emphasis or humor by inducing ambiguity because two distinct meanings are suggested by the same word (polysemy) or by two similar sounding words (homophone). See paronomasia, homonym. E.g., I hate to punish you! I hate to pun issue! E.g., I reached down thinking it was a quarter, but it's not (it's snot).

Quotation – Gnome (understanding), Noema(ta), Chreia, Sententia. (See each former synonym.) Chreia cites the quotation's author. Sententia (sentiment) is aphorism, maxim or axiom — when particulars of person, time or place are given (Noema or Noemata when plural). A Gnome (meaning understanding or knowing) encompasses all quotations and proverbs. When it comes to New Testament quotations of the Old Testament, many variances appear. According to E.W. Bullinger, there are 189 different citations of the Old Testament in the New. 105 cite the Septuagint. 21 Differ from the Septuagint. 44 differ from Septuagint and Hebrew. 19 are neutral.[149] E. W. Bullinger believes in the Holy Spirit's inspiration of both the Old and New Testaments. Hence he goes to great lengths to show the sense is retained, even if variances in words or grammar occur. The most difficult quotation is Matthew 27:9–10. E. W. Bullinger believes Jeremiah spoke it, even though Zechariah wrote it down. E.g., Socrates wrote, "By all means, marry. If you get a good wife, you'll become happy; if you get a bad one, you'll become a philosopher."

Raillery – Diasyrmos. An expression of feeling which tears away all disguise. E.g., Judas went to Jesus and said, "Hail, Rabbi!" and kissed Him. And Jesus said to him, "Friend, do what you have come for." Matthew 26:49–50. E.g., In John 7:1–9, Christ's disciples wanted Jesus to do miracles in Judea (v.3). They thought that was his mission — "For no one does anything in secret when he himself seeks to be known publicly. If You do these things, show Yourself to the world." (v.4). But Christ unveiled his mission. "My time is not yet here … The world … hates Me because I testify of it, that its deeds are evil. I do not go up to this feast [of Booths in Judea] because My time has not yet fully come" (v.6–8). Jesus knew they would kill him if he went to Judea (v.1), it was not yet that time (v.8), so he stayed in Galilee (v.9).

Redditio – see prosapodosis.

Reditus – epanodos. Return to a theme after an excursus.

---

149 Bullinger, E.W., Figures Of Speech Used In The Bible, 1898, (Mansfield Centre, Ct: Martino Publishing, 2011 Reprint edition), s.v. Gnome, p. 778–803

Redundancy – See Pleonasm.

Reduplication – Reduplicatio. See anadiplosis.

Refrication – Refricatio. Repetition or letterally "rubbing up again." To take up a thought again.

Refutatio – The 5th part of classical oration. Follows confirmatio and precedes peroratio. Here refutation is given — devoted to answering the counter arguments of one's own opponent.

Rejection – Rejectio. See Apodioxis.

Repeated Negation – Greek has two words for "no" — οὐ and μή. When both are used together a "repeated negation" is in effect. In English a repeated negative also shows emphatic resolve: "No, No." "No, I will not". E. W. Bullinger admits the Greeks did not classify this as a figure of speech, however "they used it." The combination produces a "most solemn and emphatic asseveration"[150] or emphatic statement.

1. Human use. In the Gospels, every time ordinary men use "repeated negation", **it expresses their strong wish, which fails to be true**. E.g., Regarding Christ's suffering, death and resurrection, Peter says, "God forbid it, Lord! This shall never happen to You." Matthew 16:22. But he was wrong. E.g., Regarding Jesus washing Peter's feet, Peter said to Him, "Never shall You wash my feet!" John 13:8. But Jesus washed his feet. E.g., Regarding Peter's denial, Peter said to Him, "Even if I have to die with You, I will not deny You." But he did! E.g., Doubting Thomas said "Unless I see the nail marks in His hands, and put my finger where the nails have been, and put my hand into His side, I will never believe." John 20:25. But Thomas did believe!

2. Christ's use. When Jesus uses "repeated negation," **they are always true**. E.g., "For truly I say to you, until heaven and earth pass away, not the smallest letter or stroke shall pass from the Law until all is accomplished." Matthew 5:18. E.g., "For I say to you that unless your righteousness surpasses that of the scribes and Pharisees, you will not enter the kingdom of heaven." Matthew 5:20. E.g., "Truly I say to you, you will not

---

[150] Bullinger, p. 339.

come out of there until you have paid up the last cent." Matthew 5:26. E.g., In them is fulfilled the prophecy of Isaiah: "'You will be ever hearing but never understanding; you will be ever seeing but never perceiving." Matthew 13:14. E.g., "Truly I say to you, there are some of those who are standing here who will not taste death until they see the Son of Man coming in His kingdom." Matthew 16:28. E.g., "For then there will be a great tribulation, such as has not occurred since the beginning of the world until now, nor ever will." Matthew 24:21. (E. W. Bullinger lists twenty–three more examples of this!)

Repetend – irregular recurring word or phrase. A refrain is more often and regular in appearance.

Repetitio – Frequent but irregular repetition of word or words. (Regular repetition is either Geminatio or Epizeuxis.) E.g., Ezekiel 36:23–29 repeats "you" and "your". This prophecy is about the physical return of Israel to the land of Israel. Note the land's production of food increases, before God causes the return (v.8 and 24). "But you, O mountains of Israel, you will put forth your branches and bear your fruit for My people Israel; for they will soon come" Ezekiel 36:8. "For I will take you from the nations, gather you from all the lands and bring you into your own land" Ezekiel 36:24.

Repetition – A) Repeat sounds for rhetorical effect. See alliteration, rhyme, rhythm, anaphora, assonance, climax, and pleonasm. B) Repeat one or more words: epizeuxix, polyptoton, antanaclasis, anaphora, epistrophe, symploce, epanalepsis, anadiplosis, gradatio, congeries, antimetabole, pleonasm. Germinatio. C) Repeat a phrase, a clause or an idea: auxesis, isocolon, tautology, chiasmus, antithesis, periphrasis.

Reprimand – Epitimesis, Epiplexis. Feeling expressed by rebuke, reproof or reproach. E.g., "But they [Samaritans] did not receive Him, because He was traveling toward Jerusalem. When His disciples James and John saw this, they said, "Lord, do You want us to command fire to come down from heaven and consume them?" But He turned and **rebuked** them, [and said, "You do not know what kind of spirit you are of; for the Son of Man did not come to destroy men's lives, but to save them."] Luke 9:53–56. E.g., "He said to them, "O foolish men and slow of heart to believe in all that the prophets have spoken!" Luke 24:25.

Resection – Latin for apocope. Omitting a letter or syllable at the end of a word. A kind of metaplasm.

Resumption – See Epanalepsis.

Reticentia – Latin for Aposiopesis.

Retort – Antistrophe. Turning the speaker's words back on himself. If a violent turn, it is called Biaeon, Violentum, Inversion. E.g., In Matthew 15:25–27, The Syrophoenician woman to Jesus, "Lord, help me!" And He answered and said, "It is not good to take the children's bread and throw it to the **dogs**." But she said, "Yes, Lord; but even the **dogs feed on the crumbs which fall from their masters' table**."

Retracting – Palinodia. First reproof (spoken against), then approvals.

E.g., Ephesus in Revelation 2:4–6   reproof (v.4–5), approval (v.6)

E.g., Sardis in Revelation 3:1–5   reproof (v.1–3), approval (v. 4–5).

Rhetoric – The deliberate use of eloquence to make the most persuasive effect in speaking or writing. Important in antiquity and Mediaeval education involving: elaborate categorizing of figures of speech, arts of memory, arrangement and oratorical delivery. Modern use of rhetorical dimension of a literary work looks at elements that persuade or otherwise guide the responses of readers.

Rhetorical Question – a question asked to evoke emotional response or to persuade, but not to gain information. E.g., Milton: "For what can war, but endless war still breed?"

Riddle – a puzzling indirect description of a thing, person, or idea. The way it is framed makes it a challenge to identify. But all the elements perfectly fit the solution. The riddle seems intentionally formulated to tax the ingenuity of the hearer, because it is difficult to mentally move from pieces to get the whole idea. It is far easier to get the answer then deduce the pieces.

E.g., A man without eyes, saw plums on a tree.

He neither picked plums nor left plums, now how can that be?

(Riddle Resolution: A one eyed man sees two plums.

He picks one and leaves one.)

The summed numerical value of the beast's name is 666 (Revelation 13:18) Resolve this riddle with Ionic system (where Greek letter values get assigned to each letter in the beast's name. (See "Numerology" for specific details on how to solve the 666 riddle. See *Encyclopedia Britannica,* s.v. "number" for various language letter values.

Sarcasm – Irony (q.v.). A sharp and satirical utterance designed to emotionally cut or give pain. E.g., Elijah mocked the 400 prophets of Baal, and said, "Call out with a loud voice: for he *is* a god; either he is talking (occupied NASB), or he is pursuing (gone aside NASB i.e. going to the bathroom), or he is in a journey, *or* peradventure he sleepeth, and must be awaked" 1 Kings 18:27 KJV.

Satire – squib, lampoon, words that ridicule and scorn. Intense, hard biting satire is sarcasm (q.v.)

Scesis onamaton – omission of the verb in a sentence. E.g., A maid in conversation chaste, in speech mild, in countenance cheerful, in behavior modest. Henry Peacham, *The Garden of Eloquence.*

Scheme – letterally means a shape or figure, hence a figure of speech. Today the use of the term is obsolete. Essentially a *scheme* is a departure from normal word order or phonetic sound. But in days when rhetoric was a prominent aspect of education there were two conflicting ideas about the classification of scheme. The School at Alexandria claimed schemes <u>usually</u> do NOT extend the meaning (as a trope or figure of speech does). The other school, at Antioch, claimed schemes included tropes. Latin forms are schema and schematismus. Synonym: figura I (as opposed to type which is sometimes referred to as figura II).

Sententia – One of several terms describing short, pithy sayings. Others include adage, aphorism, apothegm, dictum, gnome, maxim, motto, paroemia, pearl of wisdom, precept, proverb, saw (often with sarcasm), sententia and wisecrack. Often with the adjective "general." E.g., "The words of wise men are like goads, and masters of these collections are like well-driven nails; they are given by one Shepherd" Ecclesiastes 12:11. See Quotation.

Short Prayers – Ejaculatio (now an obsolete use of the word). Brief prayer or wish. E.g., "God forbid." "Thank God." "God be praised."

Sign – the perceptible word or object that brings into mental focus the realities behind that sign. Eucharistic bread (the sign or symbol) by remembrance of Christ's broken body on your behalf, mentally and spiritually brings you into communion with Christ (reality).

Simile – explicitly stated comparison introduced with "as" or "like". Comprehend fully the two entities and use *reflection* to gain insight on the commonality. E.g., Christ's coming for his disciples is "like lightning flashing across the sky" (obvious and open, not secretive Matthew 24:27). A Homeric (or Epic) simile as well as biblical parables are lengthy comparisons in simile form.

Similitude – an extended simile with verbs in the present tense. It is essentially a parable, except it has a timeless general truth or customary habit. Parables have a specific occurrence (or a particular example) in them and the action is in the past. Merriam–Webster Dictionary sees a similitude as have a better correspondence than a similarity which sees a weaker likeness.

Sobriquet – an alternate name. Synonyms: alias, byname, cognomen, epithet, handle, moniker (also monicker), nickname (also soubriquet), surname.

Soloecismus – grammatical error of syntax.

Somatopoeia – Zwingli's definition: Imitation of a person, depicting their supposed physical behavior. E.g., A Saturday Night Live comedian imitating the USA president (hair style, voice and speech inflection). E.g., An actor acting obese: puffs out his facial cheeks, sticks out his chest and makes a circle with his arms (finger tips touching at his belly button) pretending his belly is that large.

Spectrum – For Zwingli, a shadowy visionary image. Apparition, specter, ghost. Synonym: Phasma.

Spoonerism – swapping of initial letters between two words.
> Spoonerism: "He hissed my mystery lectures"
> Proper: "He missed my history lectures."

Status Orationis – Zwingli's definition: questions or arguments which at first appear to contradict one another. E.g., Light behaves both as a particle and as a wave. E.g., Jesus Christ has two natures — fully human and fully God, but he is only one person without dividing or mixing of those natures.

Subjection – Subjectio, Subiectum. Providing a suggestion in answer to one's own question regarding how an argument should proceed. A Latin term for anthypophora, dianoea, ypokeimenon (deprived).

Sublation – Sublatio. To remove, as to drop some letters in a word. See synaeresis.

Sudden Exclamation – Cataploce. E.g., "Then it came about after all your wickedness ('Woe, woe to you!' declares the Lord GOD), Ezekiel 16:23.

Summarizing – Eipitrochasmos, Percursio. A quick running through a summary. Akin to Asyndeton. E.g., "And what more shall I say? For time will fail me if I tell of Gideon, Barak, Samson, Jephthah, of David and Samuel and the prophets" Hebrews 11:32.

Syllepsis – syntactical yoking (zeugma) that is punning or ungrammatical. E.g., Dickens: "She went home in a flood of tears and a sedan chair." The preposition 'in' is grammatically correct "in a sedan chair." The first phrase is grammatically incorrect; to be correct it could be "with a flood of tears." E. W. Bullinger defines it as, "repetition of the sense without the repetition of the word." **One word is used, but two meanings are implied**. One word used with dual meanings understood. E.g., "they **blessed** the LORD and His people Israel." 2 Chronicles 31:8. Blessing the Lord is praising and offering Him thanks. Blessing His people is praying in His name for His blessings on them — two different aspects. E.g., "Rend your heart and not your garments" Joel 2:13. Figurative tear your heart; letterally do not tear you garment.

Syllogism – Syllogismus. Deductive logical construct of two premises sharing a common term and a conclusion. If premises are true, conclusion is true.

> All x are y   (major premise)
>
> z is x   (minor premise)
>
> therefore z is y   (conclusion).

If either premise is not stated, but the conclusion is, then it is Enthymemes (q.v.).

Syllogismus – Significatio, Ratiocinatio, Emphasis. Syllogismus has each premise, but omits the conclusion. E.g., In 1 Samuel 17:4–7B

Goliath's armor and weapons are listed, but the conclusion regarding his strength is omitted. E.g., "If anyone is not willing to work, then he is not to eat, either" 2 Thessalonians 3:10. The omitted conclusion is "Everyone must eat; therefore everyone must work."

Symbol – something that stands for something else: as a flag for a nation, the cross for Christianity. Usually the association is unstated. (Note: words are also symbols.) Usually there is no natural or associative connection of symbol with its referent, just a conventional one. As seen in numerology (q.v.) I take a very cautious approach. Basically take every Biblical figurative use of something, then see if there is an overarching sense. (E.g., See ascending enumeration where I used this method.) Apocalyptic passages, dreams and visions are particularly difficult. I accept author given and interpreted allegories. I reject interpreter allegorizations. I accept Biblical interpretations, but push no further. (So I see one author intended interpretation, but understand there may be many types of application.) E.g., see Appendix F. Symbolism of Ark Items.

E.g., **Leaven** symbolizes spreading — not evil (although evil spreads). "The kingdom of heaven is like leaven that a woman took and mixed into three measures of flour, until all of it was leavened" Matthew 13:33. E.g., **Bronze** suggests trial or judgment. "Moses made a bronze serpent and set it on the standard; and it came about, that if a serpent bit any man, when he looked to the bronze serpent, he lived" Numbers 21:9. "Four chariots were coming forth from between the two mountains; and the mountains were bronze mountains" Zechariah 6:1. E.g., Parables about **a king** symbolize God the Father as in Matthew 22:1–14B. E.g., Oil symbolizes the Holy Spirit (as in consecration, anointing or prayer for the sick James 5:14.) There are more symbols than I have offered — but be wary of inconsistent substitutions (allegorizations).

Symperasma – See "Concluding Summary."
Symploce – Intertwining, Complexio (combination), complication (folding together). Repetition of a word at both beginnings and endings. (If repetition is of phrases or sentences, it is called Coenotes)

E.g., Most true that I must fair Fidessa love,/ Most true that fair Fidessa cannot love./ Most true that I do feel the pains of love,/ Most true that I am captive unto love. Griffin, *Fidessa,* sonnet 62.

E.g., **Their land** has also been filled with silver and gold
   And there is no end to their treasures;
   Their land has also been filled with horses
   And there is no end to their chariots.
   Their land has also been filled with idols;   Isaiah 2:7–8B

Behold, My servants will eat,   **but you will** be hungry.
Behold, My servants will drink,   **but you will** be thirsty.
Behold, My servants will rejoice,   **but you will** be put to shame.
Behold, My servants will shout
   joyfully with a glad heart,   **But you will** cry out with a heavy heart,

   And you will wail with a broken spirit.
   Isaiah 65:13–14.

So also is the resurrection of the dead.
It is sown a perishable body,   **it is raised** an imperishable body;
it is sown in dishonor,   **it is raised** in glory;
it is sown in weakness,   **it is raised** in power;
it is sown a natural body,   **it is raised** a spiritual body.
If there is a natural body,   there is also a spiritual body.
   1 Corinthians 15:42–43B

Synaeresis – Sublation. When two syllables are contracted into one. A kind of metaplasm. E.g., When New Orleans is pronounced "Nawlins."

Synaesthesia – a blending or confusion of different kinds of sense–impression. E.g., To define colors as "warm" or "loud."

Synathroesmos – Coacervatio. A collection. A) A gathering up of things scattered throughout a speech (accumulatio). B) Conglomeration of many words and expressions either with similar meaning (synonym) or different meanings (congeries). Also spelled synathroesmus synathroismos, sinathrismus. Synonym: frequentatio, the heaping figure. See Enumeration for examples.

Syncatabasis – Condescension, Anthropopatheia. Ascribing human feelings, actions or attributes to God. E.g., "Has the LORD's arm been shortened?" Numbers 11:23.

Synchoresis. See Concession. Making a concession on one point to gain another.

Synchysis – a rhetorical technique to create bewilderment by scattering disconnected words or thoughts. This loss of logical thought forces the audience to consider the meaning of the words and the relationship between them.

Syncope – omit letters from word's middle. E.g., **Ta'en** thy wages. Shakespeare, *Cymbeline*, 4.2.258.

Syncrisis – (judging together), Parathesis (putting beside), Comparatio (comparing). Repeated similes. Several comparisons used together. E.g., "Though your sins are as scarlet, They will be as white as snow; Though they are red like crimson, They will be like wool" Isaiah 1:18. E.g., "Each will be like a refuge from the wind And a shelter from the storm, Like streams of water in a dry country, Like the shade of a huge rock in a parched land" Isaiah 32:2. E.g., "You will be nursed, you will be carried on the hip and fondled on the knees. "As one whom his mother comforts, so I will comfort you; and you will be comforted in Jerusalem" Isaiah 66:23–24.

Synecdoche – indirect reference to something by naming some part for the whole — as "hands" for "manual laborers." Here there is transfer of a part for the whole, or the whole for a part. Sometimes a greater entity is named for a part — as "The law is here" for "the policeman is here." Synecdoche is a special type of metonymy (s.v.) often used in sports (Miami for the Miami Heat) or government (Moscow for the soviet government). Note the relationship is in the mind of the author making the association. E.g., Total disarmament is exemplified by the conversion of two weapons: "beat their swords into ploughshares, and their spears into pruning knives" (Isaiah 2:4, Micah 4:3). E.g., "All [kinds of] livestock of Egypt died" (not every livestock, but parts of the livestock!). E.g., "This cup is the new covenant in My blood, which is poured out for you" Luke 22:20 NASB. This means the cup represents the new covenant. The cup is a synecdoche which is a specialized form of metonymy (s.v.).

Synesis – phrase constructed by intended meaning (not grammar). E.g., The crowd (singular) rose to their (plural pronoun) feet.

Synezeugmenon, Adjunctum – where 2 clauses are joined or yoked together to one verb. E.g., "the people **saw the thunder and lightning**" Exodus 20:18. E.g., "That I may **know Him and the power of His resurrection and the fellowship** of His sufferings, being conformed to His death; in order that I may attain to the resurrection from the dead." Philippians 3:10–11.

Synoeceiosiss – See Cohabitation.

Synonymia – Use of several synonyms together to amplify or explain a given subject. Repetition adds emotional force or intellectual clarity. Synonymia often occurs in parallel fashion. E.g., "You blocks, you stones, you worse than senseless things!" Shakespeare, *Julius Caesar* 1.1.2. The Latin synonym, Interpretatio, suggests the expository and rational nature of this figure, while another Greek synonym, congeries, suggests the emotive possibilities of this figure. E.g., "But the sons of Israel were **fruitful and increased greatly, and multiplied, and became exceedingly mighty**, so that the land was **filled with them**." Exodus 1:7.

Syntheton – See Combination.

Tautology – needless repetition of the same idea in different words; pleonasm on the level of a sentence or sentences. E.g., If you have a friend, keep your friend, for an old friend is to be preferred before a new friend, this I say to you as your friend. Henry Peacham, *Garden of Eloquence*, 49.

Thaumasmos – See Wondering.

Tmesis – See Mid–cut. Interjecting a word or phrase between parts of a compound word or between syllables of a word. E.g., **a** whole **nother** story.

Topographia – Description of Place. E.g., New Jerusalem Revelation 21:9–22:3B.

Transition – See Metabasis.

Transumption – see metalepsis.

Trope – a somewhat archaic word used to describe figurative speech. Anything that can be construed in a letteral sense is NOT a trope. The tropological sense is the figurative sense of a word. Not all rhetoricians agree that **tropes** are figures of *thought,* whereas **schemes (q.v.)** are *figures of speech.* Generally they do agree that schemes rearrange the normal order of word meanings; whereas tropes change the meanings of words by a 'turn' of sense. Major figures of speech that are usually classified as tropes are: metaphor, simile, metonymy, synecdoche, irony, personification, and hyperbole. Disputed figures that may be called tropes are: litotes and periphrasis. The method of tropology is typology — it seeks common intrinsic characteristics in associated objects. To understand a trope, first understand the letteral meaning of the figure. Then reflect on the similarities between the two parts. In modern terms using the "road of life," "life" is the <u>tenor</u> or primary literary term; "road" is the <u>vehicle</u> or secondary figurative term.

Type – in the hermeneutic of typology, a type is the common characteristic between two entities. E.g., Slavery is a common characteristic shared by Hagar, Mount Sinai, and Jerusalem in Galatians 4:25, "Hagar is Mount Sinai in Arabia, and corresponds to the present Jerusalem, for she is in slavery with her children."

Typological Hermeneutic – Seeks common intrinsic characteristics between two (people, events, or objects) to form an associative relationship. Both comparisons are paradoxically retained with all their similarities and differences. Both entities retain all their history and reality (particulars and essence.) "This bread is my body" understood with the method of typology means, "This bread resembles my body" for both are broken for you. Both the bread and the body are held onto, and the associative connection is the broken nature of both. (In contrast see Allegorical method.)

Understatement – See meiosis and litotes.

Vain Repetition – See Battologia.

Wishing – Hoping for a thing. Oeonismos (Greek) means divining by the flight of birds. Often they saw what they looked for. Optatio (Latin) expresses hope or ardent desire. The phrase "Oh that" often introduces this figure. E.g., "O that they were wise, that they understood this, that they would consider their latter end!" Deuteronomy 32:20 (KJV). E.g., "I wish that those who are troubling you would even mutilate themselves" Galatians 5:12.

Wondering – Thaumasmos. Statement of marveling. (This is not a statement of fact. This is not an exclamation which is Ecphonesis.) E.g., "How fair are your tents, O Jacob, Your dwellings, O Israel!" Numbers 24:5. E.g., "Now when Jesus heard this, He **marveled** and said to those who were following, "Truly I say to you, I have not found such great faith with anyone in Israel." Matthew 8:10. E.g., "Oh, the depth of the riches both of the wisdom and knowledge of God! How unsearchable are His judgments and unfathomable His ways!" Romans 11:33.

Word–clashing – Antanaclasis, Anaclasis, Antistasis, Homonym, Dialogia, Refractio, Reciprocatio. Repetition of same word in same sentence with two **different** meanings. The two words must be spelled the same but carry different meanings. E.g., "At the signing of the Declaration of Independence, Ben Franklin seriously joked, "We must all **hang** together, or most assuredly we shall all **hang** separately." {See Paronomasia which has 2 similar sounding (but different) words. Antanaclasis (q.v.) is akin to Ploce (word folding) (q.v.) but in Ploce the same word is used but with heightened meaning. E.g., "His wife is a wife indeed." "Caesar was Caesar." Shakespeare, *Julius Caesar.*} E.g., Whoever hath her wish, thou has thy **Will**,/ And **Will** to boot, and **Will** in overplus---Shakespeare *Sonnets*, 135. E.g., Your argument is **sound** … all **sound**, Benjamin Franklin — meaning your argument is reasonable … all air. E.g., "If you aren't **fired with enthusiasm**, you will be **fired with enthusiasm**." Vince Lombardi. E.g., "Follow Me, and allow the **dead** to bury their own **dead**" Matthew 8:22 means," Let the spiritually dead bury those that have died." E.g., "They are not all **Israel** who are descended from **Israel**" Romans 9:6 means "they are not all [spiritual] Israel who are descended from [physical] Israel. See Homonym.

Word–picture – Hypotyposis. Lively description of a word-picture such as an action, event, person, condition, passion, etc. used for creating the illusion of reality. Also spelled hypotiposis. Synonyms: demonstration, evidentia, adumbratio, representation, the counterfait representation, Diatyposis (thoroughly impress),

Enargeia (vivid description), Phantasia (making visible by words to the mind), Icon (image), Imago (imitation, copy), Eicasia (likeness, image). E.g., Israel's blessings Deuteronomy 28:1–14, Israel's curses Deuteronomy 28:15–45 & Isaiah 1:6–9; captivity and scattering of Israel Deuteronomy 28:45– 68. Christ's sufferings Psalm 22, Isaiah 53; Christ's return as warrior Revelation 19:11–16. E.g., The healed "blind man" still goes by that name (John 9:17).

Word–portrait – Effiction. Representing or fashioning a word portrait. Describing the physical body in such a way that you know who the speaker is talking about. E.g., Regarding Messiah, the suffering servant, "He has no stately form or majesty That we should look upon Him, Nor appearance that we should be attracted to Him. He was despised and forsaken of men, "man of sorrows and acquainted with grief; And like one from whom men hide their face. He was despised, and we did not esteem Him." Isaiah 53:2–3.

Working Out – Exergasia. Repetition to work out or illustrate what has already been said.

Epexergasia (working out upon), Expolitio (polishing up, to strengthen and embellish). This figure of speech is overwhelmingly used, because of Hebrew parallelism (the second line repeats the thought of the first). E.g.,

> A| I called out of my distress to the LORD,
>> B| And He answered me.
> A| I cried for help from the depth of Sheol;
>> B| You heard my voice.
> C| For You had cast me into the deep,
>> D| Into the heart of the seas,
>> D | And the current engulfed me.
> C| All Your breakers and billows passed over me. Jonah 2:2–3

Zeugma – a specialized ellipsis [brachylogy] with a syntactic 'yoking' of two phrases with one word (verb, noun, adjective or preposition). E.g., "I give you milk to drink, [I give you] not solid food" 1 Corinthians 3:2. Syllepsis sometimes is used as a synonym of zeugma, but Baldick prefers to make syllepsis a subset of zeugma reserved for puns or ungrammatical linking. (See syllepsis.) E.g.,

Shakespeare 128th Sonnet: "Give them thy fingers, me thy lips to kiss." There are several technical forms of zeugma.

Where the **verb does the yoking**, that position yields a special terminology:
A) Begin–yoke: Antezeugmenon (q.v.), protozeugma, proepizeuxis, and Injunctum.
B) End–yoke: hypozeugma (q.v.).
C) Middle–yoke: mesozeugma (q.v.), synzeugma and Conjunctum;
D) connected–yoke: synezeugmenon (q.v.), Adjunctum.

If the **noun does the yoking**, then specialized zeugma occur.
A) diazeugma (q.v.) defines a single subject which governs several verbs or verbal constructions.
B) hypozeuxis is when every clause (in a series of parallel clauses) has its own (different) verb. E.g., As Virgil **guided Dante** through Inferno, the Sibyl **Aeneas Avernus**. Roger D. Scott. Meaning: "As Virgil <u>guided</u> Dante <u>through</u> Inferno, the Sibyl [guided] Aeneas [through] Avernus."

[END OF FIGURES OF SPEECH]

F. SYMBOLISM OF ITEMS IN THE ARK

The **ark of the covenant** symbolizes the earthly throne of God. He spoke to Moses "from above the mercy seat, from between the two cherubim which are upon the **ark of the testimony** (Exodus 25:22). Testimonial items in the ark demonstrated how the nation of Israel failed God. A deep analysis of the temptations of Jesus shows how he righteously overcame the temptations by quoting scripture which referenced each testimonial incident. Thus these testimonial symbols work together to show Jesus is the sinless Messiah who enables the new covenant.

The ark held three items: a pot of manna, Aaron's rod, and the (replaced) commandment tablets (Hebrews 9:4). Each was a reminder of Israel's failure to keep God's word. In his temptations, Jesus resisted each temptation, quoting from Deuteronomy. Each quote referred to an incident out of which the testimonial item arose. Hence these ark items testify that Jesus is the Messiah. Therefore Jesus is without fault (spotless, without blemish 1 Peter 1:19) and without sin (Hebrews 9:14). He is the "Lamb of God who takes away the sin of the world" (John 1:29). God did this "to perfect the author of their [the sons of glory] salvation through sufferings (Hebrews 2:10).

Jesus Quotes Scripture to Combat Satan's Temptations

Deut 8:3 He humbled you and let you be hungry, and fed you with manna which you did not know, nor did your fathers know, that He might make you understand that **man does not live** by bread alone, but man lives by everything that proceeds out of the mouth of the LORD.

Deut 6:16 You shall not put the LORD your God to the test, as you **tested** Him at Massah.

Deut 6:13 You shall fear only the LORD your God; and you shall **worship** Him and swear by His name.

Figure 8
How Ark Items are Connected to Israel and Jesus

Testimonies put in ark (Exodus 25:21)	Matt 4	Luke 4	Christ Quotes	Incident
Turn stone to bread. divinity to aid humanity Man does not live by bread alone, but.. Pot of manna put in ark Exodus 16:33–34	1–4	1–4	Dt 8:13	Exodus 16:1–7
Throw self off temple pinnacle. Test God Put God to the test at Massah Aaron's rod put in ark Numbers17:10–11	5–7	9–12	Dt 6:16	Numb 17:1–17
Bow to Satan. Bypass God's plan of atonement Worship only God. Tablets broken at gold calf Law Tablets put in ark (Dt 10:5, 1 Kings 8:9)	8-11	5–8	Dt 6:13 Dt 9:15,17	Exodus 32:19

Types of sin correlated

A. 1 John 2:16 For all that is in the world, the lust of the flesh and the lust of the eyes and the boastful pride of life, is not from the Father, but is from the world.

B. Genesis 3:4–6 The serpent said to the woman, "You surely will not die! For God knows that in the day you eat from it your eyes will be opened, and you will be like God, knowing good and evil." When the woman saw that the tree was good for food, and that it was a delight to the eyes, and that the tree was desirable to make one wise, she took from its fruit and ate; and she gave also to her husband with her, and he ate.

Figure 9
Broad Categories (or Types) of Sin

Fallen World 1 John 2:16	Eden Genesis 3:4–6	Ark of the Testimony	Temptations of Jesus
lust of flesh	good food	manna	turn stone into bread
lust of the eye	delight to eye	gold calf/ broken law	bow to Satan
pride of life: test God	makes one wise	Aaron's rod	throw self off tower

A YouTube video presents this material: Hilary Arthur Nixon, Ark of the Testimony (28.09).

No wonder after Satan's failure to get Jesus to sin, God expels Satan from heaven. Satan fell from heaven like lightning (Luke 10:18). God as creator had fashioned **the sinless man who survived temptation.** Satan no longer could accuse God of failure to have a man "on the earth, a blameless and upright man, fearing God and turning away from evil." Job 1:8

Consider Satan and Job

Twice God allowed Satan to test Job in very specific ways.

In the first trial, all of Job's wealth vanished and his children died.

> Despite all this, Job did not sin, nor did he blame God   Job 1:22
>
> Job still maintained his integrity   Job 2:3.

> In the second trial, Job lost his health   Job 2:7
>
> Satan failed to have Job curse God   Job 2:5
>
> Satan bet that Job's love for God was brotherly love.
>
> Job loves God, because God blesses him. Satan was wrong.

Job sinned when he lost his integrity. In pride he claimed

> "I am righteous, But God has taken away my right"   Job 34:5

The Lord said to Job, "Will the faultfinder contend with the Almighty?

> Let him who rebukes God give an answer"   Job 40:1–2

> Thus Job confessed to the Lord, "**Therefore I retract**   Job 42:6
> **and repent**"
>
> 2 I know that You can *do* all things, And that no plan is impossible for You.
>
> 32 'Who is this who conceals advice without knowledge?'
>
> Therefore I have declared that which I did not understand,
>
> Things too wonderful for me, which I do not know.
>
> 4 'Please listen, and I will speak; I will ask You, and You instruct me.'
>
> 5 "I have heard of You by the hearing of the ear; But now my eye sees You;
>
> 6 **Therefore I retract, And I repent**, *sitting* on dust   Job 42:2–6
> and ashes."

[My bold words.]

Through these trials, Job discovered a stubborn agape love for God.

> Yes he said, "The LORD gave and the LORD has taken away.   Job 1:20
> blessed be the name of the LORD."

But his mind in pride thought: God is unjust.
    He had no right to take my blessing away
In repentance Job's attitude toward God changed.

It is this agape love with which "God so loved the world,   John 3:16
that he gave His only Son, so that everyone who believes in
Him will not perish, but have eternal life."

G. GLOSSARY

Allegorical Hermeneutic – Imparting meanings into a text the author
did not intend. Eisegesis. Usually uses substitution of one element for
another; with this substitution the reality or history of one element
becomes destroyed. For instance, in Amillennial theology, instead
of "Israel", they plug in (or substitute) "the church"; as a result they
see none of God's future plans for Israel. When the "body of Christ"
gets substituted for bread, the reality of the bread is destroyed. (In
contrast see Typological hermeneutic.)

Though historically done; this non–author intended allegorization
should NOT be used. It may trigger different thought patterns than
the author intended. Ironically the allegorical method is quick
and easy to use, because of the substitution. It can come up with
interesting insights, but like insight, the result may have no validity
to it! Verification of the validity, coherence and correspondence of
the insight must rely upon typology.

Antitype – representation which is opposite of someone or something.
E.g., Christ is the messiah; antichrist is false one who claims to be
the messiah. In biblical typology: a type is the shadow, an escalation
is a heightening of that shadow, and the antitype is the prophetic
fulfilment which causes the shadow to cease. E.g., The Tabernacle
is the mobile shadow of God's heavenly temple. Solomon's Temple
and Ezekiel's future Temple are escalations of the Tabernacle.
The prophetic fulfilment is with the New Jerusalem when God
permanently dwells with His people. See Archetype.

Archetype – Original pattern by which copies are made. In Platonic
philosophy, reality is the perfect ideal (or form — Plato's "eidos").

E.g., The Roman Times font has many different sized fonts (inferior particulars) but its essence is in the ideal form — the concept. In Jungian psychology, archetypes are the collectively-inherited unconscious idea, pattern of thought, or image that is universally present in individual psyches. E.g., Abraham is an archetype hero of faith. [Note caution may be needed when reading philosophy or religious books older than 100 years — especially if they embrace Platonism. They may reverse definitions of the modern type/ antitype. The antitype might be used as the archetype, and the type then becomes the inferior manifestation of it.]

Atonement – from the blood sprinkled upon the mercy seat [kapper]: Harmony (at–one–ment) between the Holy God and Sinners because of the sin sacrifice of Christ Jesus which propitiated and expiated God to assuage His wrath at our sin. That vertical vector is complicated enough but there is much, much more! There is the horizontal vector: sinner to priest (Leviticus 10:17), congregation and offended. Atonement [kipper] also embraces cleansing (washing away defilement) as Ezekiel's annual temple cleansing (Ezekiel 45:18–20) and initial altar consecration (Ezekiel 43:25–26).

Cleansing – purifies or washes away defilement and sin.

Coherence – the quality of being logically integrated, or complete. When analogates (or types) are very similar to each other, then more coherence exists. (See footnote 128 for examination of coherence in Joel 2:28–31.)

Consecration – makes something or someone "set apart" from sin and unto God

Consubstantiation – Lutheran view of the Lord's Supper: As one eats the bread, he along with eating bread, partakes of Christ.

Correlation – the relationship between two analogates

Correspondence – the intrinsic qualities of each analogate, or subject of typological analogy.

Covenant – Relationship as in marriage, business, or God with His people. Theologically the Old Testament is the Old Covenant (the law written on tablets of stone). The New Testament is the New Covenant (where the law is written upon one's own heart.) Testament is a legal term implying death must occur before the will and testament can take effect.

Eisegesis – reading into the text ideas or formats alien to the original author's intent.

Epiclesis – epiklesis. (Greek word letterally means "to call upon.") When the priest elevates the element and prays <u>to call upon</u> God to change the substance of the element (be it bread or wine) to the substance of Christ, that prayer is called the epiclesis. In high mass, the bells are rung at this time. This is the time that the priest invokes the Holy Spirit. Eastern Orthodox theologians hold that the epiclesis is essential to the Eucharist — without it, the miraculous transubstantiation will not occur. Catholics hold that the prayer is not absolutely essential.

Eschatology – study of last things, the future prophetic final events.

Eucharist – A transliterated Greek word, which means to "give thanks." Paul uses this word in 1 Corinthians 11:24 to describe the prayer Jesus gave to the Father for the bread.

Excursus – a digression in which some point is discussed at length; or an appendix devoted to detailed examination of some topic held over from the main body of the text. This treatise required a lengthy explanation on Allegorical interpretation (See Appendix B.3.). Rather than interrupt the focus on Catholicism, I chose to put the excursus in the appendix.

Exegesis – Getting the author's intending meaning from the text. Adjective: exegetical

Expiation – removes sin and transgression as if by covering over or washing the sin away.

Extreme Unction – Catholic practice of praying for and anointing a person in danger of death. The practice arises from James 5:13–15, the "prayer of faith". Protestants also pray for and sometimes anoint with oil, but they do not elevate the practice to that of a sacrament as the Catholics do.

Haggadah – Hebrew word of explaining scripture such as the Talmud Haggadah. The content is non–legal often devotional, practical. It may contain history, prophecy, exhortations, personal experiences, prayers. It can also mean telling, like Passover Haggadah which retells the Passover account. Midrash may contain Haggadah.

Halakah – Jewish word describing anything dealing with the Law. Technically it is the body of Jewish oral laws supplementing written law which regulates religious practice. Midrash may contain Halakah.

Hallel – Letterally it is Hebrew for Praise. Hallelujah means Praise God. In Jewish tradition, the Hallel are a special group: Psalm 113–118. Sometimes these are called the "Egyptian Hallel" because they were sung during the killing of the Passover lambs. At certain points they would stop and read a praise. During Jesus' earthly ministry, pilgrims read these Psalms of praise as they ascended to Jerusalem during three appointed festivals: Pesach (Passover), Shavuot (Pentecost), Sukkot (Feast of Tabernacles). Today's Jews also read them at Hanukkah and Rosh Chodesh (the new moon).

Hermeneutics – the principles and theory of interpretation concerned at getting to understand the meaning of a text. Methods of interpreting God's Word.

Idealism – akin to Platonism and Neoplatonism. Reality rests in the ideal, not any particular physical manifestation of the ideal.

Justification – God's declaration, "it is Just–as–if–I never sinned".

Letteral – Grammatically the sense of a phrase without using figures of speech or idioms. Hermeneutically forcing an author's intended figure of speech into nonfigurative language.

Literal – The sense an author intended so it may use figures of speech. (Often literal is understood as grammatically the simplest sense of a phrase without using figures of speech. This is my definition of Letteral.)

Mass – Letterally it means the sending. Hence Christmas is the sending of Christ [His birth]. In Catholic Mass, after the Priest calls upon God to change the elements (the epiclesis), this is the time that Christ is miraculously sent, transforming the substance of the bread (or wine) into both the body and blood of Christ.

Midrash – Jewish collection which may be haggadah and or halakah.

Neoplatonist – Plato's philosophy is the basis, but Plotinus and his followers made modifications. By the fall of the Roman Empire Platonic and Neoplatonic elements were indistinguishable. Philo, Clement of Alexandria, Origen, and Saint Augustine were deeply immersed in this system. Basically reality is in the ideal (spirit) and anything perceptible was a fogging or distraction from that ideal. See Platonism.

Papists – Catholics, derived from their earthly head being the Pope or the papacy.

Parasceve – The day of preparation for a Jewish Sabbath or some other feast day.

Pasch – sometimes Pesach. Hebrew for Passover

Paschal – the lamb slain at Passover

Passover – The 10th and final Mosaic plague on Egypt. Houses that obeyed Moses by placing blood on the lintel and sides of their front doors, found the destroying angel passed over (did not kill) the firstborn child in the house.

Platonism – Plato's doctrines that reality is in transcendent universals (ideals), that anything the mind remembers is reminiscent of those ideals and everything perceived by the senses are not completely real, but rather participate in the reality of those ideals. Hence every particular horse is not real, but horse–ness (the ideal of a horse) is. Every physical table is not real, but the ideal of table–ness is. Aristotle disagreed; the reality is in the particular horse, and what the mind perceives is an abstraction of that reality.

Propitiation – the offering of a sacrifice to appease God's divine wrath. Hence the offering of the sacrifice and death of Jesus in heaven, appeased God's justice effecting reconciliation between God and His people.

Reconciliation – to restore to fellowship, compatibility and harmony.

Redemption – liberation by payment of a price, a ransom. Sin holds us in the pawnshop of hell, but Christ ransomed us back to freedom, with the ransom of His life.

Sacrifice – the Old Testament Law demanded specific types of offerings to God: animal, vegetable, drink, incense, even spiritual sacrifices of prayer and praise.

Sanctification – is the process of making one holy.

sensus plenior – Latin "many senses." Holders of this viewpoint think there are more than one author intended meaning.

Synoptic – Comparing by overview the similarities and differences in the various accounts of the Eucharist. The First 3 Gospels (Matthew,

Mark and Luke) have many similarities; hence they are called the Synoptic Gospels.

Testament – a legal term implying death of a testator so that the last will and testament can be established. Hence the division of the Old Testament (covenant of Law on Mosaic Tablets) and the New Testament (Christ's death effected a new covenant where the Law of God is written on the hearts of the believers.)

Transubstantiation – Catholic view of the Eucharist, or Mass: As one appears to be eating the specie of bread, he partakes of the substance of Christ. The substance of the bread is by miracle transformed into the Body and Blood of Christ.

Type – in the hermeneutic of typology, a type is the common characteristic between two entities. E.g., Slavery is a common characteristic shared by Hagar, Mount Sinai, and Jerusalem in Galatians 4:25, "Hagar is Mount Sinai in Arabia, and corresponds to the present Jerusalem, for she is in slavery with her children." See Antitype and Archetype.

Typological Hermeneutic – Seeks common intrinsic characteristics between two (people, events, or objects) to form an associative relationship. Both comparisons are paradoxically retained with all their similarities and differences. Both entities retain all their history and reality (particulars and essence.) "This bread is my body" understood with the method of typology means, "This bread resembles my body" for both are broken for you. Both the bread and the body are held onto, and the associative connection is the broken nature of both. Test types with correspondence, correlation, and coherence. (In contrast see Allegorical Hermeneutic.)

Ubiquitous – omnipresent, God's characteristic of potentially being present everywhere — even if not manifested. Lutherans stress: Christ's human body takes on the divine attribute of omnipresence. Hence the God-man's flesh is present everywhere his deity is.

Viaticum – Catholic administration of Christian Eucharist given to a person in danger of dying. Letterally it means provisions as for a journey.

Virtualism – the bread and wine remain unchanged, but while receiving the elements the faithful receive the virtue, the benefits, the power of the new life in Christ Jesus and are spiritually united with Christ, God and the other Saints. Advocated by John Calvin and Zwingli.

H. BIBLIOGRAPHY

Anderson, Robert. *The Silence of God.* 1897

Augustine. *De Doctrina Christiana.*

Augustine. *De Trinitas.*

Bainton, Roland. H. *Here I stand. A Life of Martin Luther.* New York: Abingdon–Cokesbury Press, 1950.

Baldick, Chris. *The Concise Oxford Dictionary of Literary Terms.* New York: Oxford University Press, 1991.

Berkhof, Louis. *The History of Christian Doctrines.* Carlisle, Pa.: Banner of Truth Trust, 1975.

Blair, Hugh. *Lectures on Rhetoric and Belles Letters,* 1783.

Boehmer, H. *Luther in the Light of Modern Research.* Tr. E. Potter. New York: Dial Press,1930.

Bullinger, E. [Ethelbert] W. [William] *Figures of Speech Used in the Bible Explained and Illustrated.* London: Eyre and Spottiswoode, 1898. Reprint Mansfield Center, Ct: Martino Publishing, 2011.

Bullinger, [Heinrich] and Calvin. *Consensus Tigurinus,* 1549. Zurich Accord on Lord's Supper; 26 articles.

Bullinger, Heinrich. *Second Helvetic Confession.* 1562. Revised 1564. Adopted in Scotland 1566.

Buswell, James Oliver. *A Systematic Theology of the Christian Religion.* 2 volumes. Grand Rapids, Michigan: Zondervan, 1962.

Calvin, John. *Institutes of the Christian Religion.* ed. John T. McNeill. 2 volumes. Philadelphia: Westminster Press, 1960.

Catechism of the Catholic Church. Second edition, 2019. Libreria Edeitrice Vaticana - United States Conference of Catholic Bishops, Washington, DC. ISBN 978-1-60137-649-7 (Abbreviated CCC). Readable online.

Chaucer, Geoffrey. *The Reeve's Tale* in *Canterbury Tales.* 1387–1400.

Chemnitz, Martin. *The Two Natures of Christ,* trans. By J. A. O. Preus. St Louis: Concordia Publishing House, 1971.

Cicero. *Rhetorica Ad Herennium.*

Creeds of the Churches. Ed. John H. Leith. Richmond, Virginia: John Knox Press, rev. ed.., 1973.

Dana, H(arvey) E(ugene) and J(ulius) R. Mantey. *A Manual Grammar of the Greek New Testament.* N.Y.: Macmillan, 1957.

Davis, John J(ames). *Biblical Numerology*, a Basic Study of the Use of Numbers in the Bible. Grand Rapids: Baker, 1968.

Dix, Gregory. *The Shape of the Liturgy*. London: Dacre Press, 1945.

Dr. Martin Luther's Small Catechism with an American Translation text. New Haven, Missouri: Leader Publishing Co., 1971. Copyright holder is *Luther's Small Catechism* © 1943, 1971 Concordia Publishing House.

Encyclopedia Britannica CD 1999.

Erickson, Millard J. *The Word Became Flesh*. Grand Rapids, Michigan: Baker Book House, 1985.

Evans, Craig. *Holman QuickSource Guide to the Dead Sea Scrolls*. Nashville, Tenn.: B&H Publishing Group, 2010.

Fisher, George Park. *History of Christian Doctrine*. N.Y.: Charles Scribner's Sons, 1899.

Gospel parallels a Synopsis of the First Three Gospels. Ed. Burton H. Throckmorton, Jr. New York: Thomas Nelson and Sons, 2nd ed., 1952.

Griffin. *Fidessa*. 1596.

A Harmony of the Gospels. Ed. Robert L. Thomas, associate ed. Stanley N. Gundry. Chicago: Moody Press, 1978.

Hooper, John. *A defense of the True Doctrine and Use of the Lord's Supper*. The English form of this document is translated from the Latin by Elio Cuccaro, *Monument to Memorialism John Hooper's Defense of the Lord's Supper a Translation and Analysis*, a Ph. D. thesis presented to Drew University 1987.

The Interpreter's Bible. Ed. George Arthur Buttrick.. 12 volumes. New York: Abington Press, 1956

Joyce, James. *Ulysses* Paris: Sylvia Beach, 1922.

Jeremias, Joachim. *The Eucharistic words of Jesus*. New York: Scribner, 1966.

Jeske, John C. "The Communication of Attributes in the God-man Christ Jesus." Essay delivered at metropolitan North pastoral Conference at St. Matthew Evangelical Lutheran Church, Milwaukee, Wisconsin, September 16, 1974. (No longer available online.)

Kelly, J.N.D. *Early Christian Doctrines*. N.Y.: Harper and Row, 1960.

Lampe, G. W. H. "The Reasonableness of Typology," *Essays on Typology.* London: SCM Press, 1957.

Lipson, Eric–Peter. *Passover Haggadah.* A Messianic Celebration. San Francisco: JFJ Publishing, 1986.

Melanchthon, Philipp. *Elementorum Rhetorices Libri.*

Mickelsen, A. Berkeley. *Interpreting the Bible.* Grand Rapids, Michigan: Eerdmans, 1963.

Milton, John. *Paradise Lost.* 1667

Morris, Leon. *The Apostolic Preaching of the Cross.* Grand Rapids, Michigan: Eerdmans, 1974.

The New Bible Dictionary. Grand Rapids, Michigan: Wm. B. Eerdmans Publishing Co., 1962.

The New International Dictionary of New Testament Theology. Ed. Colin Brown. 3 vol. Grand Rapids, Michigan: Zondervan, 1978.

Nixon, Hilary A[rthur]. *Suggested Principles for New Testament Allegory,* a M.S.T. thesis presented to Biblical School of Theology, Hatfield, Pa., 1972. (The name of the school has changed twice. In 1978 it became Biblical Theological Seminary. In October 2018 it changed again to Missio Seminary, which is now located in Philadelphia, Pa.)

Nixon, Hilary Arthur. *The Mystery of Ezekiel's Temple Liturgy.* Why Ezekiel's Temple Practices Differ From Levitical Law. Bloomington, Indiana, WestBow Press, 2018 [rev(ision) date 05/08/2019].

Nixon, Hilary. Ark of the Testimony. YouTube video. 28.09 (minutes:seconds).

Ark of the testimony is the ark of the covenant which held three items. Each item pointed to Israel's failure. When tempted by Satan, Jesus quoted from Deuteronomy using passages that directly relate to each article. Hence the ark items bear witness (or testify) that Jesus is God's righteous and Holy One, the Messiah or Christ. The outline for this video can be found In Appendix F. Symbol-ism of Items in the ark .

Oxford Dictionary of the Christian Church. Eds. F. L. Cross and F. E. A. Livingstone. London: Oxford University Press, 1974.

Peacham, Henry. *The Garden of Eloquence.* 1577.

Philo. *Legum Allegoria.*

Potter, G. R. *Zwingli.* New York: Cambridge University Press, 1976.

Puttenham, George. *The Arte of Prosie.* 1589.

Radbertus, Paschasius. *De Corpore et Sanguine Domini.* 831, revised 844.

Richards, I. A. *The Philosophy of Rhetoric.* New York: Oxford University Press, 1936.

Robertson, A. T. *A Harmony of the Gospels.* New York: Harper and Row, 1950.

Roman Missal. English translation. Philadelphia: Eugene Cummiskey, 1st rev. ed., 1867.

Schaff, Philip. *Creeds of Christendom.* 3 volumes. New York: Harper and Row, 6th ed., 1931. Online version: https://ccel.org/ccel/schaff/creeds1

Schaff, Philip. *History of the Christian Church.* 8 vol. New York: C. Scribner's sons, 1916-23.

Shakespeare, William.

All's Well that Ends Well	1602–1605
As You Like It	1599–1600
Antony and Cleopatra	1606c <= 1606c = circa 1606
Edward III	1596
Hamlet	1600c
Henry IV	Part 1 1596–97, Part 2 1597–98
Henry V	1599
Henry VIII	1612
Julius Caesar	1599
King John	1596 (Or The Life and Death of King John)
King Lear	1606
Love's Labor Lost	1597
Macbeth	1606c
Measure for Measure	1604
The Merchant of Venice	1597
The Merry Wives of Windsor	1602
Othello	1603
The Rape of Lucrece	1594
Richard II	1595c

Richard III	1590–96
Sonnets	
The Tempest	1610

Seeberg, Reinhold. *Text-book of the History of Doctrines.* 2 vols. Grand Rapids, Michigan: Baker Book House, 1966.

Spenser, Edmund. *The Faerie Queene.* 1596.

Star Wars (Movie series 1977–2019)

Sydney, Philip. *Astrophil and Stella.* circa 1580s.

Theological Dictionary of the New Testament. Ed. Kittel, trans. G. W. Bromiley. 10 volumes. Grand Rapids: Eerdmans, 1964.

Thiel. Ep. Pontif. *De duabus naturis in Christo.* A modern work with the quote is Reinhold Seeberg, *Text-book of the History of Doctrines.* 2 volumes. Translated by Charles E Hay. Grand Rapids, Michigan: Baker Book House, 1966, vol. II, p. 34.

Thomas Aquinas. *Summa Theologica.*

Throckmorton Jr., Burton H. editor. *Gospel parallels.* A Synopsis of the First Three Gospels. 2nd ed. New York: Thomas Nelson and Sons, 1952.

Thurian, Max. *Eucharistic Memorial, Part 2,* [Louisville?]: John Knox Press, 1961.

Webster's Third New International Dictionary. Springfield, Mass.: G & C Merriam Co. Pub., 1959.

Westminster Confession of Faith. The larger and shorter catechisms with scripture proofs at large. Originally convened 1643–47. Issued by the publications committee of the Free Presbyterian Church of Scotland, 1967,

Williams, Professor Grant, https://www.academia.edu/6535222/Figures

Woolcombe, Kenneth John. "The Biblical Origins and Patristic Development of Typology," *Essays on Typology.* London: SCM Press, 1957.

Wright, Ernest Vincent. *Gadsby.* Wetzel Publishing Company, 1939.

The Zondervan Pictorial Encyclopedia of the Bible. Merrill C. Tenney general editor. 5 volumes. Grand Rapids, Michigan: Zondervan Publishing House, 3rd printing 1978.

Zwingli. Fidei Ratio., June 1530.

Zwingli and [H.] Bullinger, Editor: G.W. Bromiley. Library of Christian Classics vol. XXIV. Philadelphia: Westminster Press, 1953. (This book contains Zwingli's work on the Lord's Supper.)

Huldreich Zwinglis Sämtliche Werke, h. v. E. Egli, G. Finsler, W. Köhler, O. Farner, F. Blanke, L. v. Muralt, E. Künzli, R. Pfister, J. Staedtke, F. Büsser. Corpus Reformatorum vol. 88–95 (Berlin/Leipzig/Zurich, 1905–) (In progress). [7 volumes]

Zwingli, Huldrych. *Huldreich Zwinglis Samtliche Werke*, vols. I–XIV. Zürich, Theologischer Verlag, 1982.

I. Index